the columbus world tourist attractions

ISBN: 1-902221-40-0

© 2000 Columbus Publishing Limited

All rights reserved. No part of this publication may be reproduced or utilised in any form or by any means, including photocopying, or by any information storage and retrieval system, without prior permission in writing from the publishers:

Columbus Publishing Limited, Jordan House, 47 Brunswick Place, London N1 6EB, UK
Tel: +44 (0)20 7608 6666
Fax: +44 (0)20 7608 6569
E-mail: booksales@columbus-group.co.uk

Project Editor • *Charlotte Kershaw*
Editor • *Mark Schatzker*
Sub-Editor • *Sarah Chatwin*
Cartographer • *David Burles*
Publisher • *Pete Korniczky*

*Designed & produced by Space Design and Production Services, London EC2A.
Printed & bound by Thanet Press, Margate.*

The publishers would like to thank all the organisations and individuals who have assisted in the preparation of this publication.

Whilst every effort is made by the publishers to ensure the accuracy of the information contained in this edition of the Columbus Guide to World Tourist Attractions, *the publishers can accept no responsibility for any loss occasioned to any person acting or refraining from acting as a result of the material contained in this publication, nor liability for any financial or other agreements which may be entered into with any organisations or individuals listed in the text.*

introduction

WELCOME TO the first edition of the *Columbus Guide to World Tourist Attractions,* the only reference work of its kind to cover the world's most important tourist attractions. This book contains practical and descriptive information, covering well-known icons like the Eiffel Tower and the Statue of Liberty alongside more obscure, though equally dramatic, attractions such as Sri Lanka's Temple of the Tooth. The title is designed to complement other travel guides produced by Columbus, such as the *World Travel Guide, Columbus City Guide – Europe* and the *World Travel Atlas.*

The guide is organised by continental groups – the Americas, Europe, Africa and the Middle East, and Asia and Australasia. Within each continental grouping, individual attractions are arranged alphabetically by country. Each entry contains: a contact address; the physical location of the attraction; transportation information; opening times; the price of admission; the number of visitors received annually; and, where appropriate, information on the special needs of the disabled as well as any restrictions that may apply.

Individual attraction entries can be found either by locating the continent group and country in which the attraction is found, or by the alphabetical and category listings at the back of the book. Attractions are named according to how they are most commonly known in English. Thus Beijing's Summer Place is named as such, however the Arc de Triomphe is known as the 'Arc de Triomphe', not the 'Arch of Triumph'.

Attractions usually fall into one of six categories. The 'historical' symbol denotes attractions whose popularity is based primarily on their historical significance, such as Hadrian's Wall or Independence Hall. The 'man-made' group is for attractions that represent a triumph of building and engineering, such as the Great Pyramids or the Hoover Dam. Attractions accompanied by the 'amusement' symbol attract visitors primarily in search of fun – Walt Disney World or the London Eye, for example.

The 'cultural' symbol denotes attractions such as art galleries and museums. A 'natural' symbol, on the other hand, recognises attractions of uncommon natural beauty, such as Yellowstone National Park. 'Religious' attractions signify churches, mosques and other places of worship. *World Tourist Attractions* also contains three appendices: world festivals, such as Mardi Gras and Bastille Day; international and national travel associations, such as ABTA; and international dialling codes.

It must be stressed that the entries included in this book can only be a *selection* of the thousands of tourist attractions worldwide. Entries have been chosen to reflect a number of different criteria, and those that appear are not necessarily the most popular attractions in their given country. Columbus Travel Guides believes, however, that the attractions listed are representative of many of the world's unique places and thus demonstrate some of the motivating factors encouraging today's generation of travellers.

Columbus Travel Guides would like to thank the many tourist offices, embassies, high commissions, consulates, chambers of commerce, and public relations departments that assisted in the preparation of this edition. If there is anything that you would like to see expanded, clarified or included for the first time, or if you come across any information that is no longer accurate, please write to:

The Editor
Columbus Guide to World Tourist Attractions
Jordan House
47 Brunswick Place
London N1 6EB
United Kingdom
Tel: 44 (0)20 7608 6565
Fax: 44 (0)20 7608 6593
E-mail: kmeere@columbus-group.co.uk

contents

Americas

Maps	2-3

ARGENTINA
Iguaçú Falls	4
Los Glaciares National Park	4
Nahuel Huapi National Park	5

BOLIVIA
Lake Titicaca	5

BRAZIL
Iguaçú Falls	6
Statue of Christ the Redeemer	6
Sugar Loaf Mountain	7

CANADA
Algonquin Provincial Park	8
Banff National Park	8
CN Tower	9
Niagara Falls	10
Old Quebec	10

CHILE
Easter Island	11
Costa Rica	
Arenal Volcano	12
Monteverde Cloud Forest	12

CUBA
Old Havana	13

ECUADOR
Galapagos Islands	14

GUATEMALA
Tikal	14

JAMAICA
Dunn's River Falls	15

MEXICO
Chichén Itzá	15
Copper Canyon	16
Monte Alban	16
National Museum of Anthropology	17
Palenque	17
Teotihuacán	18

PANAMA
Panama Canal	19

PARAGUAY
Iguaçú Falls	19

PERU
Lake Titicaca	20
Machu Picchu	20

USA
Alcatraz Island	21
Central Park	22
Death Valley	22
Empire State Building	23
Freedom Trail	23
Golden Gate Bridge	24
Graceland	25
Grand Canyon	25
Hawaii Volcanoes National Park	26
Hollywood Walk of Fame	26
Hoover Dam	27
Independence National Historical Park	28
Kennedy Space Center	28
Las Vegas Strip	29
Lincoln Memorial	30

Contents

Metropolitan Museum of Art	30
Mount Rushmore National Memorial	31
National Air and Space Museum	32
Niagara Falls	32
Rock and Roll Hall of Fame	33
Statue of Liberty	33
Universal Studios Florida	34
Walt Disney World	35
White House	35
Yellowstone National Park	36
Yosemite National Park	36

VENEZUELA
Angel Falls	37

Europe

Maps	40-41

AUSTRIA
Giant Ferris Wheel	42
Hofburg Palace	42
Kunsthistorisches Museum	43
Schönbrunn Palace	43

BELGIUM
Flanders Fields	44
Manneken-Pis	45

CZECH REPUBLIC
Charles Bridge	45
Prague Castle	46

DENMARK
Legoland	46
Little Mermaid	47
Tivoli Gardens	47

ENGLAND
Big Ben	48
Blackpool Pleasure Beach	49
British Airways London Eye	49
British Museum	50
Cambridge University	50
Canterbury Cathedral	51
Hadrian's Wall	52
Millennium Dome	52
National Gallery	53
Oxford University	53
Roman Baths and Pump Room	54
St Paul's Cathedral	55
Stonehenge	55

Tower of London	56
Westminster Abbey	56
York Minster	57

FRANCE
Arc de Triomphe	58
Bayeux Tapestry	58
Cave of Lascaux	59
Chartres Cathedral	59
Château de Chenonceau	60
Château de Versailles	60
Cité des Sciences et de l'Industrie	61
Disneyland Paris	61
Eiffel Tower	62
Musée du Louvre	63
Musée d'Orsay	63
Notre Dame Cathedral	64
Pont du Gard	64
Pont St-Bénézet	65

GERMANY
Brandenburg Gate	65
Cologne Cathedral	66
Englischer Garten	66
Neuschwanstein Castle	67
Pergamon Museum	67
Reichstag	68

GREECE
Acropolis	69
Delphi	69
Knossos	70
National Archaeological Museum of Athens	70

HUNGARY
Buda Castle Palace	71
Budapest Central Synagogue	71
Fisherman's Bastion	72

ICELAND
Geysir	73
Perlan	73

IRELAND
Blarney Castle	74
Cliffs of Moher	74
Glendalough	75
Trinity College Dublin	75

ITALY
Colosseum	76
Doge's Palace	77
Florence Duomo	77
Pantheon	78

v

Contents

Pompeii	78
Ponte Vecchio	79
Roman Forum	79
St Peter's Basilica	80
Sistine Chapel	80
Tower of Pisa	81
Uffizi Gallery	81

MALTA
Hagar Qim	82

NETHERLANDS
Anne Frank House	83
Keukenhof Gardens	83
Rijksmuseum	84
Van Gogh Museum	84

NORTHERN IRELAND
Giants Causeway	85

NORWAY
Bryggen	86
Hardanger Fjord	86

POLAND
Auschwitz	87
Wawel Royal Castle	87

PORTUGAL
Castle of St George	88
Tower of Belém	89

RUSSIA
Kremlin	89
St Basil's Cathedral	90
State Hermitage Museum	90

SCOTLAND
Edinburgh Castle	91

SPAIN
Alhambra	91
Guggenheim Museum Bilbao	92
La Sagrada Familia	93
Monasterio de San Lorenzo de El Escorial	93
Prado Museum	94
Roman Aqueduct at Segovia	94
Santiago de Compostela Cathedral	95
Seville Cathedral	95

SWEDEN
Drottningholm Palace	96
Museum of National Antiquities	96

SWITZERLAND
Jet d'Eau	97
Jungfraujoch	98

TURKEY
Blue Mosque	98
Ephesus	99
St Sophia	99
Topkapi Palace	100
Troy	100

WALES
Caernarfon Castle	101

Africa & the Middle East

Maps	104-105

BOTSWANA
Moremi Wildlife Reserve	106

EGYPT
Abu Simbel	106
Egyptian Museum	107
Pyramids and Sphinx	107
Temple of Karnak	108
Valley of the Kings	108

ISRAEL
Masada	109
Temple Mount	109
Western Wall	110

JORDAN
Petra	111

KENYA
Maasai Mara Game Reserve	111
Mount Kenya National Park	112

MOROCCO
Medina in Fez	113
Tour Hassan	113

SOUTH AFRICA
Cape Point	114
Kruger National Park	114
Robben Island	115
Table Mountain	116

TANZANIA
Kilimanjaro National Park	116
Serengeti National Park	117

Contents

TUNISIA
Carthage 118
Medina in Tunis 118

YEMEN
Old City of Sana'a 119

ZAMBIA
Victoria Falls 119

ZIMBABWE
Great Zimbabwe Ruins 120
Victoria Falls 121

Asia & Australasia

Maps 124-125

AUSTRALIA
Kakadu National Park 126
Sydney Opera House 126
Uluru-Kata Tjuta National Park 127

CAMBODIA
Angkor Wat 127

CHINA
Forbidden City 128
Great Wall of China 129
Summer Palace 129
Terracotta Army 130
Three Gorges of the Yangtze River 130
Victoria Peak 131

INDIA
Ellora Temple Caves 131
Ghats at Varanasi 132
Indian Museum 133
Kaziranga National Park 133
Khajuraho 134
Palace of the Winds 134
Red Fort 135
Taj Mahal 135

INDONESIA
Prambanan Temples 136

JAPAN
Meiji Shrine 137
Mount Fuji 137
Sanjusangen-do Temple 138
Sensoji Temple 138

MALAYSIA
Batu Caves 139

Petronas Towers 139

NEW ZEALAND
Fiordland National Park 140
Tongariro National Park 141

PHILIPPINES
Banau Rice Terraces 141

SINGAPORE
Raffles Hotel 142

SRI LANKA
Sigiriya 143
Temple of the Tooth 143

THAILAND
Phang Nga Bay 144
Royal Barges National Museum 144
Royal Grand Palace 145

TIBET
Potala Palace 146

Appendices

Festivals 148
Travel Associations 154
International Dialling Codes 157

Index

Alphabetical 160
By Category 163

vii

section one
the americas

The numbers alongside the attractions below correspond to their locations on the maps overleaf, and not to the page numbers on which information on the attractions appear. Note that some attractions which straddle national frontiers and which have more than one entry in the text will likewise have more than one reference number on the map. For more detailed locations of these attractions consult the World Travel Atlas.

1	Iguaçú Falls (Argentina)	29	Machu Picchu
2	Los Glaciares National Park	30	Alcatraz Island
3	Nahuel Huapi National Park	31	Central Park
4	Lake Titicaca	32	Death Valley
5	Statue of Christ the Redeemer	33	Empire State Building
6	Iguaçú Falls (Brazil)	34	Freedom Trail
7	Sugar Loaf Mountain	35	Golden Gate Bridge
8	Algonquin Provincial Park	36	Graceland
9	Banff National Park	37	Grand Canyon
10	CN Tower	38	Hawaii Volcanoes National Park
11	Niagara Falls (Canada)	39	Hollywood Walk of Fame
12	Old Quebec	40	Hoover Dam
13	Easter Island	41	Independence National Historical Park
14	Arenal Volcano	42	Kennedy Space Center
15	Monteverde Cloud Forest	43	Las Vegas Strip
16	Old Havana	44	Lincoln Memorial
17	Galapagos Islands	45	Metropolitan Museum of Art
18	Tikal	46	Mount Rushmore National Memorial
19	Dunn's River Falls	47	National Air and Space Museum
20	Chichén Itzá	48	Rock and Roll Hall of Fame
21	Copper Canyon	49	Niagra Falls (USA)
22	Monte Alban	50	Statue of Liberty
23	National Museum of Anthropology	51	Universal Studios Florida
24	Palenque	52	Walt Disney World
25	Teotihuacán	53	White House
26	Panama Canal	54	Yellowstone National Park
27	Iguaçú Falls (Paraguay)	55	Yosemite National Park
28	Lake Titicaca	56	Angel Falls

The Americas – **Maps**

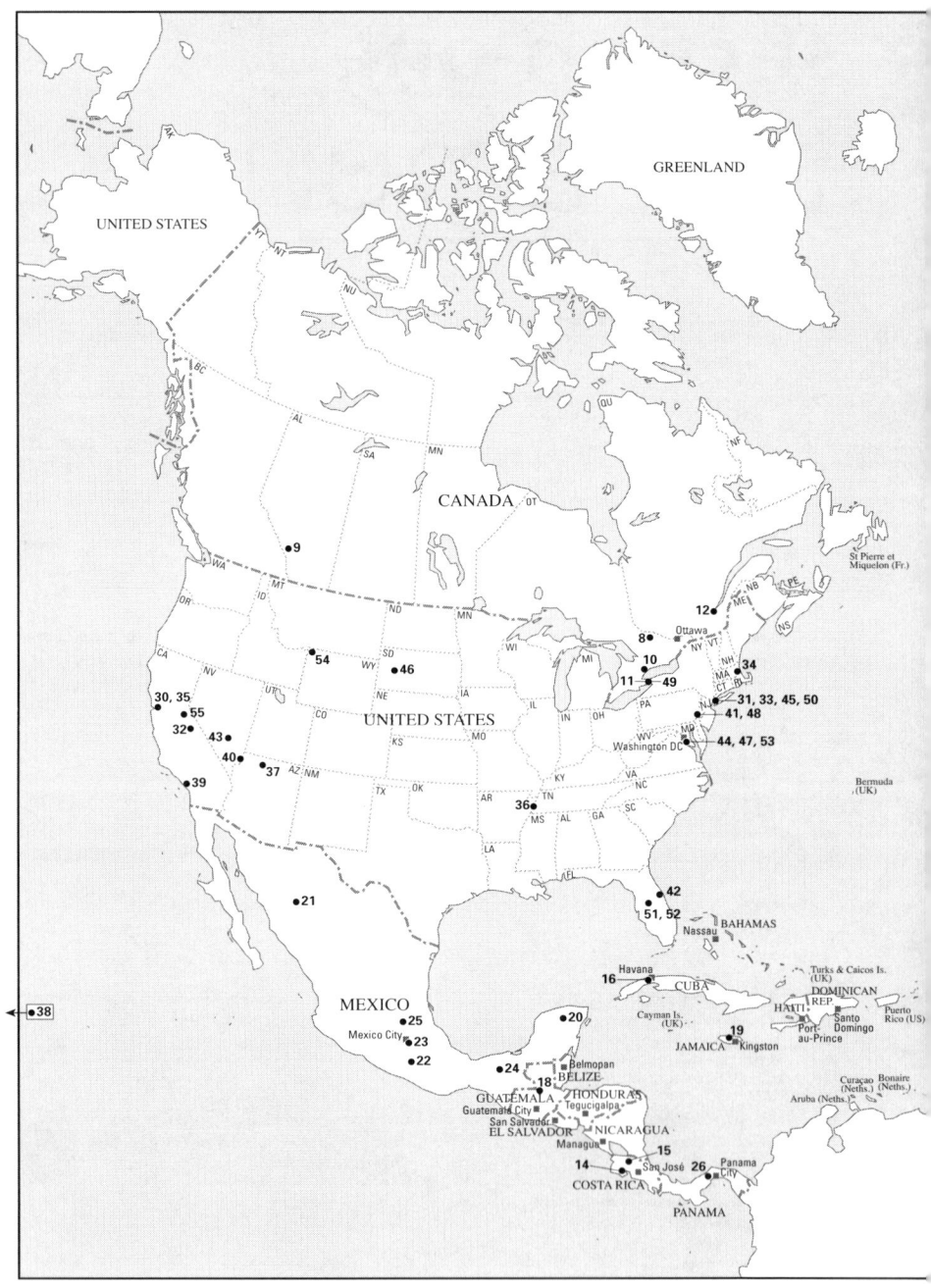

The Americas – **Maps**

3

ARGENTINA

Iguaçú Falls – see also Brazil

Contact Address
Iguaçú National Park, Victoria Aguirre Street 66, 3379 Puerto Iguazu, Province Misiones
Tel: (37) 57 42 07 22. Fax: (37) 57 42 03 82.

Location
1400km (870 miles) north of Buenos Aires, sharing the borders of Brazil, Argentina, and Paraguay.

Transportation
Air: Ministro Pistarini Airport (Buenos Aires). Coach: services from Buenos Aires.

Opening Times
Daily 24 hours.

Admission Fees
US$5.

Visitors Annually
Not available.

Special Needs
None.

Restrictions
None.

Description
Iguaçú Falls fittingly receives its name from the Guarani Indian word meaning 'great waters'. Surrounded by the virgin jungle of Iguaçú National Park, home to 2000 species of flora and 400 species of bird, the Iguaçú River divides into 275 separate falls, the highest reaching 70m (230ft). Besides taking in the stunning view, visitors may partake in kayaking, canoeing and other water sports. Nearby historic Jesuit Mission ruins are also popular.

Los Glaciares National Park

Contact Address
Avenida del Libertador 1302, 9405 El Calafate, Province Santa Cruz
Tel: (11) 29 02 49 10 05.

Location
48km (30 miles) from El Calafate.

Transportation
Air: Ministro Pistarini Airport (Buenos Aires). Coach: services from El Calafate.

Opening Times
Daily 24 hours.

Admission Fees
US$5.

Visitors Annually
Not available.

 Cultural Natural Religious

The Americas – **Argentina/Bolivia**

Special Needs
None.

Restrictions
None.

Description
Some 40 per cent of *Los Glaciares National Park*'s 6600 sq kilometres (2548 sq miles) is covered by vast ice fields that hold 47 major glaciers. The most important glacier is *Upsala*, but the most popular is the mighty *Moreno* glacier, where massive chunks of ice shear off and fall into *Lago Argentino*, the largest lake in Argentina, to form icebergs.

Nahuel Huapi National Park

Contact Address
Administrative offices, Avenida San Martin 24, 8400 San Carlos de Bariloche, Rio Negro Province
Tel/fax: (29) 44 43 04 76.

Location
Province of Rio Negro, Patagonia, Argentina.

Transportation
Air: Ministro Pistarini Airport (Buenos Aires). Coach: services from San Carlos de Bariloche.

Opening Times
Daily 24 hours.

Admission Fees
US$5.

Visitors Annually
Not available.

Special Needs
None.

Restrictions
Restricted areas exist.

Description
Occupying 710,000 hectares (2741 sq miles), *Nahuel Huapi National Park* is something like the Yosemite of South America. The main city, *Bariloche*, is renowned in Argentina as a resort destination, offering such alpine activities as skiing, trout fishing, and golf. The park, however, offers trekkers and sightseers bountiful natural beauty, including an extinct volcano called *Tronador*, a sprawling glacial lake, alpine meadows and amazing fauna.

BOLIVIA

Lake Titicaca – see *Peru*

> Please see the map at the front of each section
> for the location of attractions.

🏛 Historical   Man-made   Amusement

BRAZIL

Iguaçú Falls – see also Argentina

Contact Address
Iguaçú National Park, Catarata's Road, BR369
Tel: (45) 572 1900 *or* (0800) 451 516 (Visitor Centre). Fax: (45) 572 2027.
Web site: www.iguassu.com.br

Location
1480km (920 miles) south of Rio de Janeiro, sharing the borders of Brazil, Argentina, and Paraguay.

Transportation
Air: Foz de Iguaçú International Airport. Coach: services from Curitiba. Car: BR-277 from Curitiba, then BR-469.

Opening Times
Daily 0800-1800 (except Mon am).

Admission Fees
R$6.

Visitors Annually
1,000,000 (from Brazil).

Special Needs
Elevator access for disabled.

Restrictions
None.

Description
Iguaçú Falls fittingly receives its name from the Guarani Indian word meaning 'great waters'. Surrounded by the virgin jungle of Iguaçú National Park, home to 2000 species of flora and 400 species of bird, the Iguaçú River divides into 275 separate falls, the highest reaching 70m (230ft). Besides taking in the stunning view, visitors may partake in kayaking, canoeing and other water sports. Nearby historic Jesuit Mission ruins are also popular.

Statue of Christ the Redeemer

Contact Address
Embratur Tourist Office, Rua Uruguaiana 174, Rio de Janeiro, CEP 20.050-090
Tel: (21) 509 6017. Fax: (21) 509 7381.
E-mail: rio@embratur.gov.br
Web site: www.embratur.gov.br

Location
Corcovado Mountain, Tijuca National Park, Rio de Janeiro.

Transportation
Air: Rio de Janeiro International Airport. Coach: Novo Rio coach station.

Opening Times
Daily dawn-dusk.

Admission Fees
Free.

The Americas – **Brazil**

Visitors Annually
Not available.

Special Needs
None.

Restrictions
Summit not wheelchair accessible.

Description
The *Statue of Christ the Redeemer*, standing tall, overlooking the city of Rio de Janeiro with outstretched, welcoming arms, is perhaps the best-known symbol of this lively city. The statue sits atop Corcovado (hunchback) Mountain, and is located in *Tijuca National Park*, a lush spot for picnics and ambling. Visitors can access the base of the statue, which, at 709m (2326ft), affords superb views of Sugar Loaf Mountain, downtown Rio de Janeiro, and Rio's beaches.

Sugar Loaf Mountain

Contact Address
Embratur Tourist Office, Rua Uruguaiana 174, Rio de Janeiro, CEP 20.050-090
Tel: (21) 509 6017. Fax: (21) 509 7381.
E-mail: rio@embratur.gov.br
Web site: www.embratur.gov.br

Location
Praia Vermelha, Rio de Janeiro.

Transportation
Air: Rio de Janeiro International Airport. Coach: Novo Rio coach station.

Opening Times
Daily 0800-2200 (cable car).

Admission Fees
R$12 (cable car).

Visitors Annually
Not available.

Special Needs
None.

Restrictions
None.

Description
Shaped like a Victorian sugar loaf and 396m (1299ft) tall, *Sugar Loaf Mountain* stands as a natural welcome post to the city of Rio de Janeiro in Guanabara Bay. It offers excellent views of the city spread out below, and sunsets are said to be particularly spectacular. A cable car takes visitors to the top.

 Health? Currency? Passport Requirements? Contact Addresses? Airports? Public Holidays? Accommodation? Festivals? Nightlife? Climate? Duty Free? Visas? Excursions? Journey Times? Sport? – for all this, and more besides, consult the *World Travel Guide*.

Historical Man-made Amusement

CANADA

Algonquin Provincial Park

Contact Address
Algonquin Provincial Park, PO Box 219, Whitney, Ontario, K0J 2M0
Tel: (705) 633 5572 (information) *or* (1888) 668 7275 (reservations).
E-mail: info@algonquinpark.on.ca
Web site: www.algonquinpark.on.ca

Location
300km (186 miles) north of Toronto.

Transportation
Air: Pearson International Airport (Toronto). Coach: services from Toronto to Huntsville. Rail: Huntsville. Car: numerous entry points.

Opening Times
Daily 0800-2100; may vary seasonally.

Admission Fees
$10 (per vehicle per day); campers require extra permits; concessions available.

Visitors Annually
900,000.

Special Needs
Certain facilities and areas wheelchair accessible.

Restrictions
None.

Description
Algonquin Provincial Park was established in 1893 to develop a wildlife sanctuary in a rugged, beautiful part of southern Ontario. Soon after, it became popular with outdoors enthusiasts and canoeists because of its beautiful lakes, forests, bogs, rivers, cliffs and beaches. For campers and day visitors, *Highway 60* is the centre of events, offering campgrounds, walking trails, conducted hikes, and access to public wolf-howling sessions. Visitors can also soak up the history of the park in the *Logging Museum*, or in the *Algonquin Gallery*, which focuses on the artist Tom Thomson's (1877-1917) famous group of painters, the *Group of Seven* (Canada's first national school of painting).

Banff National Park

Contact Address
Banff Lake Louise Tourism Bureau, Box 1298, Banff, Alberta, T0L 0C0
Tel: (403) 762 8421. Fax: (403) 762 8163.
E-mail: info@BanffLakeLouise.com
Web site: www.BanffLakeLouise.com

Location
128km (80 miles) west of Calgary.

Transportation
Air: Calgary International Airport. Coach: services from Calgary. Car: Trans-Canada Highway 1.

Opening Times
Daily 24 hours.

 Cultural *Natural* *Religious*

The Americas – **Canada**

Admission Fees
$5 (per person per day); concessions available.

Visitors Annually
4,500,000.

Special Needs
Wheelchair accessible. Facilities for the hearing impaired.

Restrictions
None.

Description
Canada's first national park, *Banff National Park* was created by the Canadian government in 1885 in recognition of the area's natural beauty and wildlife. Visitors continue to be awestruck by the stunning vistas of the *Rocky Mountains* and the sight of elk grazing only metres away. The park has 6641 sq kilometres (2564 sq miles) of mountains, rivers, forests, lakes, glaciers and hot springs, and is home to wolves, mountain goats, eagles and grizzly bears, along with the notorious – and sometimes dangerous – elk. The most famous man-made addition to the area is the *Banff Springs Hotel*, completed in 1888.

CN Tower

Contact Address
301 Front Street West, Toronto, Ontario, M5V 2T6
Tel: (416) 360 8500. Fax: (416) 601 4713.
Web site: www.cntower.ca

Location
301 Front Street West, Toronto.

Transportation
Air: Pearson International Airport (Toronto). Rail: Union Station. Subway: Union Station.

Opening Times
Sun-Thurs 0900-2200; Fri and Sat 0900-2300; daily 1100-1900 (entertainment centre).

Admission Fees
C$15.99; plus C$4.75 (Sky Pod); C$7.50 (entertainment centre); concessions available.

Visitors Annually
2,000,000.

Special Needs
Wheelchair accessible.

Restrictions
None.

Description
As the world's tallest free-standing structure, the *CN Tower* is the defining figure of Toronto's lakefront skyline. Completed in 1976, the 550m (1804ft) tower offers stunning views of Toronto and Lake Ontario. Visitors may enjoy a meal at the revolving *360 Restaurant*, walk across a glass floor on the 113th storey or get an even better view from the *Sky Pod*. There is also a collection of entertainment venues at the base of the tower, including two motion simulator rides.

> Please see the map at the front of each section
> for the location of attractions.

Historical   *Man-made*   *Amusement*

The Americas – **Canada**

Niagara Falls – see also USA

Contact Address
Niagara Falls Tourism, 5515 Stanley Avenue, Niagara Falls, Ontario, L2G 3X4
Tel: (905) 356 6061.
E-mail: info@niagarafallstourism.com
Web site: www.niagarafallstourism.com

Location
130km (81 miles) west of Toronto, Ontario.

Transportation
Air: Buffalo Niagara Airport; Pearson International Airport (Toronto). Car: QEW.

Opening Times
Not applicable.

Admission Fees
Not applicable.

Visitors Annually
14,000,000.

Special Needs
Wheelchair accessible.

Restrictions
None.

Description
Niagara Falls has attracted millions of visitors ever since the first human inhabitants set eyes on it, and it is now one of the most popular tourist destinations in North America. Niagara is not the highest waterfall in the world, but it carries a staggering volume of 168,000 cubic metres (219,600 cubic yards) of water per minute over a drop of 51m (167ft), making it one of the natural wonders of the world. The surrounding town, a notorious North American honeymoon destination, offers a wealth of visitor activities, including a casino, as well as land and boat tours of the falls.

Old Québec

Contact Address
Tourisme Québec, PO Box 979, Montreal, Québec, H3C 2W3
Tel: (514) 873 2015 or (877) 266 5687. Fax: (514) 864 3838.
E-mail: lafayette@vieux-quebec.com
Web site: www.vieux-quebec.com

Location
North shore of the St Lawrence River, city centre of Québec.

Transportation
Air: Jean-Lesage International Airport. Rail: Gare du Palais.

Opening Times
Not applicable.

Admission Fees
Not applicable.

Visitors Annually
Not available.

 Cultural  Natural Religious

The Americas – **Canada/Chile**

Special Needs
Certain areas wheelchair accessible.

Restrictions
None.

Description
The only walled city north of Mexico, Québec was settled in 1608 as a fur trading post. Its fortified exterior and strategic position high above the St Lawrence River is a testament to the historical territorial tensions between the French and English that culminated in the Battle of the Plains of Abraham. Divided into two sections, *Haute* and *Basse*, the old town seems like an island of old Europe, with winding cobblestoned streets, seventeenth- and eighteenth-century buildings and churches, squares, parks and numerous monuments. The *Château Frontenac*, a Canadian landmark, is its most prominent building.

CHILE

Easter Island

Contact Address
SERNATUR, Tourist Information, Tuu Maheke s/n, esquina Apina, Easter Island
Tel: (32) 100 255. Fax: (32) 100 105.

Location
Pacific Ocean, 3800km (2360 miles) west of mainland Chile.

Transportation
Air: Mataveri Airport, Easter Island.

Opening Times
Not applicable.

Admission Fees
Not applicable.

Visitors Annually
20,000.

Special Needs
None.

Restrictions
None.

Description
A lonely volcanic island in the middle of the Pacific Ocean, as far away from Chile as from Tahiti, *Easter Island* is famous for its mysterious stone statues, or *moais*, that form an almost unbroken ring around the coast. Three hundred statues and related items of stonework grace the island, and scientists still speculate as to how its native inhabitants designed and forged the massive sculptures from volcanic rock, not to mention transporting them to the coast from inland quarries. About 2000 people inhabit the island, most living in the town of *Hanga Roa*.

Cardboarding? Harmattan? Chondla? Midnight Sun Coast? Gîte? Dude Ranch? Consolidation? Zorbing? Code Sharing?
– for all this, and more besides, consult the *World Travel Dictionary*.

Historical   *Man-made*   *Amusement*

COSTA RICA

Arenal Volcano

Contact Address
Arenal Observatory Lodge, PO Box 321-1007, Centro Colón, Costa Rica
Tel: 257 9489 *or* 695 5033. Fax: 257 4220.
E-mail: info@arenal-observatory.co.cr
Web site: www.arenal-observatory.co.cr

Location
90km (56 miles) northwest of San José.

Transportation
Air: Juan Santamaria International Airport (San José). Coach: services from San José and Ciudad Quesada. Car: Pan-American Highway.

Opening Times
Daily 0800-1600; night tours depart La Fortuna at 1800.

Admission Fees
US$15 (at gate); US$7 (in advance).

Visitors Annually
Not available.

Special Needs
Not applicable.

Restrictions
None.

Description
One of the world's most active volcanoes, *Arenal*, with its classic cone-shaped crater, can be seen from anywhere in the surrounding area, even the cafés of nearby town La Fortuna. Research centre *Arenal Observatory Lodge* provides excellent views and *Arenal Volcano National Park* offers trails around the slopes and views of the summit; there are also hot spring spas with views in the area. The volcano's intermittent daily eruptions create vast clouds of ash in the sky and huge booms. At night, the view is even more spectacular, as molten rocks and lava tumble down the slopes, creating a pretty 'firework' display that is fortunately always at least five kilometres away.

Monteverde Cloud Forest

Contact Address
Monteverde Cloud Forest Preserve, Apdo 55-5655, Monteverde, Puntarenas, Costa Rica
Tel: 645 5122. Fax: 645 5034.
E-mail: montever@sol.racsa.co.cr
Web site: www.cct.or.cr *or* www.cloudforestalive.org

Location
Six kilometres (3.6 miles) southeast of Santa Elena de Monteverde.

Transportation
Air: Juan Santamaria International Airport (San José). Coach: services from Puntarenas to Santa Elena, and from San José to Monteverde. Car: Pan-American Highway to Kilometre #149.

 Cultural  *Natural*   *Religious*

The Americas – **Costa Rica/Cuba**

Opening Times
Daily 0700-1600.

Admission Fees
US$8.75; concessions available; US$15.25 (guided tours).

Visitors Annually
55,000.

Special Needs
Not applicable.

Restrictions
None.

Description
Straddling the Continental Divide and covering 170 sq kilometres (66 sq miles), this forest has its head – and its feet – in the clouds. The ever-present drizzle and mist is home to six different vegetation habitats, over 100 mammal species, 400 bird species, 120 amphibian species and at least 2500 plant species. Access to the high level of biodiversity is through extensive trails, shelters deep within the forest for overnight camping, and a 300-ft suspension bridge that takes visitors from ground level high up into the canopy of the forest. There is also a *Visitor Centre*, *Butterfly Centre*, *Orchid Garden*, *Serpentarium* and *Hummingbird Gallery*.

CUBA

Old Havana

Contact Address
Infotur, 5ta Avenida esq.112, Miramar, La Habana
Tel: 247 036. Fax: 243 977.

Location
Havana city centre.

Transportation
Air: Havana Jose Marti International Airport.

Opening Times
Not applicable.

Admission Fees
Not applicable.

Visitors Annually
1,600,000.

Special Needs
Wheelchair accessible.

Restrictions
None.

Description
Old Havana, with its overhanging balconies and smart hotels, harks back to Cuba's days as a colonial outpost and its subsequent era as a glamorous, sophisticated Caribbean hub. Many of its colonial buildings, majestic boulevards, elegant plazas and tiny side streets have been restored, attracting more and more visitors with each passing year. The *Plaza de la Catedral*, dominated by the towers of the *Catedral de San Christobal de La Habana*, perhaps best captures Old Havana's spirit and history and is filled with handicraft makers on weekends.

Historical Man-made Amusement

The Americas – **Ecuador/Guatemala**

ECUADOR

Galapagos Islands

Contact Address
Avenue Eloy Alfaro, N32-300 y Carlos Tobar, Quito, Ecuador
Tel: (2) 228 304 *or* (5) 520 489. Fax: (2) 229 330.

Location
966km (600 miles) off the west coast of Ecuador, Pacific Ocean, on the Equator.

Transportation
Air: Isla Baltra Airport.

Opening Times
Not applicable.

Admission Fees
Not applicable.

Visitors Annually
60,000.

Description
Comprising 13 large and six small islands, the *Galapagos Islands* are historically famous for being the inspiration for Charles Darwin's theory of evolution. Nowadays, however, the most famous residents are probably the giant tortoises, after whom the islands were named. There is also abundant unusual wildlife of many kinds, including birds, iguana, sea lions and dolphins, making the area an ecological wonderland.

GUATEMALA

Tikal

Contact Address
Guatemala Tourism Commission (INGUAT), Apartado postal 1020-A, 001004 Guatemala City
Tel: 331 1333. Fax: 331 4416.
E-mail: inguat@guate.net
Web site: www.guatemala.travel.com.gt

Location
50km (30 miles) north of Flores; 300km (190 miles) north of Guatemala City.

Transportation
Air: Guatemala City La Aurora International Airport. Car: Main road from Flores.

Opening Times
Daily 0600-1800.

Admission Fees
Free.

Visitors Annually
Not available.

 Cultural   *Natural*   *Religious*

The Americas – **Guatemala/Jamaica/Mexico**

Description
Unlike many other ancient Mayan sites, the wonders of *Tikal* are hidden deep within the rainforest. Visitors gaze at its towering 44m-high (144ft) pyramid and ancient plazas to an accompaniment of jungle sounds from monkeys, tree frogs, parrots and whatever else happens to be lurking in the treetop canopy. At its zenith, the settlement was home to an estimated 100,000 Maya. Now located in *Tikal National Park*, there is much wildlife to be seen, as well as an on-site museum.

JAMAICA

Dunn's River Falls

Contact Address
Dunn's River Falls and Park, Ocho Rios, St Ann, Jamaica
Tel: (876) 974 2857.

Location
Ocho Rios, Jamaica.

Transportation
Air: Norman Manley International Airport. Car: A3 North Coast Highway.

Opening Times
Daily 0900-1700.

Admission Fees
US$6; concessions available.

Visitors Annually
1,000,000.

Special Needs
None.

Restrictions
None.

Description
Dunn's River Falls bring to mind a lush Caribbean idyll. The area consists of a large number of waterfalls cascading over rock terraces on their way down to a nearby beach. The falls are shallow enough to allow visitors to climb all 183m (600ft) of them under a tropical shower.

MEXICO

Chichén Itzá

Contact Address
Secretaria de Turismo (SECTUR), Presidente Mazaryck 172, Colonia Polanco, 11570 Mexico DF, Mexico
Tel: (5) 254 8920. Fax: (5) 254 0942.

Location
193km (120 miles) west of Cancún.

 Historical   Man-made   Amusement

The Americas – **Mexico**

Transportation
Air: Mexico City International. Coach: services from Cancún or Mérida. Car: Autopista from Cancún or Mérida.
Opening Times
Daily 0800-1700.
Admission Fees
US$4; free Sun.
Visitors Annually
Not available.
Description
Deep within the jungles of Yucatan lies *Chichen Itza*, one of the best sites of the mysterious Mayan civilisation. It flourished, the site of countless human sacrifices, until about the year 1200, when it was mysteriously abandoned. Highlights of the site include the largest Mayan ball court ever discovered, an astronomical observatory, a sacred well and a large, astronomically aligned pyramid.

Copper Canyon

Contact Address
Secretaria de Turismo (SECTUR), Presidente Mazaryck 172, Colonia Polanco, 11570 Mexico DF, Mexico
Tel: (5) 254 8920. Fax: (5) 254 0942.
Location
386km (240 miles) south of El Paso.
Transportation
Air: Mexico City International Airport. Rail: Copper Canyon Railway from Los Mochis or Chihuahua City to Creel. Coach: services from Chihuahua City to Creel. Car: Highway 16 to Creel.
Opening Times
Not applicable.
Admission Fees
Not applicable.
Visitors Annually
130,000.
Description
One of the largest canyon systems in the world, *Copper Canyon* is a land of mountains, rivers, waterfalls, desert and forest. Four of the canyons are deeper than Arizona's famous Grand Canyon, although none of them are as wide. Perhaps the most famous attraction for visitors is the *Chihuahua al Pacífico Railway*, a scenic journey that crosses 36 major bridges, travels through 87 tunnels and climbs to a height of 2438m (8000ft) before descending to sea level.

Monte Alban

Contact Address
Office of Administration, Archaeological Site, Pino Suarez 715, Centro, CP 68000
Tel: (9) 516 1215.
Web site: www.montealban.org.mx

 Cultural   Natural   Religious

The Americas – **Mexico**

Location
Ten kilometres (six miles) from Oaxaca.

Transportation
Air: Mexico City International Airport. Coach: shuttle services from Oaxaca. Car: access from Oaxaca.

Opening Times
Daily 0800-1800.

Admission Fees
US$2.50; free Sun.

Visitors Annually
Not available.

Description
Another of Mexico's famous ancient ruins, *Monte Alban* was at one time home to 50,000 Zapotec people. The builders of Monte Alban artificially levelled the mountaintop on which it sits and which overlooks the three valleys of Oaxaca. The site features a Zapotec ball court, a labyrinth of tunnels and a prominent central plaza.

National Museum of Anthropology

Contact Address
Paseo de la Reforma, Chapultepec Park, Mexico City
Tel: (5) 553 1902.

Location
Chapultepec Park, Mexico City.

Transportation
Air: Mexico City International Airport. Metro: Auditorio or Chapultepec.

Opening Times
Daily 0900-1900.

Admission Fees
US$2.50; free Sun.

Visitors Annually
400,000.

Description
Mexico's *National Museum of Anthropology* is one of the world's great museums, known not only for its vast and rich collection, but also for its simplicity of design. Opened in 1964, the exhibition halls surround a shallow pond shaded by a square concrete umbrella supported by a single pillar. The halls themselves house Mexico's greatest archaeological collection, celebrating the country's pre-Columbian inhabitants and its existing indigenous peoples.

Palenque

Contact Address
Tourist Office, Plaza de Artesanías, Avenue Juárez, Palenque
Tel: (9) 345 0356.
Or: Secretaria de Turismo (SECTUR), Presidente Mazaryck 172, Colonia Polanco, 11570 Mexico DF, Mexico
Tel: (5) 254 8920. Fax: (5) 254 0942.

 Historical   *Man-made*   *Amusement*

The Americas – **Mexico**

Location
Palenque National Park, 14.5km (nine miles) from Palenque, in the state of Chiapas.

Transportation
Air: Mexico City International Airport. Coach: services from Palenque. Car: access from Palenque.

Opening Times
Daily 0800-1730.

Admission Fees
US$2.50; free Sun.

Visitors Annually
Not available.

Description
Located in Chiapas, *Palenque* is one of the grandest of all Mayan ruins. Situated on a ledge picturesquely overlooking swampy plains to the north, and set in a backdrop of lush, green mountains, Palenque's most notable structures are the *Palace* and the *Temple of Inscriptions*. The site has yielded countless archaeological finds, and its broad, angular design has influenced various periods of architecture.

Teotihuacán

Contact Address
Secretaria de Turismo (SECTUR), Presidente Mazaryck 172, Colonia Polanco, 11570 Mexico DF, Mexico
Tel: (5) 254 8920. Fax: (5) 254 0942.

Location
50km (31 miles) northeast of Mexico City.

Transportation
Air: Mexico City International Airport. Coach: services from Mexico City. Car: main road from Mexico City.

Opening Times
Daily 0900-1800.

Admission Fees
US$2.50.

Visitors Annually
Not available.

Description
Teotihuacán grew to be the largest of Mexico's pre-Hispanic cities, with an estimated population of 200,000 during its zenith in the sixth century AD. Known for the geometric and symbolic arrangement of its monuments, its greatest building is the *Pyramid of the Sun*, standing at a height of 63m (207ft). It is joined on the Avenue of the Dead, Teotihuacán's main street, by another building of enormous size, the *Moon Pyramid*, which was originally part of a 'Moon Plaza'.

 Flight Times? Climate? Theme Parks? Time Zones? Museums? UNESCO Heritage Sites? Railways? Ski Resorts? Game Parks? – for all this, and more besides, consult the *World Travel Atlas*.

18   *Cultural*   *Natural*   *Religious*

PANAMA

Panama Canal

Contact Address
Panama Canal Authority, PO Box 5413, Miami, FL 33102
Tel: 1 (507) 272 3165. Fax: 1 (507) 272 1657.

Location
Runs for 69km (43 miles) northwest to southeast from the Atlantic to the Pacific oceans, across the Isthmus of Panama.

Transportation
Air: Tocument International Airport. Car: Inter-American Highway.

Opening Times
Daily 24hours; (Visitor Centre) daily 0900-1700.

Admission Fees
Free.

Visitors Annually
300,000.

Special Needs
Visitor Centre wheelchair accessible.

Restrictions
None.

Description
The idea of building a canal across the Isthmus of Panama was first raised as far back as the 1600s. It was not until 1880, however, that the French got around to making an attempt and failed miserably, with over 22,000 workers dying from malaria and yellow fever. The United States took a shot at it in 1904, and the first ship made its way across ten years later. Today, this 80km (50-mile) stretch of water is one of the most important and fantastic in the world, providing passage for over 12,000 ships every year. An open-air balcony at *Miraflores Locks* offers visitors good views of the electrical locomotives or 'mules' pulling giant ships through as water levels are balanced.

PARAGUAY

Iguaçú Falls – see Argentina and Brazil

Health? Currency? Passport Requirements? Contact Addresses? Airports? Public Holidays? Accommodation? Festivals? Nightlife? Climate? Duty Free? Visas? Excursions? Journey Times? Sport? – for all this, and more besides, consult the *World Travel Guide*.

Historical Man-made Amusement

19

*The Americas – **Peru***

PERU

Lake Titicaca

Contact Address
Dirección Regional de Tourismo, Jr. Ayacucho 682, Puno
Tel: (054) 351 261.

Location
Forms a natural border between Peru and Bolivia.

Transportation
Air: Lima Jorge Chavez International Airport. Car: Highway 3.

Opening Times
Not applicable.

Admission Fees
Not applicable.

Visitors Annually
Not available.

Special Needs
None.

Restrictions
None.

Description
At an elevation of 3820m (12,533ft), *Lake Titicaca* is one of the world's highest navigable lakes. It is named after the native word for 'rock of the puma', and its shape bears a likeness to this animal when viewed from above. Measuring 233km (145 miles) from northwest to southeast, it stands out as a refreshing patch of clear, blue water in its dry surroundings. *Sun Island* is the most mysterious spot on the lake, with a variety of Inca sites as well as an archaeological museum. The lake has been revered in history, featuring prominently in Inca creation myths.

Machu Picchu

Contact Address
Oficina de Información, Avenida de la Cultura 734, Cusco
Tel: (084) 263 176. Fax: (084) 223 761.
E-mail: direccion@tourcusco.com
Web site: turismo@tourcusco.com

Location
112km (70 miles) northwest of Cusco.

Transportation
Air: Lima Jorge Chavez International Airport. Rail: services from Cusco to Puente Ruinas train station, Machu Picchu. Coach: shuttle service from train station to citadel. Car: Highway 101.

Opening Times
Daily 0730-1700.

The Americas – Peru/United States of America

Admission Fees
US$17 (four-day trail); US$12 (two-day trail); US$10 (arrival by train); concessions available.

Visitors Annually
270,000.

Special Needs
Wheelchair access possible with Peruvian guide.

Restrictions
None.

Description
This famous Inca site is the most mysterious, most spectacular and best known in South America. Its existence was known only to a few locals until an American explorer happened upon it in 1911. Numerous archaeological visits have been made since; however, much of the site remains a mystery, even though it is virtually intact, right down to the high quality of its stonework. *Machu Picchu* possesses the last *Inihuatana* (sundial) remaining in South America; it is also located within an incredible cloud forest; trekking along the Inca Trail is possible.

UNITED STATES OF AMERICA

Alcatraz Island

Contact Address
National Park Service, Alcatraz Island, Golden Gate National Recreation HQ, Fort Mason, Building 201, San Francisco CA94123
Tel: (415) 705 1042 *or* 556 0560.

Location
San Francisco Bay, San Francisco, California.

Transportation
Only access is by Blue and Gold Fleet Ferry from Pier 41, Fisherman's Wharf, San Francisco; reservations required.

Opening Times
Daily 0930-1830 (summer); 0930-1630 (winter).

Admission Fees
US$14.50; concessions available.

Visitors Annually
1,350,000.

Special Needs
Wheelchair accessible.

Description
Alcatraz is the notorious American super-prison located on *Alcatraz Island*, a remote rocky outcrop in San Francisco Bay. The prison was used between 1934 and 1963, designed to remove kidnappers, racketeers and predatory criminals far from the outside world. The prison was home to some very illustrious alumni, including famous gangsters Al Capone, 'Machine Gun' Kelly and Robert 'The Birdman' Stroud. Today, the island is a venue for tourists rather than criminals, although a few former prisoners and guards can be heard on the prison's audio tour.

Historical    Man-made   Amusement

The Americas – **United States of America**

Central Park

Contact Address
Central Park Conservancy, 14 East 60th Street, New York, NY 10022
Tel: (212) 364 3444 *or* 794 6564 (Dairy Visitor Centre).
Web site: www.centralparknyc.org

Location
Between 59th and 110th streets; Dairy/Visitor Centre mid-Park at 65th Street, New York.

Transportation
Air: La Guardia International Airport or John F Kennedy International Airport. Rail: Grand Central Station. Subway: Fifth Avenue, 59th Street Columbus Circle.

Opening Times
Park: daily 24 hours. Dairy: Tues-Sun 1000-1700 (Apr-Oct), 1000-1600 (Oct-Mar).

Admission Fees
None.

Visitors Annually
Not available.

Special Needs
Certain areas wheelchair accessible.

Restrictions
None.

Description
Completed in 1873, *Central Park* was originally designed to be 341 hectares (843 acres) of rural paradise in what was then the out-of-the-way northern reaches of New York. Now, almost in the dead centre of the city, Central Park is part of the very fabric of New York. Apart from being a refreshing patch of green space in the middle of a very dense and busy city, Central Park has a cultural side, with public programmes offered by the Central Park Conservancy, as well as a zoo, dairy visitor centre, fountains and a skating rink.

Death Valley National Park

Contact Address
PO Box 579, Death Valley, CA 92328
Tel: (760) 786 2331. Fax: (760) 786 3283.
Web site: www.nps.gov/deva

Location
Southeastern California and parts of Nevada.

Transportation
Air: McCarran International Airport (Las Vegas). Car: Highway 190, Highway 95, Interstate 15.

Opening Times
Visitor Centre: 0800-1800.

Admission Fees
US$10 (per vehicle, valid for seven days).

Visitors Annually
Not available.

Special Needs
None.

 Cultural   *Natural*    *Religious*

Restrictions
None.

Description
Although only a national park since 1994, *Death Valley* has long been prized for its unique wildlife and austere desert beauty. Today, the park covers 13,500sq kilometres (5212 sq miles), the majority of which is wilderness. Although there are occasional winter storms, Death Valley's summers are notorious for temperatures in excess of 48°C (120°F). Nevertheless, Death Valley attracts many visitors to view wildflowers, snow-covered peaks, sand dunes and abandoned mines.

Empire State Building

Contact Address
350 Fifth Avenue, New York, NY 10118
Tel: (212) 736 3100 *or* 279 9777 (Skyride). Fax (212) 947 1360.
E-mail: info@esbnyc.com
Web site: www.esbnyc.com

Location
350 Fifth Avenue, Manhattan, New York.

Transportation
Air: La Guardia International Airport or John F Kennedy International Airport. Rail: Grand Central Station. Coach: Port Authority Bus Terminal. Subway: 34th Street.

Opening Times
Daily 0930-2400.

Admission Fees
US$7; concessions available.

Visitors Annually
Not available.

Special Needs
Wheelchair accessible.

Restrictions
None.

Description
Completed in 1931, the *Empire State Building* is an enduring symbol of New York City and the USA. Built during an era of skyscraper wars, the Empire State Building (at 443.3 metres/1453 feet) overtook the then world's tallest building and fellow Art Deco gem, the nearby Chrysler Building. The building cost $40,948,900 in total, including the purchase of the land, and was completed (ahead of schedule) in one year and 45 days. Visitors may visit the two observatories, one on the 86th and one on the 102nd floor, as well as a virtual-reality movie theatre with *Skyride*.

Freedom Trail

Contact Address
Freedom Trail Foundation, 3 School Street, Boston, MA 02108
Tel: (617) 227 8800. Fax: (617) 227 2498.
E-mail: ftfoffice@aol.com
Web site: www.thefreedomtrail.org

 Historical    Man-made   Amusement

The Americas – United States of America

Location
Trail begins at Boston Common, central Boston.

Transportation
Air: Logan International Airport. Subway: Park Street. Car: Massachusetts Turnpike.

Opening Times
Most sites daily 0930-1700 (summer); 1000-1600 (winter); some exceptions.

Admission Fees
Free; except for three sites charging under US$3.

Visitors Annually
3,000,000.

Special Needs
Most sites wheelchair accessible.

Restrictions
None.

Description
The *Freedom Trail* consists of a four-kilometre (2.5-mile) walking tour of historic Boston and Charlestown, encompassing 16 sites and structures of historical significance to both the city and the United States. Sites include: the ship, the *USA Constitution*, which saw battle against France and Britain; *Paul Revere House*, the one-time home of the quintessential American Patriot; and *Granary Burying Ground*, where famous Declaration of Independence signers Samuel Adams, Robert Treat Paine and John Hancock are buried.

Golden Gate Bridge

Contact Address
PO Box 9000, Presibio Station, San Francisco, CA 94129
Tel: (415) 921 5858. Fax: (415) 457 2892.
Web site: www.goldengatebridge.org

Location
San Francisco Bay, San Francisco, California.

Transportation
Air: San Francisco International Airport. Car: US-101.

Opening Times
Daily 24 hours (roadway and bicycle access); 0500-2100 (pedestrian east sidewalk).

Admission Fees
US$3 (southbound toll per car).

Visitors Annually
9,000,000.

Special Needs
Certain areas wheelchair accessible.

Restrictions
No rollerskating or rollerblading.

Description
San Francisco's best-known landmark, the *Golden Gate Bridge*, stretches 1966m (6,50ft) across San Francisco Bay, connecting the city with the Northern Counties. The suspension towers reach a height of 227m (746ft) and the clearance over the channel below is 67m (220ft). Viewing areas are located at both ends of the pedestrians' east sidewalk. Bicycles can use the sidewalk 24 hours a day, while cars have 24-hour access to the bridge.

Cultural   Natural   Religious

The Americas – **United States of America**

Graceland

Contact Address
PO Box 16508, Memphis, TN 38186
Tel: (901) 332 3322. Fax: (901) 332 1636.
E-mail: graceland@ixlmemphis.com
Web site: www.elvis-presley.com

Location
16km (ten miles) from Memphis, Tennessee.

Transportation
Air: Memphis International Airport. Car: exit 5-B off I-55.

Opening Times
Mon-Sat 0830-1700; Sun 0930-1600; closed Tues (Nov-Feb).

Admission Fees
US$12 (Mansion tour); US$22 (Platinum tour); concessions available.

Visitors Annually
600,000.

Special Needs
Mostly wheelchair accessible. Facilities for the hearing impaired.

Restrictions
None.

Description
Graceland is America's monument to one of its favourite musicians and icons, Elvis Presley. The 'King' died in 1977 and Graceland has been open to the public since 1982, becoming a shrine to his music and his legacy. The site now includes far more than just Elvis' home. Visitors can tour Elvis' two jet planes, shop at *Graceland Plaza* or stay overnight at the *Heartbreak Hotel*.

Grand Canyon

Contact Address
PO Box 129, Grand Canyon, Arizona, 86023
Tel: (520) 638 7888.
Web site: www.thecanyon.com *or* www.nps.gov/grca

Location
129km (80 miles) from Flagstaff, Arizona.

Transportation
Air: Grand Canyon Airport (local), McCarran International Airport (Las Vegas) or Phoenix Sky Harbor International Airport. Coach: services from Phoenix. Car: 4-5 hours from Phoenix or Las Vegas.

Opening Times
Daily 24 hours (South Rim: all year; North Rim: mid-May to mid-Oct).

Admission Fees
US$20 (per vehicle); US$10 (per pedestrian or cyclist).

Visitors Annually
5,000,000.

 Historical    *Man-made*   *Amusement*

The Americas – **United States of America**

Special Needs
Some areas wheelchair accessible.

Restrictions
Explorations of the canyon can be physically challenging.

Description
One of the seven natural wonders of the world, the *Grand Canyon* is a stunning geological formation that is synonymous for many with the majestic desert landscape of America's west. The canyon flows (in terms of river miles) for 365km (227 miles) and reaches a vertical depth of 1829m (6000ft) and a width of 29km (18 miles). Visitors can take in the breathtaking view from the rim or make prolonged explorations within the canyon as well. Visitors should be aware that the Grand Canyon is divided into three geographically separated areas: the South Rim, the North Rim and the inner canyon.

Hawaii Volcanoes National Park

Contact Address
PO Box 52, Hawaii Volcanoes National Park, HI 96718
Tel: (808) 985 6000. Fax: (808) 967 8186.
Web site: www.nps.gov/havo

Location
48km (30 miles) from Hilo, Hawaii.

Transportation
Car: Highway 11.

Opening Times
Daily 24 hours.

Admission Fees
US$10 (per vehicle); US$5 (per pedestrian or cyclist).

Visitors Annually
2,500,000.

Special Needs
Certain facilities and areas wheelchair accessible.

Restrictions
None.

Description
Established in 1916, *Hawaii Volcanoes National Park* embraces 878 sq kilometres (339 sq miles) and ranges from sea level to the top of *Mauna Loa*, the world's tallest volcano at 4169m (13,677ft). Seventy million years of volcanic activity is on display, encompassing the creation of Hawaii out of the ocean to the evolution of its complex and unique ecosystems. The park also offers visitors views of *Kilauea*, the world's most active volcano.

Hollywood Walk of Fame

Contact Address
Hollywood Chamber of Commerce, 7018 Hollywood Boulevard, Hollywood, CA 90028
Tel: (323) 469 8311.
Web site: www.hollywoodchamber.net

Location
Hollywood Boulevard from Gower Street to La Brea Boulevard, Vine Street from Yucca Street

Cultural   *Natural*   *Religious*

The Americas – **United States of America**

to Sunset Boulevard, Los Angeles.

Transportation
Air: Los Angeles International Airport. Car: 101 Freeway.

Opening Times
Not applicable.

Admission Fees
Not applicable.

Visitors Annually
20,000,000.

Special Needs
Wheelchair accessible.

Restrictions
None.

Description
In 1958, the *Hollywood Walk of Fame* was envisioned as a means of enshrining the memory of the Hollywood greats. Today, it is the defining emblem of Los Angeles and one of its most popular tourist attractions. Two hectares (five acres) of bronze stars embedded in pink and charcoal terrazzo squares honour famous luminaries from the beginning of cinema right up to the present day, as well as behind-the-scenes figures. The Walk of Fame takes visitors on a tour of Hollywood's entertainment industry, in particular when it passes in front of the famous *Mann's Chinese Theatre*, where stars have literally made their mark, with their hand- and footprints.

Hoover Dam

Contact Address
DOI Bureau of Reclamation, Visitor Services, PO Box 60400, Boulder City, NV 89006
Tel: (702) 294 3524. Fax: (702) 597 9685.
Web site: www.hooverdam.com

Location
48km (30 miles) southeast of Las Vegas, Nevada.

Transportation:
Air: McCarran International Airport (Las Vegas). Car: US-93.

Opening Times
Daily 0800-1745.

Admission Fees
US$8; concessions available.

Visitors Annually
1,000,000.

Special Needs
Wheelchair accessible.

Restrictions
Visitors with defibrillators or pacemakers are not recommended to take the tour because of possible electromagnetic interference.

> Please see the map at the front of each section for the location of attractions.

 *Historical*  *Man-made* *Amusement*

The Americas – **United States of America**

Description
Completed in 1935, the *Hoover Dam* is a modern engineering marvel that stretches 380m (1247ft) across the Colorado River, holding, in the form of *Lake Mead,* enough water to store the river's flow for two years. The dam itself contains 2,486,250 cubic metres (3,250,000 cubic yards) of concrete, and functions primarily as a power generator, supplying electricity to Nevada as well as nearby California and Arizona. Visitor tours examine the construction of the dam and explore its hydroelectric generating facilities.

Independence National Historical Park

Contact Address
313 Walnut Street, Philadelphia, PA 19106
Tel: (215) 597 8974 (Visitor Centre).
Web site: www.nps.gov/inde/

Location
Visitor Centre, Dock Street, off Third Street, between Chestnut Street and Walnut Street, central Philadelphia.

Transportation
Air: Philadelphia International Airport. Rail: 30th Street Station. Subway: Fifth Street Station or Market Street Station. Car: I-95 or I-76 to I-676.

Opening Times
Daily 0900-1700; may vary seasonally.

Admission Fees
Most buildings free of charge.

Annual Visitor Figures
1,600,000 (Liberty Bell); 800,000 (Independence Hall).

Special Needs
Certain areas wheelchair accessible.

Restrictions
None.

Description
The *Independence National Historical Park* contains important monuments to the history of America. Most significant is *Independence Hall*, considered the birthplace of the United States – where both the Declaration of Independence and the US Constitution were signed. Nearby, the famous *Liberty Bell* is a hugely popular symbol of American freedom, first named in the nineteenth century by the abolitionists who sought to end slavery. The park also reflects the period 1790-1800, when Philadelphia was the capital of America, since it contains the home of the US Supreme Court (Old City Hall) and the meeting place of the US Congress (Congress Hall) for that time.

Kennedy Space Center

Address
Kennedy Space Center Visitor Complex, Delaware North Park Services, Mail Code DNPS
Kennedy Space Center, FL 32899
Tel: (321) 452 2121.
Web site: www.kennedyspacecenter.com

 Cultural  *Natural*  *Religious*

The Americas – **United States of America**

Location
56km (35 miles) east of Orlando, Florida.

Transportation
Air: Orlando International Airport. Car: US-1.

Opening Times
Daily 0900-dusk.

Admission Fees
US$24 (maximum access).

Visitors Annually
3,000,000.

Special Needs
Wheelchair accessible.

Restrictions
None.

Description
Visitors to the *Kennedy Space Center* Visitor Complex find a mix of space-age technology and nature. The Centre is primarily known as the home of the *Space Shuttle*, where spectacular launches can be viewed from a safe distance. Visitors can also tour the *Apollo/Saturn Visitor Center* and experience *Astronout Encounter*, an interactive show hosted by real astronauts. Other facilities include a *Rocket Garden* and an *I-MAX* cinema. The centre is located on the Merritt Island National Wildlife Refuge, home to bald eagles, alligators, otters and sea turtles. Visitors can take wildlife walks or drives and view exhibits.

Las Vegas Strip

Contact Address
Las Vegas Convention and Visitors Authority, 3150 Paradise Road, Las Vegas, NV 89109
Tel: (702) 892 0711. Fax: (702) 892 2824.
Web site: www.lasvegas24hours.com

Location
Las Vegas city centre, Nevada.

Transportation
Air: McCarran International Airport (Las Vegas). Car: I-15.

Opening Times
Not applicable.

Admission Fees
Not applicable.

Visitors Annually
Not applicable.

Special Needs
Wheelchair accessible.

Restrictions
None.

> Please see the map at the front of each section for the location of attractions.

 Historical    Man-made   Amusement

29

The Americas – **United States of America**

Description
The *Strip* in Las Vegas is, perhaps, the defining symbol of American excess in the name of money. Here, massive casino–hotel complexes vie for supremacy in an ongoing competition to be the biggest and the best. The *Luxor*, a 36-storey bronze and glass pyramid based on an Ancient Egypt theme, draws attention to itself by shining the most powerful artificial light beam ever created from its apex. Other legendary casinos include *Caesar's Palace* and the *MGM Grand Hotel and Theme Park*.

Lincoln Memorial

Contact Address
National Capital Parks-Central, The National Mall, 900 Ohio Drive, SW Washington, DC 20242
Tel: (202) 426 6841.
Web site: www.nps.gov/linc

Location
The National Mall, West Potomac Park, at 23rd Street between Constitution and Independence Avenues.

Transportation
Air: Reagan International Airport. Rail: Union Station. Metrorail: Smithsonian. Car: I-66, I-395, I-495.

Opening Times
Daily 0800-2345.

Admission Fees
Free.

Visitors Annually
Not available.

Special Needs
Wheelchair accessible.

Restrictions
None.

Description
Modelled upon a Doric temple, the *Lincoln Memorial* is a tribute to President Abraham Lincoln and the nation he fought to preserve during the Civil War (1861-1865), the nation's bloodiest conflict. Enclosed by a colonnade and complimented by a reflecting pool in front, a large statue of President Lincoln sits in solemn thought, grasping the arms of his throne-like chair. As a symbol of freedom and racial harmony, the Lincoln Memorial was the site of Martin Luther King's 'I Have a Dream' speech.

Metropolitan Museum of Art

Contact Address
1000 Fifth Avenue, New York, NY 10028
Tel: (212) 535 7710.
Web site: www.metmuseum.org

Location
Fifth Avenue and 82nd Street, New York.

 Cultural   *Natural*   *Religious*

The Americas – **United States of America**

Transportation
Air: La Guardia International Airport or John F Kennedy International Airport. Rail: Grand Central Station. Subway: 77th Street or 86th Street.

Opening Times
Tues-Thurs and Sun 0930-1715; Fri and Sat 0930-2100.

Admission Fees
US$10 (suggested donation).

Visitors Annually
5,500,000.

Special Needs
Wheelchair accessible. Facilities for the hearing impaired, visually impaired and visitors with developmental disabilities.

Restrictions
None.

Description
With a diverse collection embracing over two million works of art, the *Metropolitan Museum of Art* ranks as one of the world's great museums. Visitors could literally spend days taking in works from the USA, Europe, China, the Far East and Africa, as well as the Classical and Islamic worlds. This provides for a museum that has managed to represent numerous important periods in the history of art, including the Impressionists and the Italian Renaissance, as well as a renowned American collection.

Mount Rushmore National Memorial

Contact Address
PO Box 268, Keystone, SD 57751
Tel: (605) 574 2523. Fax: (605) 574 2307.
Web site: www.nps.gov/moru

Location
39km (24 miles) from Rapid City, South Dakota.

Transportation
Air: Rapid City. Car: Highway 16 and 244.

Opening Times
Monument: daily 24 hours; Visitor Centre: daily 0800-2200 (summer); 0800-1700 (winter).

Admission Fees
Free.

Visitors Annually
2,800,000.

Description
Mount Rushmore National Memorial is one of the USA's most renowned national monuments. Eighteen-metre-tall (60ft) faces of presidents George Washington, Thomas Jefferson, Theodore Roosevelt and Abraham Lincoln are perched 152m (465ft) in the air, carved into solid rock, and they stand as a gateway to America's majestic west. Surrounded by the *Black Hills National Forest*, the monument was dedicated in 1927, and it took 14 years of carving and fundraising for the monument to be completed. In the summer months, visitors can also enjoy exhibits, walks and lectures.

The Americas – **United States of America**

National Air and Space Museum

Contact Address
Visitor Information Centre, Smithsonian Institution, Washington, DC 20560

Location
The National Mall, near the Washington Monument, Washington, DC.

Transportation
Air: Reagan International Airport. Rail: Union Station. Metrorail: Smithsonian. Car: I-66, I-395, I-495.

Opening Times
Daily 1000-1730.

Admission Fees
Free.

Visitors Annually
9,800,000.

Special Needs
Wheelchair accessible. Some facilities for the hearing impaired and visually impaired.

Restrictions
None.

Description
Opened in 1976, the *National Air and Space Museum* celebrates the history and evolution of air and space technology. Documenting both historical and technical achievements, virtually all aircraft and spacecraft on display were actually flown or used as backup vehicles. Exhibits include the Wright Brothers' 1903 *Flyer*, Charles Lindbergh's *Spirit of St Louis*, and moon rock collected by the Apollo astronauts from the lunar surface.

Niagara Falls– see also *Canada*

Contact Address
Niagara Falls Convention and Visitors Bureau, 310 Fourth Street, Niagara Falls, NY14303
Tel: (716) 285 2400. Fax: (716) 285 0809.
E-mail: nfcvb@nfcvb.com
Web site: www.nfcvb.com

Location
130km (81 miles) west of Toronto, Ontario, Canada.

Transportation
Air: Buffalo Niagara Airport, Pearson International Airport (Toronto). Car: QEW.

Opening Times
Not applicable.

Admission Fees
Not applicable.

Visitors Annually
14,000,000.

Special Needs
Wheelchair accessible.

Restrictions
None.

The Americas – **United States of America**

Description
Niagara Falls has attracted millions of visitors ever since the first human inhabitants set eyes on it, and it is now one of the most popular tourist destinations in North America. Niagara is not the highest waterfall in the world, but it moves a staggering volume of 168,000 cubic metres (219,600 cubic yards) of water per minute over a drop of 51m (167ft), making it one of the natural wonders of the world. The surrounding town, a notorious North American honeymoon destination, offers a wealth of visitor activities including a casino, as well as land and boat tours of the falls.

Rock and Roll Hall of Fame

Contact Address
1 Key Plaza, Cleveland, OH 44114
Tel: (888) 764 7625. Fax: (216) 781 1326.
Web site: www.rockhall.com

Location
1 Key Plaza, East Ninth Street at Lake Erie, Cleveland.

Transportation
Air: Cleveland Hopkins International Airport. Waterfront Rapid: Coast Harbour station. Car: I-90.

Opening Times
Daily 1000-1730; until 2100 Wed.

Admission Fees
US$14.95; concessions available.

Visitors Annually
500,000.

Special Needs
Wheelchair accessible.

Restrictions
None.

Description
The *Rock and Roll Hall of Fame* celebrates the American pop-cultural institution of rock music by honouring its popular and influential performers, producers, songwriters and disc jockeys. The museum features a *Hall of Fame* exhibit, which includes a computerised juke-box containing nearly every song of every performer featured, their signatures etched in glass, film exhibits and displays of artefacts.

Statue of Liberty

Contact Address
Statue of Liberty National Monument and Ellis Island, Liberty Island, New York, NY 10004
Tel: (212) 363 3200. Fax: (212) 363 6304.
Web site: www.nps.gov/stli

Location
Liberty Island, harbour of New York, New York.

Transportation
Only access is by Statue of Liberty/Ellis Island Ferry.

Historical    Man-made   Amusement

The Americas – **United States of America**

Opening Times
Daily 0900-1700. May vary seasonally.

Admission Fees
US$7 (return ferry trip including access to island/statue); concessions available.

Visitors Annually
5,000,000.

Special Needs
Wheelchair accessible. Tactile exhibits for the visually impaired.

Restrictions
Not applicable.

Description
A gift to the USA from France in 1886, the *Statue of Liberty* greeted millions of immigrants seeking a better life in America from its perch in New York Harbour. It has become a defining American symbol of freedom and democracy. Visitors to the monument can make the 22-storey climb to the statue's crown, or take a lift to the pedestal observation deck, which offers excellent views of New York. Nearby Ellis Island, part of the Statue of Liberty National Monument, houses a museum devoted to the history of immigration.

Universal Studios Florida

Contact Address
1000 Universal Studios Plaza, Orlando, FL 32819
Tel: (407) 363 8000 *or* (800) 711 0080 (tickets).
Web site. www.uescape.com

Location
Southwest of Orlando, Florida.

Transportation
Air: Orlando International Airport. Car: I-4.

Opening Times
Daily 0900-1900, closing times vary by season and event.

Admission Fees
US$46 (one-day pass to either the Studios or the Islands of Adventure); US$84.95 (two-day combined pass); US$99.95 (three-day combined pass).

Visitors Annually
Not available.

Special Needs
Wheelchair accessible. Facilities for the hearing impaired and the visually impaired.

Restrictions
Height restrictions on some attractions.

Description
This 162-hectare (400-acre) site opened in 1990 and is a fully functioning TV- and movie-making facility as well as a renowned recreational attraction. There are three parks: *Universal Studios*, featuring rides and attractions based on films; *Universal Studios Islands of Adventure*, a technologically advanced theme park including many rides; and *Universal CityWalk*, an evening and night-time entertainment complex.

Please see the map at the front of each section
for the location of attractions.

 Cultural   *Natural*   *Religious*

The Americas – **United States of America**

Walt Disney World

Contact Address
PO Box 10040, Lake Buena Vista, FL 32830
Tel: (407) 824 2222 *or* 934 7639 (tickets).
Web site: www.disney.com

Location
40km (25 miles) southwest of Orlando, Florida.

Transportation
Air: Orlando International Airport. Car: I-4.

Opening Times
Daily 0900-2400; varies seasonally according to park.

Admission Fees
US$46 (one-day, one-park pass); concessions available.

Visitors Annually
Not available.

Special Needs
Wheelchair accessible. Some facilities for the visually impaired.

Restrictions
Certain rides restricted.

Description
The world's largest theme park, *Walt Disney World* covers a space twice the size of Manhattan, delivering the Disney promise of magical escapism and thrilling rides. It is divided into four parks: *Magic Kingdom*, providing traditional Disney rides and attractions; *Animal Kingdom*, an animal park; *Disney-MGM Studios*, a Hollywood-themed park featuring rides, shows and tours; and *EPCOT Center*, which explores the world and its communities of tomorrow.

White House

Contact Address
Visitors Center, White House, 1450 Pennsylvania Avenue NW, Washington, DC 20230
Tel: (202) 456 7041.
Web site: www.nps.gov/whho

Location
1600 Pennsylvania Avenue NW, central Washington, DC.

Transportation
Air: Reagan International Airport. Rail: Union Station. Metrorail: Federal Triangle or Metro Center. Car: I-66, I-395, I-495.

Opening Times
White House tours: Tues-Sat 1000-1200, may close for official events; Visitors Center: daily 0730-1600.

Admission Fees
Free.

Annual Visitor Figures
1,500,000.

 Historical   *Man-made*   *Amusement*

The Americas – **United States of America**

Special Needs
Wheelchair accessible. Tours can be arranged in advance for the hearing impaired and visually impaired.

Restrictions
Not applicable.

Description
The *White House* is where the President of the United States of America lives and carries out official duties as Head of State. Tours of the White House are very popular so, in peak period, from the third Tuesday in March to the end of August, visitors will have to obtain free tickets dispensed by the *White House Visitors Center*. The tour takes visitors around permitted areas of the White House, where they can view rooms that play host to official governmental functions.

Yellowstone National Park

Contact Address
PO Box 168, Yellowstone National Park, WY 82190
Tel: (307) 344 7381.
Web site: www.nps.gov/yell

Location
Northwest Wyoming, portions extending into southwestern Montana and Idaho.

Transportation
Air: Cody Airport, Jackson Airport, Bozeman Airport, Billings Airport, Idaho Falls Airport, and West Yellowstone Airport (seasonal). Car: many state and federal highways.

Opening Times
Daily 24 hours to wheeled vehicles. Many entrances operate seasonally.

Admission Fees
US$20 (per vehicle); US$15 (per snowmobile/motorcycle); US$10 (per pedestrian/cyclist). Entrance valid for seven days.

Visitors Annually
3,000,000.

Special Needs
Some areas wheelchair accessible.

Restrictions
Vehicle restrictions exist.

Description
Established in 1872, *Yellowstone National Park* is the first and oldest national park in the world. Renowned for its geothermal phenomena, the park has more geysers and hot springs than the rest of the world combined. Other natural attractions include the *Grand Canyon of the Yellowstone River* (not to be confused with *the* Grand Canyon in Arizona), fossil forests and *Yellowstone Lake*. Natural wildlife, such as bears, wolves, elk, bison and trout, abound and can often be seen from the road.

Yosemite National Park

Contact Address
PO Box 577, Yosemite, CA 95389
Tel: (209) 372 0200.
Web site: www.nps.gov/yose

 Cultural *Natural* *Religious*

The Americas – **United States of America/Venezuela**

Location
341km (212 miles) east of San Francisco, California, near the Nevada border.

Transportation
Car: routes 12, 120, 140, 41 and 120.

Opening Times
Daily 24 hours.

Admission Fees
US$20 (per vehicle); US$10 (per pedestrian/cyclist). Entrance valid for seven days.

Visitors Annually
4,000,000.

Special Needs
Limited areas wheelchair accessible.

Restrictions
None.

Description
Created in 1890, *Yosemite National Park* stretches along California's eastern flank and covers almost 3108 sq kilometres (1200 sq miles) of the central Sierra Nevada mountain range. The park is well known for its giant sequoia trees, cliffs, waterfalls, alpine meadows, lakes and rivers. The area is also home to abundant wildlife – including bears.

VENEZUELA

Angel Falls

Contact Address
Avenida v. Lecuna, Parque Central, Torre Oeste, Piso 37, Caracas, Venezuela
Tel: (2) 574 1968. Fax: (2) 574 222.

Location
600km (373 miles) south of Ciudad Bolívar; 50km (30 miles) southeast of Canaima village.

Transportation
Air: Caracas Simon Bolivar International Airport *or* Ciudad Bolívar Airport to Canaima Airport; then private tour operator's plane or boat. Car: no road access.

Opening Times
Not applicable.

Admission Fees
US$7.

Visitors Annually
100,000.

Description
At 988m (3212ft), *Angel Falls* is the tallest waterfall in the world. To many it is also the most stunning, with water spilling into a free fall of nearly one kilometre before tumbling into a pool and then springing into the misty air to form a brilliant double rainbow. Located in *Canaima National Park*, Angel Falls used to be a holy site for the Incas, and is still one today for the local Venezuelan tribes.

Historical *Man-made* *Amusement*

section two
europe

The numbers alongside the attractions below correspond to their locations on the maps overleaf, and not to the page numbers on which information on the attractions appear. For more detailed locations of these attractions consult the World Travel Atlas.

1 Giant Ferris Wheel
2 Hofburg Palace
3 Kunsthistorisches Museum
4 Schönbrunn Palace
5 Flanders Fields
6 Manneken-Pis
7 Charles Bridge
8 Prague Castle
9 Legoland
10 Little Mermaid
11 Tivoli Gardens
12 Big Ben
13 Blackpool Pleasure Beach
14 British Airways London Eye
15 British Museum
16 Cambridge University
17 Canterbury Cathedral
18 Hadrian's Wall
19 Millennium Dome
20 National Gallery
21 Oxford University
22 Roman Baths and Pump Room
23 St Paul's Cathedral
24 Stonehenge
25 Tower of London
26 Westminster Abbey
27 York Minster
28 Arc de Triomphe
29 Bayeux Tapestry
30 Cave of Lascaux
31 Chartres Cathedral
32 Château de Chenonceau
33 Château de Versailles
34 Cité des Sciences et de l'Industrie
35 Disneyland Paris
36 Eiffel Tower
37 Musée du Louvre
38 Musée d'Orsay
39 Notre Dame Cathedral
40 Pont du Gard
41 Pont St-Bénézet
43 Brandenburg Gate
44 Cologne Cathedral
45 Englischer Garten
46 Neuschwanstein Castle
47 Pergamon Museum
48 Reichstag
49 Acropolis
50 Delphi
51 Knossos
52 National Archaeological Museum of Athens
53 Buda Castle Palace
54 Budapest Central Synagogue
55 Fisherman's Bastion
56 Geysir
57 Perlan
58 Blarney Castle
59 Cliffs of Moher
60 Glendalough
61 Trinity College Dublin
62 Colosseum
63 Doge's Palace
64 Florence Duomo
65 Pantheon
66 Pompeii
67 Ponte Vecchio
68 Roman Forum
69 St Peter's Basilica
70 Sistine Chapel
71 Tower of Pisa
72 Uffizi Gallery
73 Hagar Qim
74 Anne Frank House
75 Keukenhof Gardens
76 Rijksmuseum
77 Van Gogh Museum
78 Giants Causeway
79 Bryggen
80 Hardanger Fjord
81 Auschwitz
82 Wawel Royal Castle
83 Castle of St George
84 Tower of Belém
85 Kremlin
86 St Basil's Cathedral
87 State Hermitage Museum
88 Edinburgh Castle
89 Alhambra
90 Guggenheim Museum Bilbao
91 La Sagrada Familia
92 Monasterio de San Lorenzo de El Escorial
93 Prado Museum
94 Roman Aqueduct at Segovia
95 Santiago de Compostela Cathedral
96 Seville Cathedral
97 Drottningholm Palace
98 Museum of National Antiquities
99 Jet d'Eau
100 Jungfraujoch
101 Blue Mosque
102 Ephesus
103 St Sophia
104 Topkapi Palace
105 Troy
106 Caernarfon Castle

39

Europe – **Maps**

40

Europe – **Maps**

*Europe – **Austria***

Austria

Giant Ferris Wheel

Contact Address
Prater 90, A-1020 Vienna
Tel: (01) 729 5430. Fax: (01) 7295 43020.
E-mail: wr.riesenrad@aon.at
Web site: www.wienerriesenrad.com

Location
Prater, northeast Vienna.

Transportation
Air: Vienna International Airport. U-Bahn: Praterstern. S-Bahn: Wien Nord (Praterstern) from Wien Mitte. Tram: 1.

Opening Times
Daily 1000-2300 (Apr), 0900-2400 (May-Sep), 1000-2200 (Oct), 1000-1800 (Nov-Dec).

Admission Fees
öS55.

Visitors Annually
Not available.

Special Needs
Wheelchair accessible.

Description
Located in the giant wooded park and fairground known as the *Prater*, Vienna's *Giant Ferris Wheel* is one of Austria's best-known and best-loved landmarks. The wheel was completed in 1897 at a time when other such wheels stood in cities like London, Paris and Blackpool, but it is the only one of its era still surviving.

Hofburg Palace

Contact Address
Innerer Burghof, Kaisertor, A-1010 Vienna
Tel: (01) 533 7570. Fax: (01) 5337 57033.

Location
Innerer Burghof, Vienna.

Transportation
Air: Vienna International Airport. U-Bahn: Herrengasse. Tram: B-line.

Opening Times
Daily 0900-1630.

Admission Fees
Admission prices vary for each museum.

Visitors Annually
Not available.

Special Needs
Wheelchair accessible.

 Cultural   *Natural*  *Religious*

*Europe – * **Austria**

Description
The *Hofburg Palace* was home to the Austrian Hapsburg emperors until 1918. Today, it serves as a repository for Austrian culture and history, embracing 22 separate museums, a fourteenth-century Augustinian church, the famous *Spanish Riding School*, the *National Library*, as well as the president's offices. The most popular of the museums is the *Kaisertor*, which takes visitors on a tour of the Kaiser's Imperial apartments. The *Vienna Boys' Choir* sings Sunday mass at the Royal Chapel.

Kunsthistorisches Museum

Contact Address
Marie-Theresien-Platz, 1010 Vienna
Tel: (01) 52 52 44 01. Fax: (01) 523 2770.
E-mail: info@khm.at
Web site: www.khm.at

Location
Marie-Theresien-Platz, Vienna.

Transportation
Air: Vienna International Airport. U-Bahn: Volkstheater. Tram: D-Burging/Kunsthistorisches Museum.

Opening Times
Tues-Sun 1000-1800, except Thurs 1000-2100.

Admission Fees
öS100.

Visitors Annually
Not available.

Special Needs
Wheelchair accessible.

Description
Opened in 1891 to house the imperial family's vast art collection, Vienna's *Kunsthistorisches Museum* was built in the style of the Italian Renaissance to firmly establish the building's link with history's great art. Today, the museum holds one of the most important collections in the world, which includes works by Rubens, Rembrandt, Vermeer, Dürer, Titian and Brueghel the Elder.

Schönbrunn Palace

Contact Address
Schloss Schönbrunn Kultur u. Betriebs GmbH, Schloss Schönbrunn, A-1130 Vienna
Tel: (01) 81 11 32 39. Fax: (01) 81 11 33 33.
E-mail: info@schoenbrunn.at
Web site: www.schoenbrunn.at

Location
Six kilometres (3.7 miles) west of Vienna city centre.

Transportation
Air: Vienna International Airport. U-Bahn: Schönbrunn.

Opening Times
Daily, times vary according to season and attraction.

 Historical   Man-made   Amusement

Europe – **Austria/Belgium**

Admission Fees
Varies according to attraction.

Visitors Annually
1,400,000.

Special Needs
Wheelchair accessible. Audio guides available in several languages.

Description
One of the most renowned Baroque structures in Europe, *Schönbrunn Palace* began life as a hunting lodge in the 1600s but was turned into a lavish palace by Maria Theresa. A tour offers visitors the chance to admire the site's opulent elegance, including the famous ceiling frescoes of the *Great Gallery*, and the *Hall of Mirrors* where Mozart played. The grounds of the palace include a *Flower Garden*, *Tiergarten* (a zoo dating from 1752), the *Neptune Fountain*, and a reproduction of the maze that was first designed around 1700.

Belgium

Flanders Fields

Contact Address
In Flanders Fields Museum, Lakenhallen, Grote Markt 34, b-8900 Ieper
Tel: (05) 722 85840. Fax: (05) 722 8589.
E-mail: toerisme@ieper.be
Web site: www.inflandersfields.be/english/home/

Location
Flanders, Belgium.

Transportation
Air: Brussels International Airport. Rail: Ieper station. Car: A19.

Opening Times
Not applicable.

Admission Fees
BEF250 (museum).

Visitors Annually
235,000.

Special Needs
Wheelchair accessible.

Description
Flanders Fields was the site of around half a million deaths in the horrific trenches of World War I. There are numerous military cemeteries and 'Missing Memorials' commemorating those who perished in battle, as well as the playing of the 'Last Post' every evening at 2000, under the arch of the *Menin Gate*. The *In Flanders Fields Museum* in Ypres observes major events and aspects of the war, such as the first gas attack, the Christmas Truces of 1914, and No Man's Land.

> Please see the map at the front of each section
> for the location of attractions.

44   Cultural   Natural   Religious

Europe – **Belgium/Czech Republic**

Manneken-Pis

Contact Address
Office de Tourisme et d'Information de Bruxelles, Hôtel de Ville, Grand-Place, 1000 Brussels
Tel: (02) 513 8940. Fax: (02) 513 8320.
E-mail: tourism.brussels@tib.be
Web site: www.tib.be

Location
Rue de l'Etuve, Brussels.

Transportation
Air: Brussels International Airport. Rail: Bruuxelles Centrale. Métro: Bourse.

Opening Times
Not applicable.

Admission Fees
Not applicable.

Visitors Annually
5,000,000.

Special Needs
Wheelchair accessible.

Description
The *Manneken-Pis* has the double distinction of being as funny as it is well known. Crowds of tourists patrol the meandering cobbled streets near Brussels' Grand-Place hoping to find this small statuette of a little boy in the midst of a never-ending pee. The statue is, in its own way, a typically Belgian symbol of cultural self-mockery. Fittingly, no one knows how it ever got there, but that does not stop locals from dressing him in over 600 costumes.

Czech Republic

Charles Bridge

Contact Address
Prague Information Service, Na příkope 20, 110 00 Prague 1
Tel: (02) 264 022. Fax: (02) 264 023.
E-mail: info@pis.cz
Web site: www.pis.cz

Location
Central Prague.

Transportation
Air: Praha Ruzyně International Airport. Metro: Staromestská.

Opening Times
Not applicable.

Admission Fees
Not applicable.

Visitors Annually
Not available.

 Historical   *Man-made* *Amusement*

Description
The *Charles Bridge* is Prague's most familiar monument. Built in 1357, this 520m-long (1770ft) bridge was the only connection between the two halves of Prague for four hundred years. Originally, the bridge was bare of ornamentation other than one cross, however, as the Counter Reformation took hold in Bohemia, the bridge eventually received over 30 statues. These prominent sculptures add a Baroque touch to a Gothic landmark. Craft stalls and buskers make the route across the bridge even more diverting for visitors.

Prague Castle

Contact Address
Prague Castle, 11908 Prague 1
Tel: (02) 24 37 33 68. Fax: (02) 24 31 08 96.

Location
Hrad, Prague city centre.

Transportation
Air: Praha Ruzyně International Airport. Tram: 22 to Prazsky hrad.

Opening Times
Daily 0900-1700 (summer), 0900-1600 (winter).

Admission Fees
Kc120.

Visitors Annually
Not available.

Special Needs
Many areas wheelchair accessible.

Description
The reaching spires of *Prague Castle*, the seat of Bohemian government for a thousand years, can be seen from virtually anywhere in Prague. It is actually more of a complex than a castle, covering 45 hectares (110 acres) and comprising three courtyards, fortifications and gardens. Its most famous attraction is *St Vitus Cathedral*, the country's largest church, which was begun in 1344 but not completed until 1929, and is much beloved for its stained glass. Directly behind the cathedral is the *National Gallery of Bohemian Art*.

Denmark

Legoland

Contact Address
Legoland, DK 7190 Billund
Tel: 75 33 13 33. Fax: 75 35 31 79.
E-mail: danmark@legoland.dk
Web site: www.legoland.dk

Location
One kilometre (0.6 miles) north of Billund.

Transportation
Air: Billund International Airport. Car: E-45.

 Cultural   *Natural*   *Religious*

Europe – **Denmark**

Opening Times
Daily Apr-Oct; 1000-2100 (high season), 1000-2000 (low season).

Admission Fees
DKK145 (high season), DKK135 (low season).

Visitors Annually
1,500,000.

Special Needs
Wheelchair accessible.

Description
With Lego as Denmark's most famous gift to the children of the world, it is not surprising that the country has built (literally) an amusement park from it. This renowned ten-hectare (25-acre) amusement park contains no less than 40 million plastic Lego blocks. The park features attractions, rides and shows, with the sophisticated *Port of Copenhagen* exhibit – featuring electronically controlled trains, cranes and ships – a favourite for many.

Little Mermaid

Contact Address
Wonderful Copenhagen Tourist Information, GL Kongevej 1, 1610 Copenhagen V
Tel: 33 25 74 00 *or* 33 11 13 25. Fax: 33 25 74 10.

Location
Langelinie, Copenhagen waterfront.

Transportation
Air: Copenhagen Airport. S-Bahn: Østerport.

Opening Times
Not applicable.

Admission Fees
Not applicable.

Visitors Annually
Not available.

Description
Denmark's most famous cultural symbol comes from a tale told by its most renowned author and poet, Hans Christian Andersen. In his story, the youngest daughter of the Sea King rescues a drowning prince and falls in love, but in the end gets turned into sea foam. Nevertheless, the Danes chose to commemorate her in 1913 by building a sculpture on Copenhagen's waterfront, where she stares dreamily across the water.

Tivoli Gardens

Contact Address
Vesterbrogade 3, DK 1620 Copenhagen V
Tel: 33 15 10 01. Fax: 33 93 18 81.
E-mail: tivoli@tivoli.dk
Web site: www.tivoligardens.com

Location
Vesterbrogade 3.

Transportation
Air: Copenhagen Airport. Rail: Central Station.

 Historical *Man-made*   *Amusement*

Europe – **Denmark/England**

Opening Times
14 Apr-24 Sep: Sun-Thurs 1100-2400, Fri and Sat 1100-0100; 17 Nov-23 Dec: Sun-Thurs 1100-2100, Fri and Sat 1100-2200.

Admission Fees
Dkk49 (high season), Dkk39 (low season); concessions available.

Visitors Annually
3,700,000.

Special Needs
Wheelchair accessible.

Restrictions
No dogs.

Description
Opened in 1843, *Tivoli Gardens* has outlasted the great parks of Europe that were its inspiration – the Tivoli in Paris and Vauxhall Gardens in London. Tivoli Gardens still retains a flavour of that era, seeming more like an open-air garden than it does a theme park. Visitors can stroll and listen to symphonies; but rides it certainly has, including the new *Golden Tower*, *Valhalla Castle*, a *Ferris Wheel* and a roller coaster that zooms through the treetops. All visitors, however, may enjoy the many concerts, circus acts, and theatrical performances that are staged at Tivoli.

England

Big Ben

Contact Address
House of Commons Information Office, London SW1A 0AA
Tel: (020) 7219 4272. Fax: (020) 7219 5839.
E-mail: hcinfo@parliament.uk
Web site: www.parliament.uk

Location
Palace of Westminster, Parliament Square, London SW1.

Transportation
Air: Heathrow Airport. Underground: Westminster.

Opening Times
Not applicable.

Admission Fees
Not applicable.

Visitors Annually
Not available.

Special Needs
Wheelchair accessible.

Description
Big Ben is, perhaps, the most recognisable landmark in Britain. The name, however, applies only to the bell and not the whole tower, which goes by the name *St Stephen's*. The clock tower is part of the *Palace of Westminster*, which contains the United Kingdom's Houses of Parliament. The complex was constructed in a neo-Gothic style in the nineteenth century,

 Cultural   Natural    Religious

Europe – **England**

after fire had ravaged nearly all of the previous parliament buildings. *Big Ben* rings every hour, on the hour, as well as on Armistice Day. There is no access to the clock tower for visitors, although tours of the Palace of Westminster or access to the *Strangers' Gallery* can be arranged by writing to the above address.

Blackpool Pleasure Beach

Contact Address
525 Ocean Boulevard, Blackpool, Lancashire FY4 1EZ
Tel: (0870) 444 5566. Fax: (01253) 401 098.
E-mail: marketing@bpbltd.com
Web site: www.blackpoolpleasurebeach.co.uk

Location
South Shore, Blackpool.

Transportation
Air: Manchester Airport. Rail: Blackpool North Station, Blackpool Pleasure Beach Station. Car: M55.

Opening Times
1100-2400 daily (Apr-Nov), Sat and Sun (Mar).

Admission Fees
Free (tickets for rides must be purchased separately).

Visitors Annually
7,200,000.

Special Needs
Certain rides wheelchair accessible.

Description
The city of Blackpool has been attracting holiday visitors ever since 1735, when the first guest house opened. In the nineteenth century, it became a popular working-class destination among the British and, in 1896, *Blackpool Pleasure Beach* was founded. Today, this American-style amusement park, with a distinctly British feel, has 11 roller coasters, some wooden classics, as well as the latest in steel mega-coasters and, for 2000, the world's biggest dark ride, *Valhalla*.

British Airways London Eye

Contact Address
Riverside Building, County Hall, Westminster Bridge Road, London SE1 7PB
Tel: (0870) 500 0600.
Web site: www.ba-londoneye.com

Location
South Bank, London.

Transportation
Air: Heathrow Airport. Underground: Westminster, Waterloo, Embankment.

Opening Times
Daily 0900-2200 (summer), 1000-1800 (winter); times are subject to change.

Admission Fees
£7.45 (winter), £7.95 (summer); concessions available.

 Historical   *Man-made*   *Amusement*

Europe – **England**

Visitors Annually
2,200,000.

Special Needs
Wheelchair accessible.

Description
At 135m (443ft) the *British Airways London Eye* is the world's largest observation wheel and the fourth-tallest structure in London. It differs from a ferris wheel in that it has an A-frame support structure on only one side, and the pods are located on the exterior, stabilised by internal motors that keep them horizontal as the wheel slowly moves around. Designed to be visually appealing from the exterior, the wheel itself takes passengers high into the air, providing staggering views of central London and as far afield as 40km (25 miles).

British Museum

Contact Address
Great Russell Street, London WC1B 3DG
Tel: (020) 7323 8000. Fax: (020) 7323 8616.
E-mail: information@british-museum.ac.uk
Web site: www.british-museum.ac.uk

Location
Great Russell Street, London WC1.

Transportation
Air: Heathrow International Airport. Underground: Holborn, Tottenham Court Road, Russell Square.

Opening Times
Mon-Sat 1000-1700, Sun 1200-1800.

Admission Fees
Free.

Visitors Annually
5,400,000.

Special Needs
Certain areas wheelchair accessible; some facilities for hearing impaired.

Description
Founded in 1753, the *British Museum* contains one of the world's greatest displays of antiquities, documenting the rise and fall of civilisations from all over the world. Its collection, in excess of six million objects, comprises antiquities from Egypt, Western Asia, Greece, Rome and Europe, among many others. Among the museum's most famous objects are the *Rosetta Stone* and the *Elgin Marbles*.

Cambridge University

Contact Address
Tourist Information Centre, Cambridge CB2 3QB
Tel: (01223) 322 640. Fax: (01223) 457 588.
E-mail: tourism@cambridge.gov.uk
Web site: www.cambridge.gov.uk/leisure

Location
Cambridge city centre.

 Cultural *Natural*   *Religious*

Europe – **England**

Transportation
Air: Heathrow Airport, Stansted Airport. Rail: Cambridge Station. Car: M11, A14.

Opening Times
Vary from college to college. Many colleges are closed during the exam period.

Admission Fees
£3.50 (King's College), £1.75 (St John's College), £1.75 (Trinity College, Clare College), £1.20 (Queens' College).

Visitors Annually
3,500,000.

Special Needs
Wheelchair accessible.

Restrictions
Areas may be closed to visitors depending on the academic schedule.

Description
Cambridge University is one of Britain's most famous, with alumni including Sir Isaac Newton, John Milton and Steven Hawking. The university's various colleges, many of them architectural masterpieces, are scattered throughout the cobblestoned streets of Cambridge. Highlights include *King's College Chapel*, *St John's College*, and the *Wren Library* at *Trinity College*.

Canterbury Cathedral

Contact Address
Cathedral House, The Precincts, Canterbury CT1 2EH
Tel: (01227) 762 862. Fax: (01227) 865 222.
E-mail: visits@canterbury-cathedral.org
Web site: www.canterbury-cathedral.org

Location
Canterbury city centre.

Transportation
Air: Heathrow Airport, Gatwick Airport, Manston Airport. Rail: Canterbury East Station, Canterbury West Station. Car: M2.

Opening Times
Mon-Sat 0900-1730, Sun 1230-1430 and 1630-1730 (varies seasonally).

Admission Fees
£3; concessions available.

Visitors Annually
1,500,000.

Special Needs
Wheelchair accessible. Special facilities for hearing and visually impaired.

Restrictions
Possible closures at short notice for religious services.

Description
Canterbury Cathedral's history as a religious site dates back to AD597 when Pope Gregory's missionary St Augustine was given a church in the town by King Ethelbert. The cathedral is a masterpiece of Romanesque and Gothic architecture. It was a noted place of pilgrimage for many centuries, as eloquently described by Geoffrey Chaucer in the *Canterbury Tales*. Inside, visitors find, among many other curiosities, stained glass windows dating from the twelfth century, the tomb of Edward the Black Prince, and the former site of the shrine to Thomas à Becket.

 *Historical* *Man-made* *Amusement*

Europe – England

Hadrian's Wall

Contact Address
Hadrian's Wall Tourism Partnership, Eastburn, South Park, Hexham, Northumberland NE46 1BC
Tel: (01434) 602 505. Fax: (01434) 601 267.
E-mail: hadrian@hadrians-wall.org
Web site: www.hadrians-wall.org

Location
Stretches 117km (73 miles) across the north of England, from Wallsend-on-Tyne to Bowness-on-Solway.

Transportation
Air: Newcastle International Airport. Rail: Haltwhistle Station, Hexham Station. Car: M6, A1.

Opening Times
Not applicable.

Admission Fees
Some sites charge admission, but much of the wall is free of charge.

Visitors Annually
1,250,000.

Special Needs
Certain areas wheelchair accessible.

Restrictions
Walking on the wall is discouraged.

Description
Built by order of the Emperor Hadrian in AD122, *Hadrian's Wall* is the best known and most important Roman monument in Britain. The wall was built to mark the northern boundary of the Roman Empire in the British Isles and to keep out pugilistic barbarians to the north. After the Empire's collapse in the fifth century AD, the wall was left to decay, with many of its stones being re-used in nearby buildings. Vast sections of the wall still remain, however, giving a genuine sense of its former importance and scale.

Millennium Dome

Contact Address
Greenwich, London SE10 0AX
Tel: (0870) 606 2000.
E-mail: info@newmill.co.uk
Web site: www.dome2000.co.uk

Location
Greenwich, London SE10.

Transportation
Air: Heathrow International Airport. Underground: North Greenwich. Boat: direct services from Waterloo and Blackfriars. Car: no access.

Opening Times
Sun-Thurs 0900-2000, Fri and Sat 0900-2300; site closes permanently 31 Dec 2000.

Admission Fees
£20; concessions available.

 Cultural   *Natural*  *Religious*

Europe – **England**

Visitors Annually
10,000,000 anticipated.

Special Needs
Wheelchair accessible; disabled parking; facilities for visually impaired.

Restrictions
No access by car.

Description
The *Millennium Dome*, on the banks of the River Thames in Greenwich, is the centrepiece of Britain's millennial celebrations. Covering a total of 80,000 sq metres (860,000 sq feet), 14 recreational and educational zones are contained beneath its translucent roof. Popular zones include the Body Zone, the Money Zone, the Mind Zone and the Journey Zone. A live show, with music by Peter Gabriel, tells a love story through music, pyrotechnics, and interpretative dance.

National Gallery

Contact Address
Trafalgar Square, London WC2N 5DN
Tel: (020) 7747 2885.
Web site: www.nationalgallery.org.uk

Location
Trafalgar Square, London WC2.

Transportation
Air: Heathrow Airport. Underground: Leicester Square, Charing Cross, Embankment, Piccadilly Circus.

Opening Times
Thurs-Tues 1000-1800, Wed 1000-2100.

Admission Fees
Free.

Visitors Annually
5,000,000.

Special Needs
Wheelchair accessible.

Description
Britain's *National Gallery* possesses one of the world's great collections of Western paintings. It has around 2300 pictures covering every European school from the thirteenth to the nineteenth century. Among its many recognisable masterpieces are works by Botticelli, Raphael, Leonardo da Vinci, Tintoretto, Michaelangelo, Titian and Brueghel.

Oxford University

Contact Address
Oxford Information Centre, The Old School, Gloucester Green, Oxford OX1 2DA
Tel: (01865) 726 871. Fax: (01865) 240 261.
Web site: www.oxford.gov.uk/tourism

Location
Oxford city centre.

 Historical  Man-made   Amusement

Europe – **England**

Transportation
Air: Heathrow Airport. Rail: Oxford City Station. Car: M40.

Opening Times
Colleges generally open for visitors during afternoons.

Admission Fees
Varies from college to college.

Visitors Annually
Not available.

Special Needs
Certain areas wheelchair accessible.

Restrictions
Large groups should contact colleges in advance.

Description
Founded by Henry II in 1167, *Oxford University* ranks as the oldest in England and one of the most famous in the world. Its protracted list of important alumni includes John Locke, Christopher Wren, Lewis Carroll, Jonathan Swift, Oscar Wilde, Tony Blair and Bill Clinton. The university itself is made up of a number of colleges (situated throughout the city), most displaying stunning architecture and trim lawns. Of particular interest to visitors are *Christ Church*, *University College* and the *Bodleian Library*.

Roman Baths and Pump Room

Contact Address
Museum Enquiries, Stall Street, Bath BA1 1LZ
Tel: (01225) 477 785. Fax: (01225) 477 743.
E-mail: museum_enquiries@bathnes.gov.uk
Web site: www.romanbaths.co.uk

Location
In front of the Abbey, Bath city centre.

Transportation
Air: Heathrow Airport. Rail: Bath Spa Station. Car: M4, A46.

Opening Times
Daily 0900-1800 (Apr-Jul and Sep), 0900-2130 (Aug), 0930-1700 (Oct-Dec).

Admission Fees
£6.90 (Roman Baths); free (Pump Room).

Visitors Annually
1,000,000.

Special Needs
Pump Room wheelchair accessible. Special facilities for the developmentally disabled and hearing impaired.

Description
The ancient Romans were the first to capitalise on the only natural hot spring in Britain, building a temple and bathing complex that was one of the finest in the Roman world. The healing spring was incorporated into the monastery that stood on the site in the Middle Ages, thus giving rise to the current name of the city, Bath. The Roman structure gradually fell into disrepair and it was not until a visit by the ailing Prince George in 1702 that the baths once again became a popular healing destination. Over the course of the town's redevelopment, the Roman ruins were discovered (in 1879) and restored. Visitors can now view the Georgian grandeur of the Pump House, or see the remains of the ancient Roman baths and temple.

 Cultural *Natural*  *Religious*

*Europe – **England***

St Paul's Cathedral

Contact Address
The Chapter House, St Paul's Churchyard, London EC4M 8AD
Tel: (020) 7236 4128 or (020) 7246 8348. Fax: (020) 7248 3104.
E-mail: chapterhouse@stpaulscathedral.org.uk
Web site: www.stpauls.co.uk or stpauls.london.anglican.org

Location
London EC4.

Transportation
Air: Heathrow Airport. Underground: St Paul's.

Opening Times
Sightseeing: 0830-1600 Mon-Sat (galleries from 0930). Worship: 0715-1800 Mon-Sat, 0745-1700 Sun.

Admission Fees
£5; concessions available.

Visitors Annually
Not available.

Special Needs
Certain areas wheelchair accessible.

Restrictions
Possible closures at short notice for religious services.

Description
St Paul's Cathedral is Sir Christopher Wren's most famous work. Its dome, one of the largest in Europe, stands out as one of the most distinctive features of London's skyline. There has been a cathedral dedicated to St Paul on the site for 1400 years. The present Cathedral stands on the site of an even older medieval cathedral that burned down in the Great Fire of 1666. Decorating the interior of the dome is the Whispering Gallery, so named for its incredible acoustics. Higher up, there are magnificent views across London.

Stonehenge

Contact Address
Abbey Buildings, Abbey Square, Amesbury, Wiltshire SP4 7ES
Tel: (01980) 624 715. Fax: (01980) 623 465.
Web site: www.stonehenge.org

Location
27km (17 miles) west of Andover.

Transportation
Air: Heathrow Airport. Rail: Salisbury Station. Car: A303 or A344/360.

Opening Times
Daily 0900-1900 (Jun-Aug); closes earlier seasonally.

Admission Fees
£4; concessions available.

Visitors Annually
900,000.

 *Historical* *Man-made* *Amusement*

Europe – **England**

Special Needs
Wheelchair accessible. Facilities for hearing and visually impaired.

Description
The famous circle of giant 6.7m-high (22ft) stones that is *Stonehenge* is one of the most famous sites of the ancient world. The first prehistoric construct appeared there around 3100BC. However, it was not until 2150BC that the four-tonne bluestones were brought to Stonehenge from southwest Wales – by manpower alone! One hundred and fifty years later, the sarsen stones were brought from 32km (20 miles) away, the largest weighing an astonishing 50 tonnes.

Tower of London

Contact Address
Tower Hill, London EC3N 4AB
Tel: (020) 7709 0765.
Web site: www.tower-of-london.com *or* hrp.org.uk

Location
Tower Hill, London EC3.

Transportation
Air: Heathrow Airport. Underground: Tower Hill.

Opening Times
Mon-Sat 0900-1700, Sun 1000-1700 (Apr-Oct); Tues-Sat 0900-1600, Sun and Mon 1000-1600 (Nov-Mar).

Admission Fees
£11; concessions available.

Visitors Annually
2,500,000.

Description
The infamous *Tower of London* was begun in 1078 by William the Conqueror, 11 years after his Norman invasion of England, and remained a royal residence until the sixteenth century. It was also a notorious prison where figures as important as Sir Walter Raleigh and Henry VI lost their lives. Today, it houses the *Crown Jewels* and the *Royal Armouries*. *Yeoman Warders*, or *Beefeaters*, still guard the site and take visitors on tours.

Westminster Abbey

Contact Address
The Chapter Office, Dean's Yard, Westminster Abbey, London SW1P 3PA
Tel: (020) 7222 5152. Fax: (020) 7233 2072.
E-mail: info@westminster-abbey.org
Web site: www.westminster-abbey.org

Location
London SW1.

Transportation
Air: Heathrow Airport. Underground: Westminster.

Please see the map at the front of each section
for the location of attractions.

 Cultural Natural Religious

Europe – **England**

Opening Times
Mon-Fri 0930-1645, Sat 0930-1445.

Admission Fees
£5; concessions available.

Visitors Annually
1,250,000.

Special Needs
Certain areas wheelchair accessible.

Description
England's most visited religious site, *Westminster Abbey* is a monument to British history. Inside there are buried kings, statesmen, warriors, scientists, musicians and poets. The abbey has seen the coronation of virtually every English monarch since William the Conqueror. Initially the site of a Norman abbey, Henry III built the present building in the thirteenth century to compete with the great European cathedrals of that time.

York Minster

Contact Address
York Minster Visitors Centre, St Williams College, 4-5 College Street, York YO1 2JF
Tel: (01904) 557 216. Fax: (01904) 557 201.
E-mail: info@yorkminster.org
Web site: www.yorkminster.org

Location
College Street, York city centre.

Transportation
Air: Manchester Airport. Rail: York Station. Car: A59, A64.

Opening Times
Mon-Sat 0900-dusk, Sun 1300-dusk.

Admission Fees
£3; concessions available.

Visitors Annually
2,000,000.

Special Needs
Wheelchair accessible. Facilities for hearing and visually impaired.

Description
The largest Gothic cathedral in Northern Europe, *York Minster* was constructed in 1220. For hundreds of years before this, however, the site had been of religious and political significance, featuring numerous battles between the English and the Vikings for control of the city and its cathedral. Today, half the medieval stained glass in England lies in this cathedral, with the *Great East Window* displaying over 100 scenes. Views of York can be had from the *Central Tower*.

 Flight Times? Climate? Theme Parks? Time Zones? Museums? UNESCO Heritage Sites? Railways? Ski Resorts? Game Parks? Sporting Events? Dive Sites? Travel Statistics? WTO Regions? – for all this, and more besides, consult the *World Travel Atlas*.

 *Historical*   *Man-made*   *Amusement*

*Europe – * **France**

France

Arc de Triomphe

Contact Address
Rond Point, Place Charles de Gaulle, 75008 Paris
Tel: (01) 55 37 73 77. Fax: (01) 44 95 02 13.

Location
Rond Point Place Charles de Gaulle, central Paris.

Transportation
Air: Charles de Gaulle Airport, Orly Airport. Métro: Charles de Gaulle-Étoile.

Opening Times
Daily 1000-2230 (Oct-Mar), 0930-2300 (Apr-Sep).

Admission Fees
FFr40; concessions available.

Visitors Annually
1,400,000.

Description
Commissioned by Napoleon to commemorate the victorious French Army, the *Arc de Triomphe* has been a defining symbol of Paris ever since completion in 1836. Engraved on the arch are numerous names of important and not-so-important victories and beneath it lies the *Tomb of the Unknown Soldier*. Visitors can reach the 50m-tall (164ft) top of the arch for stunning views of Paris, including the *Louvre* and the *Champs Elysées*, or tour the museum inside which charts the arch's history and construction.

Bayeux Tapestry

Contact Address
Centre Guillaume le Conquérant, Rue de Nesmond, 14400 Bayeux
Tel: (02) 31 51 25 50. Fax: (02) 31 51 25 59.

Location
Rue de Nesmond, Bayeux.

Transportation
Air: Caen-Carpiquet Airport. Rail: Bayeux station. Car: A13.

Opening Times
Daily 0900-1900 (May-Aug), 0900-1830 (Sep-Oct 15 and Mar 15-Apr), 0930-1230 and 1400-1800 (Oct 16-Mar 14).

Admission Fees
FFr40; concessions available.

Visitors Annually
430,000.

Special Needs
Wheelchair accessible.

Description
Located in the town of Bayeux is one of Europe's most singular historical records: the *Bayeux Tapestry*. Depicting the events in the 1060s which culminated in the Norman

 Cultural   *Natural*   *Religious*

Conquest of 1066, the 70m-long (231ft) tapestry begins with Harold of Wessex's voyage to Normandy; details his meeting with William; his coronation as the successor to King Edward the Confessor; and ends with his death, and William's victory, at the Battle of Hastings. Although it nearly met ruin in 1792 at the hands of French revolutionaries using it as a wagon cover, the whole extent of this remarkable tapestry is now available to view.

Cave of Lascaux

Contact Address
Simitour Perigourd, 25 Rue Wilson, 2400 Périgueux
Tel: (05) 53 35 50 10. Fax: (05) 53 06 30 94.
E-mail: semitour@perigourd.tm.fr
Web site: www.culture.fr/culture/arcnat/lascaux/en

Location
Aquitaine, near the town of Périgueux.

Transportation
Air: Périgueux-Basillac Airport. Rail: Condat-Le-Lardin station.

Opening Times
Daily 0900-1900; varies seasonally.

Admission Fees
FFr15; concessions available.

Visitors Annually
Not available.

Restrictions
Visitors must buy tickets in Montignac.

Description
Discovered in 1940 by a group of exploring teenagers, the cave paintings at Lascaux are considered to be among the world's best. The area features many such cave paintings, although the 15,000-year-old images of bulls, horses and reindeer are considered to be the best. After the discovery of the cave, increased amounts of carbon dioxide were found to be damaging the paintings. As a result, since 1963, the caves have been sealed. Visitors now may view a precise cement replica.

Chartres Cathedral

Contact Address
Office du Tourisme, Place de la Cathédrale, BP289, 28005 Chartres
Tel: (2) 37 18 26 26. Fax: (2) 37 21 51 91.
E-mail: chartres.tourism@wanadoo.fr

Location
Place de la Cathédrale, Chartres.

Transportation
Air: Charles de Gaulle Airport (Paris). Rail: services from Montparnasse Station (Paris) to Chartres. Car: A6 to A10 and A11.

Opening Times
Mon-Sat 0730-1915, Sun 0830-1915.

Admission Fees
Free.

 Historical   Man-made   Amusement

Visitors Annually
1,300,000.

Description
Chartres Cathedral is considered by many to be the finest Gothic cathedral in France, if not in Europe. After the original burned down in 1194, a papal representative managed to convince the spiritually devastated people of Chartres to build a new cathedral. What has resulted is a spectacular combination of early Gothic and high Gothic, attracting hordes of visitors every year. The cathedral is also particularly well known for its spires, stained glass and numerous religious sculptures.

Château de Chenonceau

Contact Address
Château de Chenonceau, 37150 Chenonceaux
Tel: (02) 47 23 90 07. Fax: (02) 47 23 80 88.
E-mail: chateau.de.chenonceau@wandadoo.fr
Web site: www.chenonceau.com

Location
34km (21 miles) from Tours, Loire Valley.

Transportation
Air: Charles de Gaulle Airport (Paris). Rail: St-Pierre-des-Corps (Tours). Car: A10.

Opening Times
Daily 0900-1900; closes earlier seasonally.

Admission Fees
FFr50.

Visitors Annually
850,000.

Description
Standing on the River Cher, the *Château de Chenonceau* is probably the most celebrated château of the many that are situated in the Loire Valley. Used as a working mill in the early Middle Ages, the château was built in 1513 and benefited from a succession of powerful noblewomen, who collectively imbued it with grace and charm. The interior is well known for its 59m-long gallery, for the library used by Catherine de Medici, and for the guard room.

Château de Versailles

Contact Address
Château de Versailles, RP 834, 78008 Versailles
Tel: (01) 30 83 78 00. Fax: (01) 30 83 78 90.
E-mail: www.chateauversailles.fr
Web site: www.chateauversailles.fr/en

Location
23km (15 miles) southwest of Paris city centre.

Transportation
Air: Charles de Gaulle Airport, Orly Airport. Rail: Montparnasse station. RER: Versailles-Rive-Gauche. Car: A13.

Opening Times
Château: Tues-Sun 0900-1830 (summer), 0900-1730 (winter). Gardens: daily, opening times vary according to season.

 Cultural *Natural*  *Religious*

Europe – **France**

Admission Fees
FFr45 (château); free (gardens).

Visitors Annually
3,900,000.

Special Needs
Wheelchair accessible.

Description
The Palace at Versailles began as a 'modest' hunting lodge in 1623. Louis XIV was so taken with it that by 1682 it had become the official residence of the court of France and a lavish and potent statement of monarchical power. Much of this character remains to this day, with visitors able to view the renowned 75m (250ft) *Hall of Mirrors*, the bedchambers, the grand staircase, and – perhaps most spectacularly – the gardens bedecked with extraordinarily elaborate fountains and pools.

Cité des Sciences et de l'Industrie

Contact Address
Cité des Sciences et de l'Industrie, 30 avenue Corentin-Cariou, 75930 Paris
Tel: (01) 40 05 12 12. Fax: (1) 40 05 81 90.
Web site: www.cite-sciences.fr/english

Location
Northeast Paris.

Transportation
Air: Charles de Gaulle Airport, Orly Airport. Métro: Porte de La Villette.

Opening Times
Tues-Sat 1000-1800, Sun 1000-1900.

Admission Fees
FFr50 (Explora), FFr25 (Argonaute), FFr29 (Cinaxe).

Visitors Annually
3,500,000.

Special Needs
Wheelchair accessible. Facilities for visually impaired and hearing impaired.

Restrictions
Pregnant women and children under three not admitted to certain areas.

Description
Located on a large urban renewal site devoted to culture and leisure, *Cité des Sciences et de l'Industrie* was completed in 1986 with a mandate to educate visitors about science and technology. The complex is made up of several individual sites. *Explora* offers visitors activities such as piloting an aeroplane or travelling through the human body. The *Géode* is a large geodesic dome containing a 1000-sq-metre (1196-sq-yard) screen. *Cinaxe* is a simulator outfitted with equipment used to train airline pilots.

Disneyland Paris

Contact Address
Disneyland Paris, BP100, 77777, Marne la Vallée
Tel: +44 (8705) 030 303.
Web site: www.disney.co.uk

 Historical   Man-made   Amusement

Europe – **France**

Location
32km (20 miles) east of Paris.

Transportation
Air: Charles de Gaulle Airport, Orly Airport. Rail: Eurostar or RER services to Marne-la-Vallée. Car: A4.

Opening Times
Daily 1000-1800 (low season), 0900-2300 (high season).

Admission Fees
FFr220; concessions available.

Visitors Annually
12,500,000.

Special Needs
Wheelchair accessible.

Description
Opened in 1992, *Disneyland Paris* is the Walt Disney Company's first attempt to win the hearts of Europeans as it had the hearts of its own Americans. Although locals took some time in warming to it, the Park has now reached such a point of success that a second Park, *Disney Studios*, will be opening in 2002. The original Park is very much like its American cousins, featuring sections like *Mainstreet USA*, *Discoveryland*, *Adventureland*, *Frontierland* and *Fantasyland*, however, enthusiasts rave that the more modern engineering of the French Parks can make for a superior experience.

Eiffel Tower

Contact Address
Champ de Mars, 7500 Paris
Tel: (01) 44 11 23 23. Fax: (01) 44 11 23 22.
E-mail: courrier@tour-eiffel.fr
Web site: www.tour-eiffel.fr

Location
Champ de Mars, Paris.

Transportation
Air: Charles de Gaulle Airport, Orly Airport. Métro: Bir-Hakeim, Trocadéro, Ecole Militaire. RER: Champ de Mars-Tour Eiffel.

Opening Times
Daily 0930-2300 (1 Sep-10 Jun), 0900-2400 (11 Jun-31 Aug).

Admission Fees
By lift: FFr22 (1st storey), FFr44 (2nd storey), FFr62 (3rd storey); by stairs: FFr18 (1st and 2nd storeys only).

Visitors Annually
6,400,000.

Description
Originally created as the centrepiece of Paris' *Exposition Universelle* in 1889, which was commemorating the centenary of the French Revolution, the *Eiffel Tower* went on to become the centrepiece of the city itself. The 318m-high tower that has become symbolic of Paris the world over, weighs 10,100 tonnes, contains 18,000 pieces of iron, held together by 2,500,000 rivets. Literally towering over the Champ de Mars, the third floor offers a superb view of Paris.

 Cultural   *Natural*  *Religious*

Europe – **France**

Musée du Louvre

Contact Address
Musée du Louvre, 75058 Paris
Tel: (01) 40 20 50 50. Fax: (01) 40 20 54 42.
E-mail: info@louvre.fr
Web site: www.louvre.fr

Location
Galerie du Carrousel, rue de Rivoli, central Paris.

Transportation
Air: Charles de Gaulle Airport, Orly Airport. Métro: Palais Royal-Musée du Louvre.

Opening Times
Thurs-Sun 0900-1800, Mon and Wed 0900-2145.

Admission Fees
FFr45 (until 1500); FFr26 (after 1500 and all-day Sun).

Visitors Annually
5,000,000.

Special Needs
Wheelchair accessible. Special services for the developmentally disabled and visually impaired.

Description
Constructed as a fortress in the Middle Ages and rebuilt in the mid-sixteenth century as a royal palace, it wasn't until 1793 that the *Louvre* became a museum. Today, it is the home of some of the world's most famous works of art, including the *Mona Lisa* and *Venus de Milo*. The rest of the permanent collection includes Greek, Etruscan, Roman, Egyptian and oriental antiquities, as well as sculptures, objets d'art and prints and drawings.

Musée d'Orsay

Contact Address
62 rue de Lille, 75343 Paris
Tel: (01) 40 49 48 48 *or* 45 49 11 11. Fax: (01) 42 22 71 61.
Web site: www.musee-orsay.fr

Location
62 rue de Lille, central Paris.

Transportation
Air: Charles de Gaulle Airport, Orly Airport. Métro: Solférino. RER: Musée d'Orsay.

Opening Times
Tues-Sat 1000-1800 (until 2145 Thurs), Sun 0900-1800.

Admission Fees
FFr40.

Visitors Annually
3,000,000.

Special Needs
Wheelchair accessible. Tactile exhibits for visually impaired. Sign-language tours for hearing impaired. Tours for the developmentally disabled.

Description
This magnificently restored railway station houses the French national collection of art from

 Historical   *Man-made*   *Amusement*

Europe – **France**

1848 to 1914. Since opening in 1986, the sky-lit upper level is a notorious beehive of tourist activity, attracting pilgrims from far and wide to take in the stunning collection of impressionists, which includes works by Monet, Degas, Cézanne and Van Gogh. The museum's collection also showcases the Art Nouveau movement.

Notre Dame Cathedral

Contact Address
Place du Parvis de Notre Dame, 75004 Paris
Tel: (01) 42 34 56 10 *or* 44 32 16 70 (towers). Fax: (01) 40 51 70 98.
E-mail: ecrire@catholique-paris.com
Web site: www.catholique-paris.com

Location
Ile-de-la-Cité, Paris.

Transportation
Air: Charles de Gaulle Airport, Orly Airport. Métro: Cité. RER: St-Michel-Notre-Dame.

Opening Times
Daily 0800-1845 (cathedral), 1000-1815 (towers).

Admission Fees
FFr25; concessions available.

Visitors Annually
12,000,000.

Special Needs
Wheelchair accessible.

Description
Begun in 1163 and completed in about 1345, *Notre Dame* ranks as one of France's finest examples of Gothic architecture. In its long life, besides being a resplendent medieval cathedral, Notre Dame has been reportedly set on fire and used to house livestock. However, the cathedral sill awes visitors with its massive rose windows, a 7800-pipe organ, towering spire and splayed flying buttresses. A view from the top of the west façade is available to visitors.

Pont du Gard

Contact Address
Concession Pont du Gard, Route de Pont du Gard, 30210 Vers Pont du Gard
Tel: (4) 66 37 51 12. Fax: (4) 66 37 51 50.
E-mail: accueil-pontgard@nimes.cci.fr

Location
21km (13 miles) northeast of Nimes.

Transportation
Air: Marseille-Provence Airport. Rail: Avignon or Nimes. Car: A9, N100, N86.

Opening Times
Daily 24 hours.

Admission Fees
Free.

Visitors Annually
1,250,000.

 Cultural   *Natural*   *Religious*

Europe – **France/Germany**

Restrictions
Visitors prohibited from walking along the top tier.

Description
Constructed by the son-in-law of Emperor Augustus, the stunning *Pont du Gard* is the largest surviving piece of a Roman aqueduct that spanned the *River Gardon*, northeast of Nimes. At a height of 49m (161ft) and with a length of 273m (896ft), it consists of three tiered levels of arches. At one time, it was part of a greater engineering marvel that transported water over a distance of more than 50km (35 miles). The aqueduct took over a century to complete and was constructed without mortar. There is now a new cultural centre, which contains exhibitions on Roman civilisation and the aqueduct specifically.

Pont St-Bénézet

Contact Address
Avignon Tourist Board, 41 cours Jean Jaurès, 8400 Avignon
Tel: (04) 32 74 32 74. Fax: (04) 90 82 95 03.
E-mail: information@ot-avignon.fr
Web site: www.avignon-tourisme.com

Location
Avignon city centre.

Transportation
Air: Marseilles-Provence Airport.

Opening Times
Daily 0900-1900 (Apr-Sep), 0930-1730 (Oct-Mar).

Admission Fees
Not applicable.

Visitors Annually
Not available.

Description
'Sur le pont d'Avignon on'y danse, on y danse ...' – the melody of the nineteenth-century song draws visitors to the famed bridge, formally known as the Pont St-Bénézet after the shepherd Bénézet whose heavenly vision and determination caused the bridge to be built. The 900m bridge, spanning the two channels of the River Rhone and the island in between (Ile de la Barthelasse), was built between 1177 and January 1185. Originally made of wood, it was continuously rebuilt, the only bridge linking the Mediterranean and Lyons, an important trade hub, in the Middle Ages. The river finally won the day, washing away the bridge in the mid-1600s. Today, only four of its original 22 arches and the tiny *Chapelle St-Nicholas* remain. The small *Musée des Images* offers pictures of the bridge in its former glory.

Germany

Brandenburg Gate

Contact Address
Berlin Tourist Office, Am Karlsbad 11, 10785 Berlin
Tel: (0180) 575 4040. Fax: (030) 25 00 24 24.

 Historical Man-made Amusement

Europe – **Germany**

Location
Unter den Linden, Berlin city centre.

Transportation
Air: Tegel Airport. S-Bahn: Unter den Linden.

Opening Times
Daily 24 hours.

Admission Fees
Not applicable.

Visitors Annually
Not available.

Description
Built in 1791 as an emblem of peace, the *Brandenburg Gate*, the only remaining town gate in the country, is an enduring symbol of Berlin and Germany. It has survived multiple wars, including the long Cold War, during which it was sealed off in no-man's land, becoming a symbol of division between east and west. In 1989, it was reopened to the public following the destruction of the Berlin Wall. Today, traffic passes freely through the gate and the surrounding plaza is filled with tourists.

Cologne Cathedral

Contact Address
Domforum, Domkloster 2, 50667 Cologne
Tel: (0221) 92 58 47 20. Fax: (0221) 92 58 47 21.
Web site: www.koelner-dom.de

Location
Domkloster 2, central Cologne.

Transportation
Air: Cologne/Bonn–Konrad Adenauer International Airport. Rail: Central Station.

Opening Times
Daily 0600-1930.

Admission Fees
Free (cathedral); DM3 (treasury); DM3 (tower).

Visitors Annually
4,500,000.

Description
Begun in 1248 and completed in 1880, *Cologne Cathedral* is a Gothic masterpiece, celebrating the scale and finely detailed intricacy of the style. Its twin towers stand 157m (515ft) above the city, on the left bank of the Rhine. The interior is equally impressive, with fourteenth-century stained glass, a resplendent choir, and a large gold shrine considered a masterpiece of medieval gold work.

Englischer Garten

Contact Address
Verwaltung des Englischen Gartens München, Englischer Garten 2, 80538 Munich

Location
Northeast Munich.

 Cultural   *Natural*   *Religious*

Europe – **Germany**

Transportation
Air: Flughafen München. U-Bahn: Universität, Giselastrasse or Münchener Freiheit.

Opening Times
Daily 24 hours.

Admission Fees
Free.

Visitors Annually
Not available.

Special Needs
Wheelchair accessible.

Description
Munich seems an odd place to find an English garden, but it is home to one of the most famous, the *Englischer Garten*, one of Europe's oldest urban landscaped parks. Originally laid out in 1789 as a military garden, it was soon opened to the public who found there, and still find, another cultural oddity, the *Chinesischer Turm* (Chinese Tower). Surrounding it is a beer garden popular with both tourists and locals for beer, coffee and cakes.

Neuschwanstein Castle

Contact Address
Kurverwaltung, Münchner Strasse 2, 87645 Schwangau
Tel: (08362) 81035. Fax: (08362) 8990.

Location
Near Schwangau, Bavaria.

Transportation
Air: Flughafen München. Rail: Fussen station. Coach: services from Fussen to Hohenschwangau. Car: A95, A8, A96 to B17.

Opening Times
Daily 1000-1600 (Oct-Mar), 0900-1800 (Apr-Sep).

Admission Fees
DM14; concessions available.

Visitors Annually
1,200,000.

Description
Neuschwanstein Castle is one of three castles built by 'mad' Ludwig II of Bavaria. Seemingly out of a fantasy, it sits perched among the natural splendour of the Alps, and it is not surprising that it was the inspiration for Disney's Magic Kingdom. Unfortunately, Ludwig II never witnessed its completion as he was found mentally unfit by a government commission. Visitors, however, can take tours and witness the 17 rooms that were finished, including the opulent *Singer's Hall* and majestic throne room.

Pergamon Museum

Contact Address
Bodestrasse 1-3, 10178 Berlin
Tel: (030) 20 90 55 77. Fax: (030) 20 90 55 02.
Web site: www.smb.spk-berlin.de

 *Historical*   *Man-made*   *Amusement*

67

Europe – **Germany**

Location
Bodestrasse 1-3, central Berlin.

Transportation
Air: Tegel Airport. S/U-Bahn: Friedrichstrasse.

Opening Times
Tues-Sun 1000-1800 (until 2200 Thurs).

Admission Fees
DM8.

Visitors Annually
650,000.

Special Needs
Wheelchair accessible.

Description
One of the world's great museums, the *Pergamon Museum* lies on Berlin's Museuminsel museum complex. It houses spectacular works of architectural antiquities, including collections of Greek, Assyrian, Islamic and Far Eastern art. Many objects are of a magnitude rarely found indoors, such as the *Pergamon Altar*, with a 120m (394ft) frieze, the *Market Gate of Miletus* and the *Ishtar Gate* from Babylon.

Reichstag

Contact Address
Platz der Republik 1, 11011 Berlin
Tel: (030) 22 73 21 52. Fax: (030) 22 73 00 27.
E-mail: DBT-Besucherdienst@t-online.de
Web site: www.bundestag.de

Location
Platz der Republik 1, Berlin.

Transportation
Air: Tegel Airport. S-Bahn: Unter den Linden.

Opening Times
Daily 0800-2200.

Admission Fees
Free.

Visitors Annually
2,000,000.

Special Needs
Wheelchair accessible.

Restrictions
Acces to dome only; full guided tour requires advanced reservations.

Description
The imposing neo-Renaissance *Reichstag*, located in the heart of Berlin's city centre near the River Spree and the *Brandenburg Gate*, was completed in 1894. It was home to the German parliament until 1933, when there was a fire which coincided with Adolph Hitler assuming dictatorial control of the country. It was not until 1990 that the German parliament (now called the Bundestag) again met in this historic building, and in 1999 the parliament moved permanently to a renovated and renewed *Reichstag*. A new glass dome symbolises the transparency of the democracy, and visitors can pass between its layers to watch the governmental process at work.

 Cultural   *Natural* *Religious*

Europe – **Germany/Greece**

Greece

Acropolis

Contact Address
Acropolis, Athens
Tel: (01) 321 0219 (Acropolis) *or* 323 6665 (museum). Fax: (01) 321 4172.

Location
Athens city centre.

Transportation
Air: Athens Athinai Airport. Metro: Monastiráki, Theseion.

Opening Times
Daily 0800-1900 (summer), 0830-1500 (winter).

Admission Fees
Dr2000.

Visitors Annually
Not available.

Special Needs
None.

Description
The *Acropolis* is one of the most famous sites of the ancient world. This 'Sacred Rock' rising over 60m (200ft) above Athens reached its apogee during the city's golden age under Pericles. It is the site of three different temples to Athena, the patron goddess of Athens, the most famous of which is the *Parthenon*. Completed in 438, its broad flank of Doric columns is synonymous with ancient culture throughout the world.

Delphi

Contact Address
Delphi Museum, 330 54 Greece
Tel: (0265) 82 313. Fax: (0265) 82 966.

Location
160km (100 miles) northwest of Athens.

Transportation
Air: Athens Athinai Airport. Rail: Levadia Station.

Opening Times
Daily, times vary according to season.

Admission Fees
Dr1200.

Visitors Annually
500,000.

Special Needs
Certain areas wheelchair accessible.

Description
Soaring high above the Gulf of Corinth, *Delphi* was one of the most important sites in the

*Europe – * **Greece**

Ancient Greek world, home to the sanctuary of Apollo and the seat of his oracle. The famed oracle is perhaps the best known of Delphi's ancient inhabitants, his predictions affecting matters as grand as those of warfare. Today, the site lies in ruins, although they are well-preserved and highly popular ruins.

Knossos

Contact Address
Knossos Palace, Crete
Tel: (081) 231 940.

Location
Island of Crete, eight kilometres (five miles) from north shore.

Transportation
Air: Athens Athinai.

Opening Times
Daily 0800-1700 (winter), 0800-1900 (summer).

Admission Fees
Dr1500.

Visitors Annually
1,000,000.

Special Needs
Wheelchair accessible.

Description
Located on the island of Crete, *Knossos* is the site of the most important palace of the ancient Minoans, the earliest of the Aegean civilisations. It was home to King Minos and, as tradition has it, the Minotaur, a giant bull who inhabited the perilous Labyrinth. The Minoan civilisation spread to mainland Greece to form the Mycenaean civilisation, a precursor to the Ancient Greeks. Knossos offers the modern-day visitor an abundance of ancient sites, including the *Palace of Knossos*, the *Royal Villa*, the *House of Frescoes* and the *Temple Tomb*.

National Archaeological Museum of Athens

Contact Address
Patission 44, Athens 10682
Tel: (01) 821 7717. Fax: (01) 821 3573.
E-mail: protocol@eam.culture.gr

Location
Athens city centre.

Transportation
Air: Athens Athinai Airport. Metro: Omonia.

Opening Times
Daily 0800-1900 (summer); Tues-Sun 0830-1500, Mon 1030-1700 (winter).

Admission Fees
Dr2000.

 Cultural *Natural* *Religious*

Europe – Greece/Hungary

Visitors Annually
Not available.

Description
The most important museum in this ancient yet bustling city, the *National Archaeological Museum of Athens* houses one of the richest collections of ancient Greek art in the world. Completed in 1899, the collection comprises all periods of ancient Greek civilisation. It is particularly well known for objects found at the ancient city of Mycenae, including gold death masks, ornate vessels, gold dishes and more.

Hungary

Buda Castle Palace

Contact Address
I. Budvári Palota, Dísz tér 17, Budapest
Tel: (1) 375 7533. Fax: (1) 212 2534.

Location
Buda.

Transportation
Air: Budapest Ferihegy Airport. Tram: 18. Car: no access.

Opening Times
Varies according to museum. Closed Mon.

Admission Fees
Varies according to museum.

Visitors Annually
Not available.

Description
Located in Budapest's picturesque Old Town, *Buda Castle Palace* was first inhabited by King Béla after the 1241 Mongol invasion. The palace has housed a number of monarchs and many, often damaging, wars. The result is a mixture of styles ranging from Gothic to Baroque. Today, it is home to a number of museums, including the *Ludwig Museum* and the *Hungarian National Gallery*. The Ludwig Museum is named after its patron Peter Ludwig, whose donations included Picasso, Warhol and Lichenstein, and mostly contains Eastern European painting and sculpture. The Hungarian National Gallery contains an encyclopaedic collection of Hungarian art from the tenth century to the present day.

Budapest Central Synagogue

Contact Address
VII. Dohány utca 2, Budapest
Tel: (1) 342 1335. Fax: (1) 342 8949.

Please see the map at the front of each section for the location of attractions.

 Historical   Man-made   Amusement

Europe – **Hungary**

Location
Pest.

Transportation
Air: Budapest Ferihegy Airport. Metro: Deák tér. Tram: 47 or 49.

Opening Times
Sun-Fri 1000-1500.

Admission Fees
Ft400.

Visitors Annually
Not available.

Description
The *Budapest Central Synagogue* is the largest synagogue in Europe and the second largest in the world. Completed in 1859, it was built in a Moorish-Byzantine style and today its two shining Moorish domes have been restored to their former brilliance. A *Jewish Museum* next door recounts the horrors of the Holocaust and displays exhibits dating as far back as the Middle Ages.

Fisherman's Bastion

Contact Address
Tourism Office of Budapest, 1364 Budapest, PF 215, 1052 Budapest
Tel: (1) 266 0479. Fax: (1) 266 7477.
Web site: www.hungarytourism.hu

Location
Buda.

Transportation
Air: Budapest Ferihegy Airport. Tram: 18. Car: no access.

Opening Times
Daily 24 hours.

Admission Fees
Ft100; free Mon.

Visitors Annually
Not available.

Special Needs
Not wheelchair accessible.

Description
The *Fisherman's Bastion* was built in 1905, and named after the guild of fishermen responsible for defending this stretch of wall in the Middle Ages. An almost Disney-like tower dominates this stone wall with seven turrets representing the Magyar tribes who populated the country. Excellent views across the Danube can be had, especially by climbing the tower.

 Art in Amsterdam? Romance in Rome? Metros in Madrid? Sport in Strasbourg? Drinking in Dublin? Business in Berlin? Eating out in Edinburgh? Accommodation in Athens?
– for all this, and more besides, consult the *Columbus City Guide – Europe*.

Cultural *Natural*  *Religious*

Europe – **Iceland**

Iceland

Geysir

Contact Address
Iceland Tourist Board, Laekjargata 3, 101 Reykjavik
Tel: 535 5500. Fax: 535 5001.
E-mail: info@icetourist.is
Web site: www.south.is/geysir.html

Location
Haukadalur, Biskupstungur, 801 Selfoss; 125 km southeast of Reykjavik.

Transportation
Air: Reykjavik Keflavik Airport. Car: ring road 1.

Opening Times
Not applicable.

Admission Fees
Not applicable.

Visitors Annually
200,000.

Special Needs
Certain areas wheelchair accessible.

Description
Until 1916, *Geysir* was one of the world's great geysers. Mysteriously, though, it went dormant, some say due to hundreds of tourists filling its chamber with objects, and has come to life only once in 1935. Nevertheless, the smaller *Strokker* geyser nearby makes up for its big brother's silence by erupting every five to ten minutes. The entire area is a geothermal park, with belching mud pits, hissing steam vents, hot and cold springs, warm streams and even primitive plants.

Perlan

Contact Address
Post 5252, 125 Reykjavik
Tel: 562 0200. Fax: 562 0207.
E-mail: perlan@perlan.is
Web site: www.perlan.is

Location
Öskjuhlio, Reykjavik.

Transportation
Air: Reykjavik Keflavik Airport.

Opening Times
Daily 1000-2200.

Admission Fees
Not applicable.

Visitors Annually
400,000.

Historical   *Man-made*   *Amusement*

*Europe – **Iceland/Ireland***

Special Needs
Wheelchair accessible.

Description
Perlan (the Pearl) is as much an architectural masterpiece as it is a feat of engineering. This dominating ten-storey building is geothermally heated by water forced through steel supports. Excellent views of Reykjavik can be had from the *Viewing Deck* on level four. There is a revolving restaurant in the dome at the top of the building, as well as a winter garden on the first floor.

Ireland

Blarney Castle

Contact Address
Blarney Castle, County Cork
Tel: (021) 385 252. Fax: (021) 381 518.
E-mail: info@blarneyc.ie

Location
Nine kilometres (5.5 miles) northwest of Cork.

Transportation
Air: Cork Airport. Rail: Cork Station. Car: N20.

Opening Times
Mon-Sat 0900-1900, Sun 0930-1700; may vary seasonally.

Admission Fees
Ir£3.50.

Visitors Annually
220,000.

Restrictions
Not recommended for small children.

Description
Set in idyllic Irish countryside, *Blarney Castle* is home to the famous *Blarney Stone*. Situated high in the battlements of the castle, the stone is thought to be half of the Stone of Scone, an ancient Scottish stone believed to have special powers. Kissing the stone is said to imbue visitors with the gift of eloquent speech. The castle itself began life as a tenth-century hunting lodge and was rebuilt in stone in 1210. Today, much of it lies in ruin.

Cliffs of Moher

Contact Address
Cliffs of Moher, Shannon Heritage Visitor Centre, Liscannor, County Clare
Tel: (065) 708 1171 (seasonal) *or* 708 1565 (Shannon Heritage).

Location
County Clare, west Ireland.

Transportation
Air: Shannon Airport. Rail: Ennis station, Galway station. Car: N67; N-85 from Ennis.

 Cultural    *Natural   Religious*

Europe – **Ireland**

Opening Times
Not applicable. Visitor Centre: 0930-1530 (winter), 0900-2000 (summer).

Admission Fees
Not applicable. Visitor Centre: Ir£1.05.

Visitors Annually
800,000.

Special Needs
Wheelchair accessible.

Description
The majestic *Cliffs of Moher* are one of Ireland's most spectacular and most visited tourist attractions. The cliffs rise out of the Atlantic Ocean, reaching a maximum height of 230m (755ft), and border the region called the Burren, home to interesting rock formations and rare plants and wildlife. The cliffs are best seen from *O'Briens Tower* for superb views across the rolling, blue Atlantic.

Glendalough

Contact Address
Glendalough Visitors Centre, Glendalough
Tel: (0404) 45352.

Location
24km (15 miles) west of Wicklow.

Transportation
Air: Dublin Airport. Rail: Wicklow station, Rathdrum station. Car: N11. Coach: daily services from Dublin.

Opening Times
Daily 0930-1700 (mid-Oct-mid-Mar), 0930-1800 (mid-Mar-May and Sep-mid-Oct), 0900-1830 (June-Aug).

Admission Fees
Ir£2; concessions available.

Visitors Annually
111,000.

Special Needs
Certain areas wheelchair accessible.

Description
Known in Irish as 'glenn of the two lakes', *Glendalough* is a glacially sculpted green valley of characteristic Irish beauty. During the 'Golden Age' of Ireland it was home to a monastic settlement established by St Kevin, a reclusive monk who plays a prominent role in the folklore of the area. Today, visitors can find well-preserved ruins, including a cathedral, a round tower and several churches.

Trinity College Dublin

Contact Address
Trinity College Library, College Street, Dublin 2
Tel: (01) 608 2320. Fax: (01) 608 2690.
Web site: www.tcd.ie

75

Europe – **Ireland/Italy**

Location
College Street, central Dublin.

Transportation
Air: Dublin Airport. Rail: Pearse Street Station.

Opening Times
Library and Book of Kells: daily 0930-1700 (Sunday hours vary seasonally).

Admission Fees
Ir£4.50 (library and Book of Kells).

Visitors Annually
500,000.

Special Needs
Wheelchair accessible.

Description
Founded in 1592, *Trinity College* is Ireland's most prominent university, with a list of alumni that includes Samuel Beckett, Jonathan Swift and Oscar Wilde. As well as partaking in a pleasurable stroll through the campus' lush grounds, visitors flock to the *Old Library*. Built in 1732, the Old Library houses the *Book of Kells*, one of the finest examples of medieval decorated manuscripts.

Italy

Colosseum

Contact Address
Piazza Colosseo, Formece 72, Rome
Tel: (06) 700 4261. Fax: (06) 700 4261.

Location
Rome city centre.

Transportation
Air: Leonardo de Vinci Airport. Metro: Colosseo.

Opening Times
Mon, Tues and Thurs-Sat 0900-two hours before sunset; Wed and Sun 0900-1300.

Admission Fees
L10,000.

Visitors Annually
10,000,000.

Special Needs
Wheelchair accessible.

Description
The *Colosseum* is arguably ancient Rome's most famous ambassador to posterity. Completed in AD82, this massive structure, with arch upon arch reaching 48m (157ft) into the air and measuring 190m by 155m (620ft by 513ft), held up to 50,000 boisterous citizens of Rome. The Colosseum was home to Rome's notorious gladiatorial games, featuring combat between men and animals, as well as even naval engagements. Unlike other Roman amphitheatres that are dug into hillsides, the Colosseum is a free-standing structure of stone and concrete.

 Cultural   *Natural*   *Religious*

Europe – **Italy**

Doge's Palace

Contact Address
Piazza San Marco, Venice
Tel: (041) 522 4951. Fax: (041) 528 5028.

Location
Piazza San Marco, Venice.

Transportation
Air: Marco Polo Airport. Ferry: line 1 or 82.

Opening Times
Daily 0900-1900 (summer), 0900-1700 (winter).

Admission Fees
L18,000.

Visitors Annually
1,250,000.

Description
Located in Venice's renowned *Piazza San Marco*, the *Doge's Palace* was home to the government of the former Venetian Republic. Originally built in 814, the present structure was completed in the early 1400s. The palace was a showplace for artistry, craftsmanship and architecture, and still exemplifies Venetian Gothic style, with graceful arcades and historic works of art.

Florence Duomo

Contact Address
Azienda di Promozione Turistica, Via A. Manzoni 16, 50121 Florence
Tel: (055) 23320. Fax: (055) 234 6286.

Location
Piazza del Duomo, Florence.

Transportation
Air: Amerigo Vespucci Airport. Rail: Santa Maria Novella.

Opening Times
Mon-Fri 0900-1700, Sat 1000-1645, Sun 1300-1700.

Admission Fees
Free.

Visitors Annually
5,500,000.

Description
The domed roof of Florence's *Duomo Santa Maria del Fiore*, simply known as *Duomo*, is symbolic of the meeting of Renaissance craft and culture. Taking over two centuries to build, it was one of the greatest achievements of the Italian Renaissance, affecting architectural styles that would follow. The cupola itself has a diameter of 46.5m (153ft) at the base, and the interior boasts sculptures by Renaissance names like Paulo Uccello, Andrea del Castagno, Giorgio Vasari and Federico Zuccari. The Duomo stands on the remains of an older cathedral, which can be seen in the archaeological area revealed beneath the floor.

Europe – Italy

Pantheon

Contact Address
Piazza de la Rotunda, Rome
Tel: (06) 68 30 02 30. Fax: (06) 588 3340.

Location
Piazza de la Rotunda, Rome.

Transportation
Air: Leonardo da Vinci Airport.

Opening Times
Mon-Sat 0900-1830, Sun 0900-1300.

Admission Fees
Free.

Visitors Annually
Not available.

Special Needs
Wheelchair accessible.

Description
Considered by many to be the best preserved of all great classical monuments, the *Pantheon* was dedicated in 27BC by Agrippa, the admiral who defeated Anthony and Cleopatra. Originally, the structure served as a temple for the seven Roman planetary deities, Apollo, Diana, Mars, Mercury, Jupiter, Venus, and Saturn, but was later consecrated as a Catholic church. The Pantheon possesses a dome with a span of 43.2m (142ft), the largest of its kind until the Duomo in Florence was built in the fifteenth century.

Pompeii

Contact Address
Via Satra 1, CAP 80045
Tel: (081) 850 7255. Fax: (081) 863 2401.

Location
25km (15.5 miles) south of Naples.

Transportation
Air: Naples Capodichino Airport. Rail: Pompeii Station.

Opening Times
Daily 0900-one hour before dusk.

Admission Fees
L1200.

Visitors Annually
Not available.

Special Needs
Wheelchair accessible.

Description
Once a lavish resort town for wealthy Romans, *Pompeii* was literally buried alive under hot volcanic ash and mud in AD79 during an eruption of nearby *Mount Vesuvius*. The city was eventually forgotten and it was not until the eighteenth century that it was rediscovered.

 Cultural   *Natural*   *Religious*

Now excavated, it provides an enthralling insight into the everyday lives of the ancient Romans. Visitors can view authentic villas replete with erotic and religious wall paintings, as well as actual brothels and plaster casts of fallen volcano victims.

Ponte Vecchio

Contact Address
Azienda di Promozione Turistica, Via A Manzoni 16, 50121 Florence
Tel: (055) 23320. Fax: (055) 234 6286.

Location
Florence city centre.

Transportation
Air: Amerigo Vespucci Airport. Rail: Santa Maria Novella.

Opening Times
Not applicable.

Admission Fees
Not applicable.

Visitors Annually
Not available.

Special Needs
Wheelchair accessible.

Description
This famous fourteenth-century bridge, home to Florence's gold and silversmiths, is still paved with goldsmiths and jewellers. The *Ponte Vecchio*'s genteel atmosphere dates back to the days of Cosimo de' Medici, who threw out a group of butchers who set up shop on the bridge. Above the shops that line the bridge is a secret passageway known as the *Corrodoio Vasariano*, linking the *Palazzo Vecchio*, *Uffizi Gallery* and the *Pitti Palace*, and originally built as a private passage for the Medici family.

Roman Forum

Contact Address
Via de Fori Imperiali, Piazza Santa Maria Nova 53, 00100 Rome
Tel: (06) 699 0110. Fax: (06) 678 7689.

Location
Rome city centre.

Transportation
Air: Leonardo da Vinci Airport. Metro: Colosseo.

Opening Times
Daily 0900-1800.

Admission Fees
Free.

Visitors Annually
Not available.

Special Needs
Wheelchair accessible.

 Historical Man-made Amusement

*Europe – **Italy***

Description
The *Roman Forum* was the symbolic heart of an empire that stretched from England to Carthage. Today, it requires a certain amount of imagination to picture it in its former glory, as the ravages of history have not been kind. Among the best-preserved monuments remaining are the triumphal *Arch of Septimius*, eight columns of the *Temple of Saturn* and the rectangular *House of the Vestal Virgins*.

St Peter's Basilica

Contact Address
Centro Servizi, Pellegrini e Touristi Informazioni, 00120 Vatican City
Tel: (06) 69 88 16 62.
Web site: www.christusrex.or

Location
Vatican City, Rome.

Transportation
Air: Leonardoda Vinci Airport. Metro: Ottaviano.

Opening Times
Daily 0800-1700 (Oct-Mar); 0700-1800 (Apr-Sep).

Admission Fees
L5000 (without lift); L6000 (with lift).

Visitors Annually
Not available.

Special Needs
Wheelchair accessible.

Restrictions
Visitors must be dressed appropriately, legs and shoulders must be covered.

Description
St Peter's Basilica stands in the Vatican City above the alleged resting place of the remains of St Peter. Although begun in 1506 and completed 120 years later, it replaced a previous basilica that had stood for a thousand years. Its renowned dome was designed by Michaelangelo and the interior, which includes Bernini's *Throne of St Peter* made from bronze purloined from the *Pantheon*, is an unbridled display of Renaissance grandeur.

Sistine Chapel

Contact Address
Viale Vaticano, 00120 Vatican City
Tel: (06) 69 88 38 60. Fax: (06) 69 88 59 61.
Web site: www.vatican.va

Location
Vatican City, Rome.

Transportation
Air: Leonardo da Vinci Airport. Metro: Ottaviano.

Opening Time-
Mon-Fri 1845-1600, Sun 0845-1300.

Admission Fees
L18,000.

 Cultural   Natural   Religious

Europe – **Italy**

Visitors Annually
Not available.

Special Needs
Wheelchair accessible.

Description
Renowned equally for the crowds that line up to see it as it is for its breathtaking beauty, the *Sistine Chapel* was constructed between 1475 and 1480 as a private chapel for Popes. The painting of its ceiling was charged to a reluctant Michaelangelo, whose subsequent depiction of Creation ranks among the most famous painted images of all time. The *Last Judgement*, also by Michaelangelo, hangs behind the altar, while other famous Renaissance works adorn the rest of the interior.

Tower of Pisa

Contact Address
Azienda di Promozione Turistica, Via B. Croce 26, 56125 Pisa
Tel: (050) 561 820 *or* 560 547. Fax: (050) 560 505.
Web site: torre.duomo.pisa.it

Location
Piazza del Duomo, Pisa.

Transportation
Air: Galileo Galilei Airport. Rail: Pisa Centrale.

Opening Times
Not applicable.

Admission Fees
Not applicable.

Visitors Annually
Not available.

Description
Constructed in 1173, at a time when the Pisans were enjoying an era of military success, the *Tower of Pisa* is infamous not only because of its striking beauty but because it is leaning. It has leaned almost since construction first started, thanks to the poor swampy soil beneath it. Under normal circumstances, the tower would have fallen long ago, but due to the fact that its construction was often interrupted by war and its limestone is unusually flexible, the tower still stands today, the top five metres (16ft) closer to the ground than it ought to be. The tower itself is closed to visitors, but people still flock to stare and take photographs.

Uffizi Gallery

Contact Address
Via della Ninna 5, 50122 Florence
Tel: (055) 238 8651 *or* 294 883 (ticket reservations). Fax: (055) 238 8694.
E-mail: uffizi@mac.uffizi.firenze.it
Web site: www.uffizi.firenze.it

Location
Via della Ninna 5, Florence.

Transportation
Air: Amerigo Vespucci Airport. Rail: Santa Maria Novella.

 Historical    Man-made   Amusement

Europe – Italy/Malta

Opening Times
Tues-Fri 0830-1850, Sat and Sun 0830-1900.

Admission Fees
L12,000.

Visitors Annually
1,400,000.

Description
As Italy's most important gallery, the *Uffizi Gallery* houses one of the richest and most important art collections in the world. Bequeathed to the gallery as the Medici art collection in 1737, on the condition that it never leaves the city, its works include extraordinary Renaissance masterpieces. Major works on hand include Botticelli's *Birth of Venus* and Primavera and Leonardo da Vinci's *Annunciation*, as well as pieces by Giotto, Titian, Tintoretto and Raphael.

Malta

Hagar Qim

Contact Address
Director, Museum of Archaeology, Auberge de Provence, Valetta
Tel: 221 623 *or* 239 545. Fax: 243 628 *or* 241 975.

Location
15km (nine miles) south of Valetta.

Transportation
Air: Malta International Airport. Car: Wied Zurreieq.

Opening Times
Daily 0830-1630.

Admission Fees
Lm1.

Visitors Annually
100,000.

Special Needs
Wheelchair accessible.

Description
Discovered under a mound of rubble in 1839, the Neolithic temples of *Hagar Qim*, dating from 300BC, are some of the oldest human structures in the world. Reminiscent of England's Stonehenge, the temples are built entirely of limestone rock, some towering at over six metres (20ft) high, weighing several tonnes. On the morning of the summer solstice, sunlight passes through a hole known as the 'oracle hole' and fills the apse of the temple.

 Flight Times? Climate? Theme Parks? Time Zones? Museums? UNESCO Heritage Sites? Railways? Ski Resorts? Game Parks? Sporting Events? Dive Sites? Travel Statistics? WTO Regions? – for all this, and more besides, consult the *World Travel Atlas*.

Cultural Natural Religious

Europe – **The Netherlands**

The Netherlands

Anne Frank House

Contact Address
PO Box 730, 1000 AS Amsterdam
Tel: (020) 556 7100. Fax: (020) 620 7999.
Web site: www.annefrank.nl

Location
263 Prinsengracht, Amsterdam city centre.

Transportation
Air: Amsterdam Schiphol Airport. Tram: 13, 14, 17 or 20.

Opening Times
Daily 0900-2100 (Apr-Aug), 0900-1900 (Sep-Mar).

Admission Fees
f10; concessions available.

Visitors Annually
800,000.

Special Needs
Not wheelchair accessible.

Restrictions
Access difficult for the less mobile.

Description
Anne Frank House is the historic home where Anne Frank and her family hid from the Nazis during WWII. Eventually they were betrayed to the Germans and Anne died at the Bergen-Belsen concentration camp: her father, however, survived and published her diary, which became world famous. Today, the house is a permanent exhibition dedicated to the memory of Anne Frank, where the original diary is on display.

Keukenhof Gardens

Contact Address
PO Box 66, 2160 AB Lisse
Tel: (0252) 465 564. Fax: (0252) 465 565.
E-mail: info@keukenhof.nl
Web site: www.keukenhof.nl

Location
Town of Lisse.

Transportation
Air: Amsterdam Schiphol Airport. Rail: Leiden Central Station. Car: A4, A44, N208.

Opening Times
Daily 0800-1930.

Admission Fees
f19; concessions available.

Visitors Annually
Not available.

Europe – **The Netherlands**

Special Needs
Wheelchair accessible.

Description
Keukenhof Gardens draws its name from a fifteenth-century countess who gathered herbs here, in the kitchen gardens. It was designed as a park in 1840 and the flower garden was started in 1949. Today, Keukenhof Gardens is where the Dutch love of tulips enters the realm of the surreal. Although open daily, the best time of year to visit is from the last week in March to the last week in May. These 28-hectare (69-acre) gardens are filled with over five million bulbs, planted in layers of three, of narcissi, hyacinths, and, of course, tulips.

Rijksmuseum

Contact Address
PO Box 74888, 1070 DN Amsterdam
Tel: (020) 674 7000. Fax: (020) 674 7001.
E-mail: info@rijksmuseum.nl
Web site: www.rijksmuseum.nl

Location
Stadhouderskade 42, Amsterdam.

Transportation
Air: Amsterdam Schiphol Airport. Rail: Central Station. Tram: 2, 5, 6, 7, 10, 12 or 20.

Opening Times
Daily 1000-1700.

Admission Fees
f15; concessions available.

Visitors Annually
1,300,000.

Special Needs
Wheelchair accessible.

Description
The largest and most popular museum in the Netherlands, the *Rijksmuseum* was first opened in 1800 in the Hague. It came to its present building, designed by Dutch architect Cuypers, in 1885. Today, its collection houses a large number fifteenth to nineteenth-century paintings, including notable pieces by Rembrandt and Vermeers, as well as a collection of furniture, including a stunning group of dolls' houses.

Van Gogh Museum

Contact Address
PO Box 75366, 1070 AJ Amsterdam
Tel: (020) 570 5200. Fax: (020) 673 5053.
E-mail: info@vangoghmuseum.nl
Web site: www.vangoghmuseum.nl

Location
Museumplein, entrance at Paulus Potterstraut 7, Amsterdam.

Transportation
Air: Amsterdam Schiphol Airport. Rail: Central Station. Tram: 2 or 5.

 Cultural *Natural*   *Religious*

Europe – **The Netherlands/Northern Ireland**

Opening Times
Daily 1000-1800.

Admission Fees
f15.50; concessions available.

Visitors Annually
1,300,000.

Special Needs
Wheelchair accessible.

Description
Opened in 1973, the *Van Gogh Museum* houses the collection of paintings bequeathed from Vincent Van Gogh to his brother Theo. The museum contains some 200 paintings, 500 drawings, 700 letters and the artist's own collection of Japanese prints, as well as a large collection of Van Gogh's contemporaries, including Henri de Toulouse-Lautrec and Paul Gauguin.

Northern Ireland

Giants Causeway

Contact Address
Giants Causeway Visitors Centre, 44 Causeway Road, Bushmills, County Antrim BT57 8SU
Tel: (028) 2073 1855. Fax: (028) 2073 2537.
E-mail: causeway@nitic.net

Location
Three kilometres (two miles) north of Bushmills.

Transportation
Air: Belfast International Airport. Rail: Port Rush. Car: M2 and A26.

Opening Times
Daily 24 hours.

Admission Fees
Free.

Visitors Annually
450,000.

Special Needs
Wheelchair accessible.

Description
Situated on the northern coast of Ireland, *Giants Causeway* is a unique geological feature consisting of a protrusion of basalt hexagonal columns jutting into the sea. The Causeway was formed 50-60 million years ago by the cooling of volcanic rock, although local legend maintains that the causeway was built by two giants, one in Ireland and one in Scotland, who needed to travel over the sea to fight one another.

 Art in Amsterdam? Romance in Rome? Metros in Madrid? Sport in Strasbourg? Drinking in Dublin? Business in Berlin?
– for all this, and more besides, consult the *Columbus City Guide – Europe*.

Historical  Man-made Amusement

Norway

Bryggen

Contact Address
Bergen Tourist Office, Vågsallmenningen, N-5014 Bergen
Tel: (55) 321 480. Fax: (55) 321 464.
E-mail: info@bergen-travel.com
Web site: www.bergen-travel.com

Location
Bergen harbour.

Transportation
Air: Bergen Flesland Airport.

Opening Times
Not applicable.

Admission Fees
Not applicable.

Visitors Annually
Not available.

Special Needs
Wheelchair accessible.

Description
Considered by UNESCO to be one of the world's foremost showcases of the Middle Ages, *Bryggen* consists of a series of gabled buildings standing in the old wharf of Bergen, reminiscent of Bergen's prominent role in the days of the Hanseatic League. They have survived countless threats over the last 60 years, including fires and Nazi bombings, and many of the houses have been restored to their original state. Today, Bryggen is alive with restaurants, cafés and artists' workshops.

Hardanger Fjord

Contact Address
Destination Hardanger Fjord, PO Box 66, 5601 Norheimsund
Tel: (56) 55 38 70. Fax: (56) 55 38 71.
E-mail: info@hardangerfjord.com
Web site: www.hardangerfjord.com

Location
75km (47 miles) east of Bergen.

Transportation
Air: Bergen Flesland Airport. Car: E134, E39, Route 7.

Opening Times
Not applicable.

Admission Fees
Not applicable.

Visitors Annually
Not available.

 Cultural   Natural    Religious

Europe – **Norway/Poland**

Special Needs
Limited wheelchair access.

Description
Hardanger Fjord is one of the most popular destinations for visitors to Norway. This scenic area offers virtually every kind of natural landscape available in the country, from scenic water routes, apple and cherry orchards and hiking trails, to waterfalls, mountain plateaus and year-round skiing. The area also contains *Hardangervidda*, Norway's largest national park, and the *Viking Burial Place* in Hereid.

Poland

Auschwitz

Contact Address
State Museum of Auschwitz-Birkenau, 20 Wiezniow Oswiecimia Strasse, 32-600 Oswiecim
Tel: (33) 843 2157. Fax: (33) 843 2227.

Location
70km (46 miles) west of Cracow.

Transportation
Air: Krakow-Balice John Paul II International Airport. Rail: Cracow station.

Opening Times
Daily 0800-1500 (Dec-Feb), 0800-1600 (Mar and Nov), 0800-1700 (Apr and Oct), 0800-1800 (May and Sep), 0800-1900 (Jun-Aug).

Admission Fees
Free.

Visitors Annually
Not available.

Special Needs
Wheelchair accessible.

Restrictions
No children under 14.

Description
Auschwitz is the most infamous of the Nazi death camps. It saw the death of an estimated four million victims, mostly Jewish, between 1940 and 1945. Today, the camp is a museum dedicated to the memory of those who suffered and died. Barracks and crematoria offer displays detailing the nature of the atrocities, including personal articles and photographs. A half-hour walk away is *Auscwitz II-Birkenau*, a camp even more geared to mass death than the original Auschwitz.

Wawel Royal Castle

Contact Address
Wawel 5, 31-001 Kraków
Tel: (012) 421 5155. Fax: (012) 421 1697.
Web: www.cyfronet.krakow.pl/wawel

 Historical   *Man-made*   *Amusement*

Location
Wawel, central Cracow.

Transportation
Air: Krakow-Balice John Paul II International Airport. Rail: Cracow station.

Opening Times
Tues-Thurs and Sat 0930-1500, Fri 0930-1600, Sun 1000-1500.

Admission Fees
Z12 (Royal Chambers *or* Treasury and Armoury), Z6 (The Lost Wawel *or* Oriental Art) and Z2 (Dragon's Den).

Visitors Annually
Not available.

Restrictions
Restrictions on visitor numbers.

Description
Wawel Royal Castle was the seat of Polish royalty from the eleventh century onwards. The majority of the castle is in the Renaissance style, although significant Romanesque and Gothic elements remain. Today, it functions as a museum, with some of the original Renaissance decoration still existing. Among its many treasures are the *Crown Treasury and Armoury*, the *Lost Wawel* exhibit and a collection of sixteenth-century Flemish tapestries.

Portugal

Castle of St George

Contact Address
Castelo de São Jorge, 1100-129 Lisbon
Tel: (21) 887 7244. Fax: (21) 887 5695.

Location
Lisbon city centre.

Transportation
Air: Lisbon Airport. Tram: 12 or 28.

Opening Times
Daily 0900-2100 (summer), 0900-1800 (winter).

Admission Fees
Free (gardens); Esc600 (Olisipónia); Esc300 (Tower of Ulysses).

Visitors Annually
Not available.

Description
Perched on the highest of Lisbon's seven hills, above the old Moorish quarter, the *Castle of St George* was the royal residence until the late fifteenth century. Originally built by the Visigoths, the castle was rebuilt in 1940 to a state of luxury. It offers spectacular views of Lisbon, beautiful gardens, the *Olisipónia* with its multimedia exhibits that detail the history of Lisbon, and a camera obscura in the *Tower of Ulysses*.

> Please see the map at the front of each section
> for the location of attractions.

 Cultural  Natural Religious

*Europe – **Portugal/Russia***

Tower of Belém

Contact Address
Praca do Emperio, 1400 Lisbon
Tel: (21) 362 0034. Fax: (21) 363 9145.
E-mail: mjeronimos@mail.telepac.pt

Location
Praca do Emperio, Lisbon.

Transportation
Air: Lisbon International Airport. Rail: Belém Station.

Opening Times
Tues-Sun 1000-1700

Admission Fees
Esc400.

Special Needs
Certain areas wheelchair accessible.

Description
Completed in 1515, the *Tower of Belém* is one of Lisbon's most famous sights. Built in order to provide strategic defence to the river in a time of Portugal's naval ascendancy, the tower was the last sight seen by seafarers leaving the city. A gangway leads visitors to the museum; there is also a drawbridge and bulwark, former home to cannons, as well as a terrace that offers superb views of Lisbon and its surroundings.

Russia

Kremlin

Contact Address
The State Historical-cultural Museum-preserve 'Moscow Kremlin', Kremlin, Moscow 103073
Tel: (095) 202 6649. Fax: (095) 202 3832.
E-mail: press@kremlin.museum.ru
Web site: www.kremlin.museum.ru

Location
Moscow city centre.

Transportation
Air: Sheremetyevo International Airport. Metro: Biblioteka imeni Lenina, Aleksandrovski Sad.

Opening Times
Fri-Wed 1000-1700.

Admission Fees
Rb200.

Visitors Annually
Not available.

Special Needs
Wheelchair accessible.

Europe – **Russia**

Description
The *Kremlin* (literally 'fortified town') is a walled fortress dating back to the city's founding in 1147. From 1276 to 1712 it was the seat of government for the grand princes and tsars of Russia. In 1918, the Communist government held power from within its walls, and the present government still does to this day. The redbrick walls and towers enclose many historic Russian buildings, such as the *Assumption Cathedral*, the *Annunciation Cathedral*, the *Armoury Museum* and the *Diamond Fund*.

St Basil's Cathedral

Contact Address
Krasnaya ploshchad 4, Moscow
Tel: (095) 298 3304.

Location
Red Square, Moscow.

Transportation
Air: Sheremetyevo International Airport. Metro: Kitay-Gorod.

Opening Times
Wed-Mon 1000-1630.

Admission Fees
Rb75.

Visitors Annually
Not available.

Special Needs
Wheelchair accessible.

Description
The wildly coloured, onion-shaped domes of *St Basil's Cathedral* are Russia's most famous image. Each dome has a distinctive patterning and colour scheme, creating a stunning, fantastical effect reminiscent of whipped meringue. The cathedral was built in the 1550s to commemorate Ivan the Terrible's victory over the Mongols.

State Hermitage Museum

Contact Address
Dvortzovaya nab. 34-36, St Petersburg 191186
Tel: (0812) 110 9625.
E-mail: info@hermitage.ru
Web site: www.hermitagemuseum.org

Location
Dvortzovaya nab. 34-36, St Petersburg.

Transportation
Air: Pulkovo Airport. Metro: Nevskiy Prospect, Gostiny Dvor.

Opening Times
Tues-Sat 1030-1800, Sun 1030-1700.

Admission Fees
Rb250.

Visitors Annually
Not available.

 Cultural   *Natural*    *Religious*

Europe – **Russia/Scotland/Spain**

Special Needs
Wheelchair accessible.

Description
The *State Hermitage Museum* is one of the largest museums in the world, housing over three million art objects and representing periods as diverse as prehistoric art, Oriental art, Russian culture, Western European art and antiquity. The foundation of the collection stems from a purchase in 1764 by Catherine the Great of a considerable group of Western European paintings. One of the five buildings in which it is housed is the magnificent *Winter Palace*, the former residence of the Russian Emperors.

Scotland

Edinburgh Castle

Contact Address
Castle Hill, Edinburgh EH1 2NG
Tel: (0131) 225 9846. Fax: (0131) 220 4733.
Web site: www.historic-scotland.gov.uk

Location
Castle Hill, Edinburgh.

Transportation
Air: Edinburgh Airport. Rail: Waverley Station.

Opening Times
Mon-Sat 0930-1800 (Apr-Sep), 0930-1700 (Oct-Mar).

Admission Fees
£7; concessions available.

Visitors Annually
1,000,000.

Description
Edinburgh Castle looks over the city of Edinburgh from its perch on top of an extinct volcano. The oldest building in Edinburgh and its most popular tourist attraction, the castle has served both as fortress and royal residence, and today houses the *Scottish Crown Jewels*, the *Stone of Destiny*, and *Mons Meg* (a massive fifteenth-century bombard), as well as the headquarters of the Scottish Division. Within the castle premises is *St Margaret's Chapel*, a tiny Norman building that has stood for more than 900 years. Every day, except Sunday and bank holidays, at 1300, the one o'clock gun is fired from the castle.

Spain

Alhambra

Contact Address
Patronato de la Alhambra y Generalife, Real de la Alhambra s/n, 18009 Granada
Tel: (958) 220 912. Fax: (958) 210 584.

 *Historical* *Man-made* *Amusement*

*Europe – * **Spain**

Location
Granada city centre.

Transportation
Air: Malaga Airport.

Opening Times
Mon-Sat 0900-2000 (summer), 0900-1745 (winter).

Admission Fees
Pta750.

Visitors Annually
Not available.

Description
Overlooking the city of Granada, the *Alhambra* is the most important piece of Moorish architecture in Spain. Built between 1338 and 1390 as both a palace and a fortress, the name means 'the red' in Arabic, and the building is so-called because of the colour of the bricks forming the outer walls. Among the many sights within the interior is the *Alhambra Palace*, containing the fabled *Court of the Lions*, an alabaster basin supported by 12 white marble lions.

Guggenheim Museum Bilbao

Contact Address
Abandoibarra Etorbidea 1, 48001 Bilbao
Tel: (94) 435 9080. Fax: (94) 435 9040.
E-mail: atelleria@guggenheim-bilbao.es
Web site: www.guggenheim-bilbao.es/ingles/home.htm

Location
Bilbao city centre.

Transportation
Air: Bilbao Airport. Rail: Bilbao-Abando Station. Metro: Moyua Station.

Opening Times
Tues-Sun 1000-2000.

Admission Fees
Pta1000.

Visitors Annually
Not available.

Special Needs
Wheelchair accessible.

Description
The *Guggenheim Museum Bilbao* opened in 1997 and quickly became one of the most famous museums in the world. The collection focuses primarily on American and European art of the twentieth century, featuring styles such as Pop Art, Minimalism, Arte Povera, Conceptual Art, and Abstract Expressionism, as well as artworks that contemporary European and American artists designed specifically for the museum. The building itself is designed by renowned architect Frank O Gehry and is as well known for its striking appearance as for what it contains.

> Please see the map at the front of each section for the location of attractions.

 Cultural *Natural* *Religious*

*Europe – ***Spain***

La Sagrada Familia

Contact Address
Calle Mallorca 401, 08013 Barcelona
Tel: (93) 207 3031. Fax: (93) 476 1010.
E-mail: sagfam@grupart.es
Web site: www.sagfam.deakin.edu.au

Location
Calle Mallorca 401, Barcelona.

Transportation
Air: Barcelona Airport. Metro: Sagrada Familia.

Opening Times
Daily 0900-1800 (Nov-Feb), 0900-1900 (Sep-Oct), 0900-2000 (Apr-Aug).

Admission Fees
Pta800.

Visitors Annually
1,250,000.

Special Needs
Certain areas wheelchair accessible.

Description
The *Expiatory Temple of the Holy Family* is the unfinished masterpiece of Barcelona's most celebrated architect, Antonio Gaudí. A towering example of Barcelona's modernist architecture, its eerie, snaking lines and omnipresent detail make it unique among Europe's many cathedrals. Nevertheless, it lies in a perpetual state on incompleteness, with only one of its three façades complete.

Monasterio de San Lorenzo de El Escorial

Contact Address
Monasterio de San Lorenzo de El Escorial, San Lorenzo de El Escorial
Tel: (91) 890 5902/3/4.

Location
50km (31 miles) northwest of Madrid.

Transportation
Air: Madrid Barajas Airport. Rail: El Escorial Station. Car: M505, Nacional VI Highway.

Opening Times
Tues-Sun 1000-1900 (Apr-Sep), 1000-1800 (Oct-Mar).

Admission Fees
Pta850.

Visitors Annually
Not available.

Description
The *Monasterio de San Lorenzo de El Escorial* was built in the latter half of the sixteenth century by Philip II, King of the Spanish Empire, to commemorate his victory over the

 Historical  Man-made Amusement

Europe – **Spain**

French at the battle of San Quentin. Housing a monastery, two palaces and a library, the complex was intended to serve all the functions of church and state. Although the exterior is somewhat austere, the magnificent interior houses numerous works of art, including paintings by Titian, Tintoreto, Durer, Ribera and Velasquez, as well as 40,000 volumes in its noteworthy library.

Prado Museum

Contact Address
Villanueva Building, Paseo del Prado s/n, 28014 Madrid
Tel: (91) 330 2800. Fax: (91) 330 2856.
E-mail: museo.nacional@prado.mcu.es
Web site: museoprado.mcu.es

Location
Paseo del Prado, Madrid city centre.

Transportation
Air: Madrid Barajas Airport. Metro: Atocha, Banco de España.

Opening Times
Tues-Sat 0900-1900; Sun 0900-1400.

Admission Fees
Pta700 (permanent exhibitions), Pta500 (temporary exhibitions); concessions available.

Visitors Annually
Not available.

Special Needs
Wheelchair accessible.

Description
The 213-year-old *Prado Museum* is one of Europe's great museums. It possesses a collection of 4000 artworks emphasising Spanish, Flemish and Italian art from the fifteenth to the nineteenth century, including masterpieces by Titian, El Bosco, Botticelli, Rembrandt and Fra Angelico. The museum also possesses a renowned collection of paintings by Goya, ranging from his sun-soaked, festive early paintings to the grim madness of his black period.

Roman Aqueduct at Segovia

Contact Address
Spanish Tourist Office, Plaza Mayor 10, 40001 Segovia
Tel: (921) 460 334. Fax: (921) 460 330.
Web site: www.cyberspain.com/ciudades-patrimonio

Location
Segovia city centre.

Transportation
Air: Madrid Barajas Airport. Rail: Segovia Station.

Opening Times
Not applicable.

Admission Fees
Not applicable.

Visitors Annually
Not available.

 Cultural *Natural*  *Religious*

Special Needs
Wheelchair accessible.

Description
One of the best preserved Roman constructions, the *Roman Aqueduct at Segovia* was still in use as little as 50 years ago. Constructed around AD50 out of some 200,400 granite blocks, the structure was made without concrete and stands due to an equilibrium of forces. When in use, it carried water from the River Frio to the city of Segovia over a distance of 16km (ten miles). The portion of the aqueduct that is above ground is 728m (2388ft) in length and consists of 165 arches.

Santiago de Compostela Cathedral

Contact Address
Comisión de Cultura, Praza Platerías s/n, 15704 Santiago de Compostela
Tel: (981) 560 527. Fax: (981) 563 366.

Location
Praza do Obradoiro, Santiago de Compostela.

Transportation
Air: Santiago de Compostela Lavacolla Airport. Rail: Hórreo station, Santiago de Compostela.

Opening Times
Daily 0700-2100.

Admission Fees
Free.

Visitors Annually
5,000,000.

Special Needs
Wheelchair accessible.

Description
According to legend, the *Catedral de Santiago de Compostela* holds the remains of one of Christ's apostles, St James. As such, both the cathedral and town have been the sight of a major Christian pilgrimage for over a thousand years. The cathedral was consecrated in the year 1211, but has been added to significantly over the centuries, including a fifteenth-century dome and a baroque façade called the *Obradoiro*. Within the Obradoiro is the *Gate of Glory*, considered to be Spain's finest piece of Romanesque sculpture.

Seville Cathedral

Contact Address
Centro de Información de Sevilla, Carrer Arjona 28, 41001 Seville
Tel: (954) 505 600. Fax: (954) 505 605.
E-mail: cis@sevilla.org
Web site: www.sevilla.org

Location
Plaza Virgen de los Reyes (Puerta del Lagarto), Seville.

Transportation
Air: Seville Airport.

Opening Times
Mon-Sat 1030-1700, Sun 1400-1800.

 Historical   Man-made   Amusement

Europe – **Spain/Sweden**

Admission Fees
Pta700; free Sun.

Visitors Annually
Not available.

Description
Seville Cathedral was built in the fourteenth century on top of a razed mosque used by the retreating moors. Although builders retained the minaret and patio from the former mosque, the cathedral they constructed was then – and is still now – the largest Gothic structure in the world. The main altarpiece, *Retablo Mayor*, is the largest altar in the world. The cathedral also houses the remains of Christopher Columbus.

Sweden

Drottningholm Palace

Contact Address
Drottningholm Palace, 178 02 Drottningholm
Tel: (08) 402 6280. Fax: (08) 402 6281.
Web site: www.royalcourt.se/drottningholm/eng/index.html

Location
15km (nine miles) west of central Stockholm.

Transportation
Air: Arlanda Airport. Underground: Brommaplan. Car: in central Stockholm, Drottningholmsvägen to Brommaplan.

Opening Times
Daily 1000-1630 (May-Aug); daily 1200-1530 (Sep); Sat and Sun only 1200-1530 (Oct-Apr).

Admission Fees
SKr50.

Visitors Annually
Not available.

Description
Home to the royal family since 1981, *Drottningholm Palace* is one of the most magnificent legacies of Sweden's imperial age. Work began on the present palace in 1662, and over the years the interior has been embellished and improved by successive residents and is now renowned for its Rococo interiors. Drottningholm is surrounded by splendid Baroque gardens, including the great English Park and the French formal garden.

Museum of National Antiquities

Contact Address
Statens Historiska Museum, Box 5428, S-114 84 Stockholm
Tel: (08) 51 95 56 00. Fax: (08) 667 6578.
Web site: www.historiska.se

Location
Narvavagen 13-17, Stockholm.

 Cultural   Natural   Religious

Europe – **Sweden/Switzerland**

Transportation
Air: Arlanda Airport. Underground: Karlaplan.

Opening Times
Tues-Wed and Fri-Sun 1100-1700, Thurs 1100-2000.

Admission Fees
SKr60; concessions available.

Visitors Annually
120,000.

Special Needs
Wheelchair accessible.

Description
Sweden's *Museum of National Antiquities* traces the nation's history from the Stone Age to the sixteenth century. One of its most famous attractions is the Viking exhibition and the Gold Room. The museum also houses a fine collection of European painted medieval wooden religious sculpture and medieval textiles.

Switzerland

Jet d'Eau

Contact Address
Services Industriéls de Genève, 2 ch. Du Château Bloch, 1211 Geneva
Tel: (022) 420 7092. Fax: (022) 420 9360.
Web site: www.sig-ge.ch

Location
Geneva waterfront.

Transportation
Air: Geneva International Airport. Rail: Gare de Cornavin.

Opening Times
Mar-Oct daily 24 hours.

Admission Fees
Not applicable.

Visitors Annually
Not available.

Special Needs
Wheelchair accessible.

Restrictions
Sometimes switched off.

Description
Next to chocolates, watches, bankers and cowbells, a giant fountain seems an odd symbol of Europe. That being said, Geneva's *Jet d'Eau* has been breaking the calm of this peaceful city for over a hundred years. It made its debut in 1886 at a height of 30m (98ft), but has since grown to 140m (460ft). At three times the height of the Statue of Liberty, it is Europe's tallest fountain. An estimated seven tonnes of water are blasted aloft at a speed of 200kph (124mph) by the combined force of a number of electric pumps.

Historical   *Man-made*   *Amusement*

Jungfraujoch

Contact Address
Interlaken Tourism, Hoehweg 37, 3800 Interlaken
Tel: (033) 822 2121. Fax: (033) 822 5221.
E-mail: mail@interlakentourism.ch
Web site: www.interlakentourism.ch

Location
18km (11 miles) south of Interlaken.

Transportation
Air: Berne Belp Airport. Rail: Jungfrau Station.

Opening Times
Not applicable.

Admission Fees
Not applicable.

Visitors Annually
Not available.

Special Needs
Wheelchair accessible by train.

Description
The stereotypically Swiss hiking trails and snow-covered Alps of the *Jungfraujoch* have been attracting visitors for hundreds of years. The peak of the Jungfrau reaches 4158m (13,642ft), and beneath it lies the ridge or 'joch', where visitors can take in the largest glacier in Switzerland. Skiing and alpine activities are immensely popular with visitors, however, the best way to take in the region is by train. Completed in 1912, the *Jungfraujoch Railway* reaches the highest railway station in Europe.

Turkey

Blue Mosque

Contact Address
Sultan Ahmet Camii, Sultan Ahmet Meydani, Istanbul
Tel: (212) 518 1319.

Location
Sultan Ahmet, Istabul.

Transportation
Air: Istanbul Ataturk Airport.

Opening Times
Daily.

Admission Fees
Free.

Visitors Annually
Not available.

Europe – **Turkey**

Description
So grand was Istanbul's _Blue Mosque_ when it was first built that it raised a stir because it was considered a sacrilegious attempt to rival the architecture of Mecca. Construction began in 1609, and the mosque takes its name from the blue _Iznik_ tile work that covers the interior. From the exterior, it appears as a cascade of opulent domes, surrounded by six balconied minarets. The interior features a massive dome supported by four grand columns, as well as characteristic Ottoman tile patterns.

Ephesus

Contact Address
Ataturk Mah, Agora CAR. 35
Tel: (0232) 892 6945.

Location
600km (373 miles) southwest of Istanbul.

Transportation
Air: Istanbul Ataturk Airport.

Opening Times
Daily 0830-1800.

Admission Fees
TL2,000,000.

Visitors Annually
Not available.

Special Needs
Wheelchair accessible.

Description
Ephesus is one of the grandest and best-preserved ruins of the ancient world. To the ancient Greeks, it was the most important city in Ionian Asia Minor, and housed a significant temple. To the Romans, it was a flourishing city, with fountains, pools and the second largest library outside of Alexandria. Much of it remains intact for tourists today, including the façade of the library, Roman public toilets, the _Harbour Gymnasium_ and the _Temple of Hadrian_.

St Sophia

Contact Address
Museum of Hagia Sophia, Sultan Ahmet Square, Sultan Ahmet, Istanbul
Tel: (212) 522 0989 _or_ 522 1750.

Location
Sultan Ahmet, Istanbul.

Transportation
Air: Istanbul Ataturk Airport.

Opening Times
Tues-Sun 0930-1700.

Admission Fees
TL2,000,000.

Visitors Annually
Not available.

 Historical   _Man-made_    _Amusement_

Europe – **Turkey**

Description
When *St Sophia* was inaugurated by Justinian in the year 537, it was the most impressive building in the world and remained the crowning achievement of the Byzantine world for over a millennium. In the fifteenth century, Mehmet the Conqueror converted it to a mosque, adding the minarets, tombs and fountains. In 1937, it was established as a museum, with many of its Byzantine mosaics revealed from underneath layers of Ottoman plaster.

Topkapi Palace

Contact Address
Topkapi Palace Museum, 34400 Sarayii, Sultan Ahmet, Istanbul
Tel: (212) 512 0480 *or* 512 0484.

Location
Sultan Ahmet, Istanbul.

Transportation
Air: Istanbul Ataturk Airport.

Opening Times
Wed-Mon 0930-1700.

Admission Fees
TL2,000,000.

Visitors Annually
Not available.

Description
The *Topkapi Palace* was home to the sultans from the fifteenth century to the early 1800s. Hidden behind walls up to 12m (39 ft) high is an irregular palace – by European standards – neither monumental, symmetric nor immediately grand. What remains of it confirms its vast, sprawling design, replete with many courtyards and a notorious harem that housed up to 300 concubines. Other highlights include the sultan's bathroom and the imperial treasury.

Troy

Contact Address
Hükümet Konagŝ Kat,1 Çanakkale
Tel: (0286) 217 3791 *or* 217 5012.

Location
30km (19 miles) west of Çanakkale.

Transportation
Air: Istanbul Ataturk Airport.

Opening Times
Daily summer 0800-1700.

Admission Fees
TL500,000.

Visitors Annually
Not available.

Description
Until 1871, classical scholars the world over had thought Troy the stuff of legend. That changed when a millionaire-cum-archaeologist named Heinrich Schlieman discovered the

 Cultural    *Natural*   *Religious*

city that was the site of the famous battle that is depicted in Homer's *Iliad*. Troy is the city that lends its name to the Trojan Horse, history's most odious gift. Today, the ruins of nine levels are still being excavated (dating as far back as 3000BC), the fruits of which are on display for the curious and myth-obsessed alike.

Wales

Caernarfon Castle

Contact Address
Caernarfon, Gwynedd LL55 2AY
Tel: (01286) 677 617.

Location
Caernarfon, 12km (eight miles) southwest of Bangor.

Transportation
Air: Manchester Airport. Rail: Bangor Station. Car: M56, A55.

Opening Times
Daily 0930-1800 (closes earlier in winter).

Admission Fees
£4.20; concessions available.

Visitors Annually
220,000.

Description
Built by Edward I and begun in 1283, *Caernarfon Castle* is one of Europe's great medieval castles. The design, with its high walls marked with arrow slits and its angular towers, is said to have been inspired by the great city of Constantinople. The castle was built when Edward conquered Wales and was intended to form the administrative centre of the area. Prince Charles' investiture as the Prince of Wales took place at the castle in 1969. Today, visitors can enjoy informative exhibitions and displays.

section three
africa & the middle east

The numbers alongside the attractions below correspond to their locations on the maps overleaf, and not to the page numbers on which information on the attractions appear. Note that some attractions which straddle national frontiers and which have more than one entry in the text will likewise have more than one reference number on the map. For more detailed locations of these attractions consult the World Travel Atlas.

1	Moremi Wildlife Reserve	14	Tour Hassan
2	Abu Simbel	15	Cape Point
3	Egyptian Museum	16	Kruger National Park
4	Pyramids and Sphinx	17	Robben Island
5	Temple of Karnak	18	Table Mountain
6	Valley of the Kings	19	Kilimanjaro National Park
7	Masada	20	Serengeti National Park
8	Temple Mount	21	Carthage
9	Western Wall	22	Tunis Medina
10	Petra	23	Old City of San'a
11	Maasai Mara Game Reserve	24	Victoria Falls (Zambia)
12	Mount Kenya National Park	25	Victoria Falls (Zimbabwe)
13	Medina in Fez	26	Great Zimbabwe Ruins

Africa & the Middle East – **Maps**

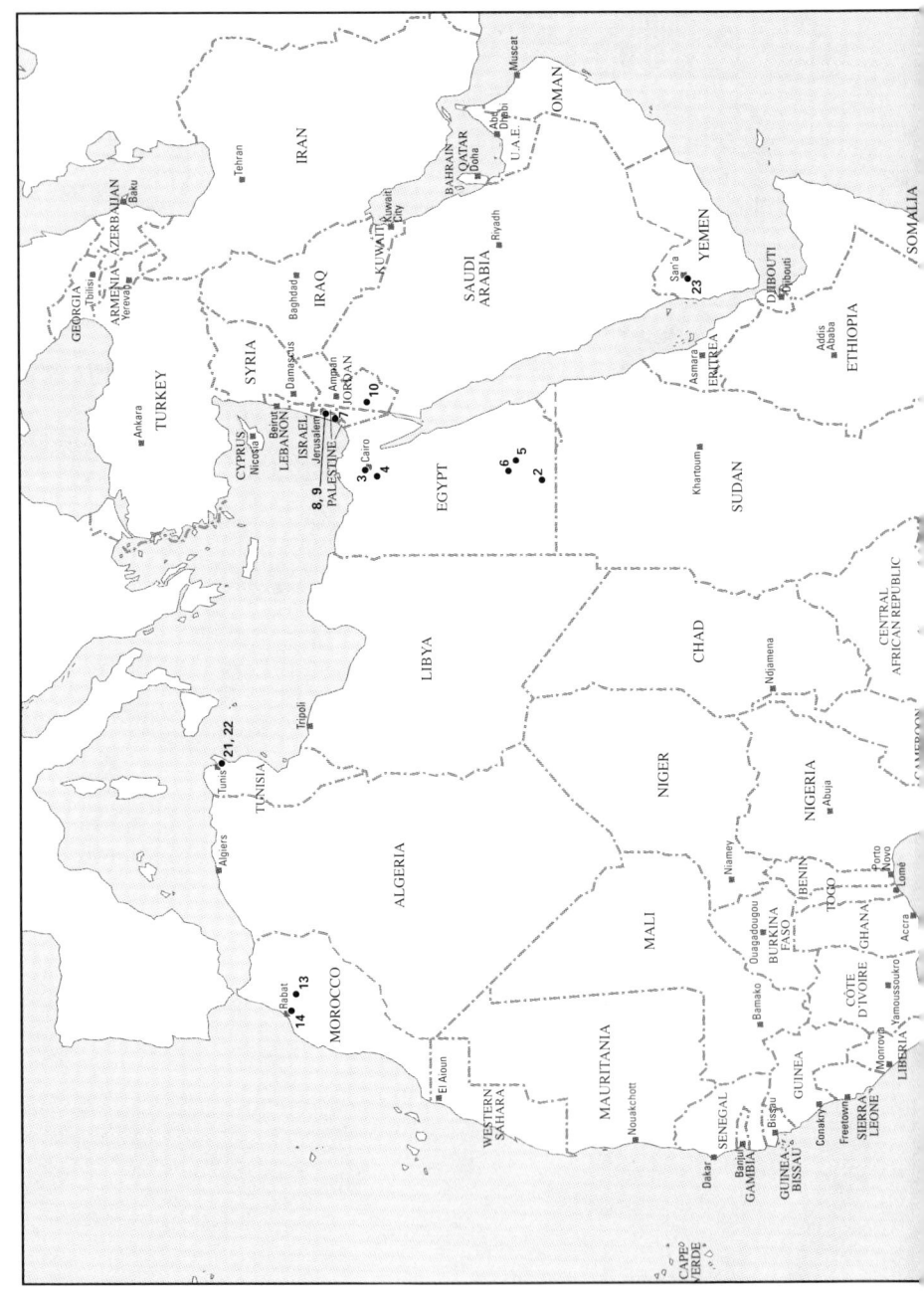

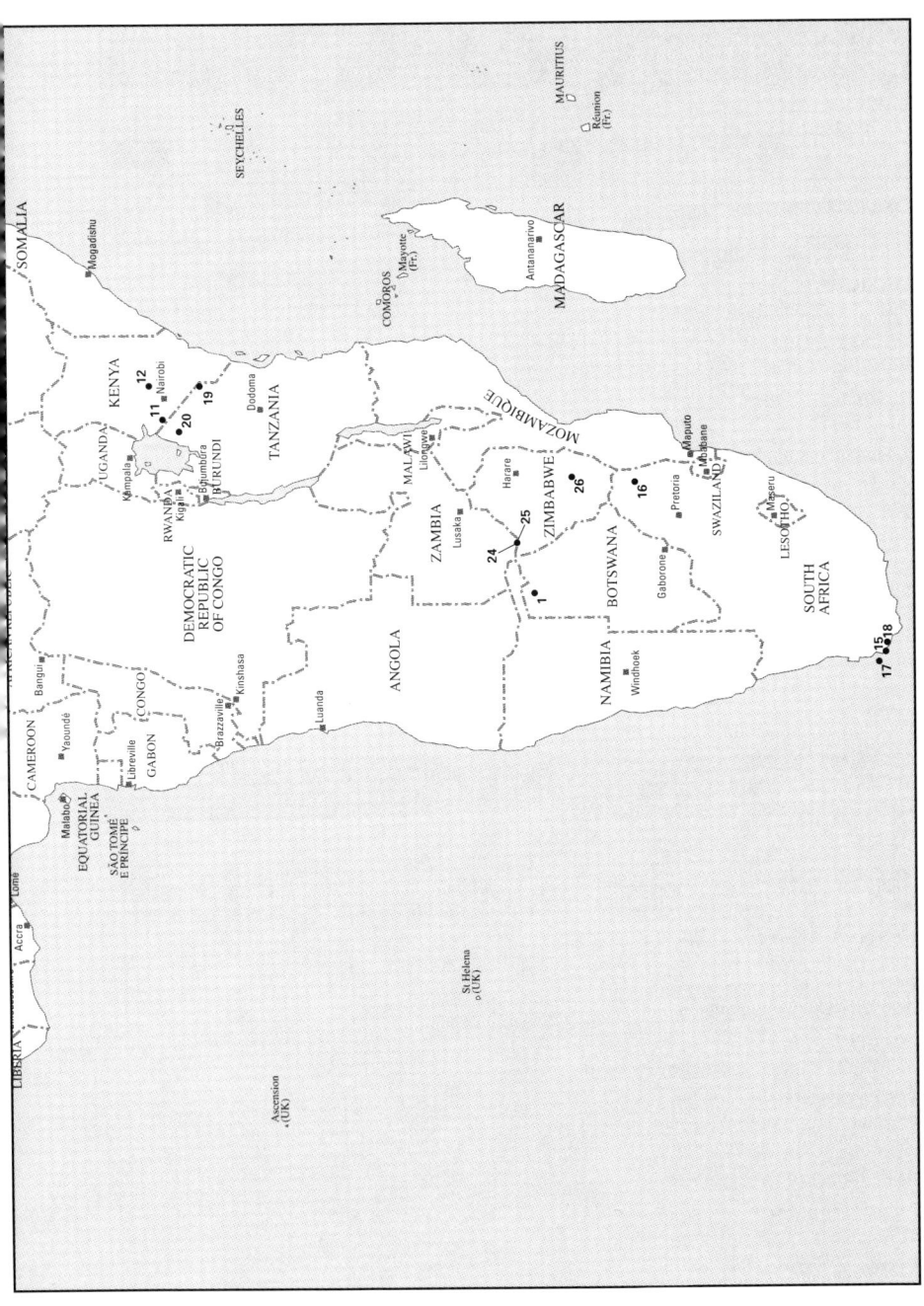

Botswana

Moremi Wildlife Reserve

Contact Address
Department of Tourism, Ministry of Commerce and Industry, Private Bag 0047, Gaborone
Tel: 353 024. Fax: 580 991.

Location
Okavango Delta, northwest Botswana.

Transportation
Air: Gaborone Sir Seretse Khama International Airport.

Opening Times
Dusk-dawn.

Admission Fees
US$11.

Visitors Annually
Not available.

Description
Botswana's *Moremi Wildlife Reserve* lies in the centre of the Okavango Delta, the largest inland delta in the world. Covering an area of 3000 sq kilometres (1170 sq miles), the reserve encompasses a wide range of habitats – from woodland, floodplain and reed beds to wetland, forest and savannah woodland. The fauna inhabiting the park is abundant and equally diverse, ranging from exotic birds, zebras, buffaloes, wildebeest and giraffes to hippos and lions.

Egypt

Abu Simbel

Contact Address
Ministry of Tourism, Misr Travel Tower, Abassia Square, Cairo
Tel: (2) 284 1707. Fax: (2) 258 9551.
Web site: www.touregypt.net

Location
280km (174 miles) southwest of Aswan.

Transportation
Air: Cairo International Airport.

Opening Times
Daily 0700-1700.

Admission Fees
E£36.

Visitors Annually
24,000.

Africa & the Middle East – **Egypt**

Description
One of the most famous ancient Egyptian monuments, *Abu Simbel* consists of two temples constructed in 1257BC by Pharaoh Ramses II. The most famous of the two features four colossal 20m-high (65ft) statues of Ramses II flanking the entrance, although they are actually dedicated to the sun god Re. The temples were cut out of the sandstone cliffs above the River Nile, and consequently were threatened by the construction of the Nasser Dam, which caused the water in Lake Nasser to rise significantly. With the support of UNESCO, an international appeal was launched and the temples were gradually relocated to a higher elevation over a four-year period between 1964 and 1968.

Egyptian Museum

Contact Address
Maydan El Tahrir, Cairo
Tel: (2) 574 2681 *or* 575 4319. Fax: (2) 579 5133.
Web site: www.tourism.egnet.net

Location
Maydan El Tahrir, Cairo city centre.

Transportation
Air: Cairo International Airport.

Opening Times
Daily 0900-1700.

Admission Fees
E£20.

Visitors Annually
1,500,000.

Description
The 107 halls of the *Egyptian Museum* were opened in 1902. The collection, however, dates back to 1835 when the Egyptian government began to halt the outflow of national treasures. The museum holds a number of ancient Egypt's greatest pieces, among them 11 mummified kings and queens. By far the most popular attractions of the museum, however, are the treasures from Tutankhamun's tomb, most famously the boy-king's golden mask.

Pyramids and Sphinx

Contact Address
Ministry of Tourism, Misr Travel Tower, Abassia Square, Cairo
Tel: (2) 284 1707. Fax: (2) 258 9551.
Web site: www.touregypt.net

Location
Giza Plateau, Greater Cairo.

Transportation
Air: Cairo International Airport.

Opening Times
Daily 0700-1930.

Admission Fees
E£31; concessions available.

 Historical   Man-made   Amusement

Visitors Annually
Not available.

Description
The *Pyramids* at Giza are among the best-known ancient monuments in the world. Of the three pyramids at Giza, the *Pyramid of Cheops* is the largest. It was built between 2589 and 2566BC, reaches a height of 140m (482ft) and consists of two million blocks of stone. The famous Sphinx stands nearby, with the body of a lion joined to the head of a man, which was carved over 4500 years ago out of a single block of sandstone.

Temple of Karnak

Contact Address
Ministry of Tourism, Misr Travel Tower, Abassia Square, Cairo
Tel: (2) 284 1707. Fax: (2) 258 9551.
Web site: www.touregypt.net

Location
1.6km (one mile) east of Luxor.

Transportation
Air: Cairo International Airport.

Opening Times
Daily 0600-1700.

Admission Fees
E£20.

Visitors Annually
Not available.

Description
The *Temple of Karnak* is a vast complex that consists of three main temples, some smaller enclosed temples, as well as several outer temples. It was built over a period of 1300 years and includes several of the finest examples of ancient Egyptian design and architecture. Among them are the *Hypostyle Hall*, considered one of the world's great architectural achievements, and the *Obelisk of Thutmose I*, a 22m (71ft) monument, the only one of four original obelisks that is still standing.

Valley of the Kings

Contact Address
Ministry of Tourism, Misr Travel Tower, Abassia Square, Cairo
Tel: (2) 284 1707. Fax: (2) 258 9551.
Web site: www.touregypt.net

Location
West bank of Luxor, seven kilometres (four miles) from the Al-Fadlya Canal junction.

Transportation
Air: Cairo International Airport.

Opening Times
Daily 0600-1700.

Admission Fees
E£20.

 Cultural   Natural    Religious

Description
The *Valley of the Kings* is a limestone valley in Thebes where the mummified bodies of many of the Egyptian pharaohs were interred. The area marks a period in ancient Egyptian history in which the pharaohs abandoned the pyramid style and chose instead tombs dug within limestone, decorated to resemble the underworld, in an effort to avert grave robbing. The tombs, although robbed centuries ago, still offer fantastic wall paintings that depict many aspects of daily life in ancient Egypt. The most famous tomb, belonging to a young pharaoh named Tutankhamun, was discovered in pristine condition by Howard Carter in 1922 – all the contents are now exhibited in the *Egyptian Museum* in Cairo. Nearby, the wall paintings in the tombs of the *Valley of the Queens* and the *Valley of the Nobles* are equally fascinating, depicting, as they do, ancient Egyptian scenes from the perspective of these 'lesser mortals'.

Israel

Masada

Contact Address
MP Yam Hamelach, Negev
Tel: (07) 658 4207. Fax: (07) 658 4464.

Location
Negev, southern coast of the Dead Sea.

Transportation
Air: Ben-Gurion International Airport. Car: Route 3199 from Arad. Cable car access.

Opening Times
Sun-Thurs and Sat 1000-1600, Fri 1000-1500.

Admission Fees
IS13.

Visitors Annually
9,000,000.

Special Needs
Wheelchair accessible.

Description
Perched high on a sheer-sided plateau, *Masada* is famous for being the site of a mass suicide by a group of Jewish people who put their religious and cultural pride before their own lives. The fortress was originally built around 35BC as a luxurious refuge for King Herod, but was taken by the Jewish people, following a Jewish revolt. When the Romans were on the brink of recapturing the town, however, all 967 men, women and children courageously took their own lives. The site now consists of a national park, reconstructed buildings of the old walled town, a museum and a cable car.

Temple Mount

Contact Address
Ministry of Tourism, PO Box 1018, King George Street 24, Jerusalem
Tel: (2) 675 4811. Fax: (2) 623 3683.
Web site: www.infotour.co.il

 Historical Man-made Amusement

Africa & the Middle East – **Israel**

Location
Old City of Jerusalem.

Transportation
Air: Ben-Gurion International Airport.

Opening Times
Sun-Thurs 0730-1030 and 1230-1330; may vary according to religious holidays.

Admission Fees
Free; IS36 (Dome of the Rock, Al Aqsa Mosque and Islamic Museum combined ticket).

Visitors Annually
Not available.

Description
Temple Mount, a walled section of the Old City of Jerusalem, is a site of tremendous religious significance to Jews, Muslims and Christians. Today, the *Dome of the Rock* dominates this site. The area is believed to be the place where Abraham offered Isaac for sacrifice and where Muhammad ascended to heaven. Temple Mount is also home to the *Al Aqsa Mosque*, a Muslim place of worship, as well as the *Islamic Museum*, which houses a collection of Korans as well as Islamic artefacts and relics.

Western Wall

Contact Address
Ministry of Tourism, PO Box 1018, King George Street 24, Jerusalem
Tel: (2) 675 4811. Fax: (2) 623 3683.
Web site: www.infotour.co.il

Location
Jerusalem city centre.

Transportation
Air: Ben-Gurion International Airport. Bus: 1or 2 to the Dung Gate.

Opening Times
Daily 24 hours.

Admission Fees
Not applicable.

Visitors Annually
Not available.

Special Needs
Wheelchair accessible.

Restrictions
Modest clothing mandatory. During the Sabbath and Jewish holidays, visitors may not arrive by car or take pictures of the wall.

Description
The *Western Wall*, known to non-Jews as the Wailing Wall, is a 584m (1916ft) stretch of wall that is all that remains of the *Second Temple of Jerusalem*. The holiest of Jewish places, it attracts thousands of Jews each year to pray, and consequently many hundreds of non-Jews to watch. The wall is 20m (60ft) in height, 50m (160ft) across and is made of chiselled stones. It now forms part of a larger wall surrounding the *Dome of the Rock* and *Al Aqsa Mosque*.

> Please see the map at the front of each section
> for the location of attractions.

Cultural *Natural* *Religious*

Jordan

Petra

Contact Address
Jordan Tourism Board, Unit 11, Blades Court, 121 Deodar Road, London SW15 2NU
Tel: (020) 8877 4524. Fax: (020) 8874 4219.
Web site: www.mota.gov.jo

Location
188km (117 miles) south of Amman.

Transportation
Air: Queen Alia International Airport. Coach: Abdali and Wahdat bus stations. Car: Desert or King's Highway.

Opening Times
Daily 0600-1800.

Admission Fees
JD20 (one-day pass); JD25 (two-day pass); JD30 (three-day pass).

Visitors Annually
Not available.

Special Needs
Wheelchair accessible.

Description
Jordan's best-known tourist attraction, *Petra*, is one of the great wonders of the Middle Eastern world – a city that was carved straight into solid rock. That it unfolds grandly after a two-kilometre (1.2-mile) walk through a very narrow chasm only adds to its mystery and grandeur. Built in the fifth and sixth centuries BC, Petra is the ruined capital of the Nabatean Arabs. Its immense façades had been lost for centuries and were only rediscovered by the Swiss traveller Johan Ludwig Burckhardt in 1812.

Kenya

Maasai Mara National Reserve

Contact Address
PO Box 40, Narok
Tel: (02) 0305 2189 *or* 0305 2487.
E-mail: tourism@kws.org

Location
200km (125 miles) southwest of Nairobi.

Transportation
Air: Jomo Kenyatta International Airport. Car: road from Nairobi to Mai Mahiu, Narok and Ewaso Nyiro.

Opening Times
Daily 0630-1900.

 Historical  Man-made   Amusement

Africa & the Middle East – **Kenya**

Admission Fees
US$27; concessions available.

Visitors Annually
120,000.

Special Needs
Certain areas wheelchair accessible.

Description
Opened in 1974, the *Maasai Mara National Reserve* is the most popular game park in Kenya. Occupying a 320-sq-kilometre (124-sq-mile) chunk of the famous Serengeti plains, the Maasai Mara is inhabited by many of Africa's most popular wild animals, such as lions, cheetahs, elephants, leopards, black rhinos and hippos. However, the reserve is best known for the annual migration of thousands of wildebeest across crocodile-infested waters.

Mount Kenya National Park

Contact Address
Kenya Wildlife Service, PO Box 40241, Nairobi
Tel: (02) 501 081 *or* 501 082. Fax: (02) 505 866.
E-mail: kws@kws.org
Web site: www.mountkenya.com

Location
175km (109 miles) northeast of Nairobi.

Transportation
Air: Jomo Kenyatta International Airport, Wilson Airport. Car: road to Nanyuki.

Opening Times
Daily 0630-1900.

Admission Fees
US$15; concessions available; guides or porters extra.

Visitors Annually
16,000.

Special Needs
Certain areas wheelchair accessible.

Description
Mount Kenya is Africa's second highest mountain at 5199m (17,058ft). Opened as a national park in 1949, the mountain, with its gleaming white peaks, has been revered by local inhabitants for generations. For visitors, the park offers exotic mountain scenery, beginning with upland forest near the bottom section of the park and progressing to mountain forest, bamboo forests and glacier peaks. A wide variety of fauna inhabits the mountain, some unique to it, including Sykes monkeys, buffaloes, elephants, black rhinos, leopards, Bongo antelopes and giant forest hogs.

 Health? Currency? Passport Requirements? Contact Addresses? Airports? Public Holidays? Accommodation? Festivals? Nightlife? Climate? Duty Free? Visas? Excursions? Journey Times? Sport? – for all this, and more besides, consult the *World Travel Guide*.

*Africa & the Middle East – **Morocco***

Morocco

Medina in Fez

Contact Address
Moroccan National Tourist Office, Second Floor, 205 Regent Street, London W1R 7DE
Tel: (020) 7437 0073. Fax: (020) 7734 8172.
E-mail: mnto@btconnect.com
Web site: www.tourism-in-morocco.com

Location
Fez city centre.

Transportation
Air: Mohammed V Airport, Saïss Airport. Rail: Fez Station.

Opening Times
Not applicable.

Admission Fees
Not applicable.

Visitors Annually
Not available.

Description
Fez is the oldest of Morocco's imperial cities, founded shortly after the Arabs first entered North Africa. Its *medina*, the ancient quarter or the old city, is also the largest medina in Morocco. For the visitor, it offers an enchanting, winding, medieval maze of mosques, food markets and covered bazaars filled with crafts, such as metalwork objects and rugs. The medina is also home to the theological university, built in 1350.

Tour Hassan

Contact Address
Moroccan National Tourist Office, Second Floor, 205 Regent Street, London W1R 7DE
Tel: (020) 7437 0073. Fax: (020) 7734 8172.
E-mail: mnto@btconnect.com
Web site: www.tourism-in-morocco.com

Location
Rabat city centre.

Transportation
Air: Mohammed V and Rabat Salé airports. Rail: Rabat Agdal and Rabat Ville stations.

Opening Times
Not applicable; the minaret cannot be entered.

Admission Fees
Not applicable.

Please see the map at the front of each section for the location of attractions.

 Historical    Man-made   Amusement

Africa & the Middle East – **Morocco/South Africa**

Visitors Annually
Not available.

Description
The *Tour Hassan*, the grandiose minaret of a vast yet incomplete mosque, is Rabat's most famous landmark. Begun in 1195, the minaret was intended to be the largest in the Muslim world, but construction was abandoned upon the death of the sultan, Yacoub al-Mansour. Today, the site also houses the *Mausoleum of Mohammed V*, the grandfather of the present king of Morocco.

South Africa

Cape Point

Contact Address
Cape Peninsula National Park, PO Box 37, Constantia, 7848 Cape Town
Tel: (021) 713 0260. Fax: (021) 713 0604.
E-mail: capepeninsula@park-sa.co.za
Web site: www.capepeninsula.co.za

Location
60km (37 miles) southwest of Cape Town.

Transportation
Air: Cape Town International Airport. Car: M3.

Opening Times
Daily dawn-dusk.

Admission Fees
R20; concessions available.

Visitors Annually
800,000.

Special Needs
Certain areas wheelchair accessible.

Description
Part of the *Cape Peninsula National Park*, *Cape Point* is an 8000-hectare (31-sq-mile) narrow promontory of land that juts into a stretch of open sea popularly believed to be the meeting point of the Atlantic and Indian oceans. The peninsula is characterised by towering sea cliffs, the highest in South Africa, which reach a height of 249m (817ft). Known for its spectacular walks and trails, the area offers whale watching, tidal pools, over a thousand species of indigenous plants and a variety of mammals, such as baboon and buck.

Kruger National Park

Contact Address
National Parks Board, PO Box 787, Pretoria 0001
Tel: (012) 343 1991. Fax: (012) 343 0905.
E-mail: reservations@parks.sa.co.za
Web site: www.parks-sa.co.za

Location
Northeast South Africa, between Northern Province and Mpumalanga.

114

Africa & the Middle East – **South Africa**

Transportation
Air: Johannesburg International Airport, Skukuza Airport. Car: Mpumalanga Highway.

Opening Times
Daily 0530-1830; varies seasonally.

Admission Fees
R30 (per person), plus R24 (per private vehicle); concessions available.

Visitors Annually
Not available.

Special Needs
Wheelchair accessible.

Description
At 20,000 sq kilometres (7722 sq miles), *Kruger National Park* is the largest game reserve in South Africa, boasting the world's highest concentration of species. Created in 1898, the park is named after its original proponent, President Paul Kruger. Today, it boasts a wealth of wildlife, including cheetahs, leopards, lions, rhinos, wildebeest, buffaloes, elephants, giraffes, antelope and impala. The park is also popular for its cultural heritage sites, including many indigenous rock art sites.

Robben Island

Contact Address
Robben Island Museum, Robben Island 7400
Tel: (021) 419 1300. Fax: (021) 419 1057.
E-mail: info@ robben-island.org.za
Web site: www.robben-island.org.za

Location
Atlantic Ocean, 11km (seven miles) north of Cape Town harbour.

Transportation
Air: Cape Town International Airport. Ferry: Autfhumato, Makana.

Opening Times
Daily 0900-1500.

Admission Fees
R100; concessions available.

Visitors Annually
Not available.

Special Needs
Wheelchair accessible.

Description
Robben Island was the notorious island prison used to incarcerate thousands of anti-apartheid figures between 1961 and 1991. Its most famous inmate was Nelson Mandela, who referred to it as a 'harsh, iron-fisted outpost'. Used as a prison as far back as 1525, it has also housed the mentally ill and lepers. Since 1996, visitors have benefitted from a *National Museum* and cultural centre on the island, where they can see, among other things, the cell where Nelson Mandela was imprisoned.

Please see the map at the front of each section
for the location of attractions.

Historical  *Man-made*   *Amusement*

Table Mountain

Contact Address
Cape Peninsula National Park, PO Box 37, Constantia, 7848 Cape Town
Tel: (021) 713 0260. Fax: (021) 713 0604.
E-mail: capepeninsula@parks-sa.co.za
Web site: www.cpnp.co.za

Location
Cape Town city centre.

Transportation
Air: Cape Town International Airport. Car: M3.

Opening Times
Daily dawn-dusk.

Admission Fees
R65; concessions available.

Visitors Annually
600,000.

Special Needs
Wheelchair accessible.

Description
Like Cape Point, *Table Mountain* is part of the strip of land forming *Cape Peninsula National Park*. Table Mountain, however, stands in the middle of Cape Town and defines the downtown area. So named for its flat summit, Table Mountain rises to a height of 1086m (3562ft); a cable car carries visitors up to the summit, which offers spectacular views of the city and its beaches. The mountain is also home to an indigenous rodent-like creature called the Rock Hyrax or 'dassie', the closest surviving species related to modern elephants.

Tanzania

Kilimanjaro National Park

Contact Address
Tanzania National Parks, PO Box 3174, Arusha
Tel: (57) 503 471 *or* 504 082. Fax: (57) 508 216.
E-mail: tanapa@habari.to.tz
Web site: www.tanganyika.com

Location
Northeast Tanzania, near Kenya border.

Transportation
Air: Dar-es-Salam International Airport.

Please see the map at the front of each section
for the location of attractions.

 Cultural Natural  Religious

Africa & the Middle East – **Tanzania/Tunisia**

Opening Times
Daily 0600-1800.

Admission Fees
US$25.

Visitors Annually
15,000.

Restrictions
Extreme caution must be used when climbing the mountain; official tour operators only should be used.

Description
Kilimanjaro National Park is the home of *Mount Kilimanjaro*'s equatorial snow-capped peaks, which form one of the most famous images of Africa. At 5895m (19,340ft), Mount Kilimanjaro is the highest mountain in Africa and one of the largest free-standing mountains in the world. It is actually an active volcano and possesses the highest walkable summit in the world. Visitors climbing to the top pass through hot savannah, alpine tropics and finally an arctic moonscape at the very top. A game reserve since 1921, the area was designated a national park in 1973.

Serengeti National Park

Contact Address
Tanzania National Parks, PO Box 3174, Arusha
Tel: (57) 503 471 *or* 504 082. Fax: (57) 508 216.
E-mail: tanapa@habari.to.tz
Web site: www.tanganyika.com

Location
Northeast Tanzania.

Transportation
Air: Dar-es-Salam International Airport.

Opening Times
Daily 0600-1800.

Admission Fees
US$25.

Visitors Annually
Not available.

Description
A game reserve since 1921 but made a national park in 1951, *Serengeti National Park* is the largest in Tanzania and one of the most famous in the world. Fittingly, Serengeti means 'endless plain' in the local Maasia tongue and at 14,763 sq kilometres (5700 sq miles), it features a diversity of environments ranging from savannah and grass plains to woodland and black clay plains. The glory of the Serengeti, however, is its wildlife. The park is most famous for the annual migration of two million wildebeest and zebra: it also teems with lions, elephants, gazelles and ostriches.

 Health? Currency? Passport Requirements? Contact Addresses? Airports? Public Holidays? Accommodation? Festivals? Nightlife? Climate? Duty Free? Visas? Excursions? Journey Times? Sport? – for all this, and more besides, consult the *World Travel Guide*.

 Historical  Man-made   Amusement

Tunisia

Carthage

Contact Address
Site de Carthage, Carthage
Tel: (1) 730 036.

Location
15km (nine miles) north of Tunis.

Transportation
Air: Tunis-Carthage International Airport.

Opening Times
Daily 0830-1730.

Admission Fees
TD4.

Visitors Annually
500,000.

Special Needs
Wheelchair accessible.

Description
The city of *Carthage* was, for many years, the arch-enemy of the ancient Roman empire. From the middle of the third century to the middle of the second century AD, the two great cities were embroiled in a series of wars that saw Hannibal's famous attack on Rome, and Rome's subsequent sacking of Carthage. The Romans eventually settled in the conquered city, which went on to become the administrative capital of Roman Africa. Today, it is mainly Roman sites, including theatres, temples, villas and baths, which can be seen by visiting tourists. However, an impressive collection of Punic objects survive for inspection in the *National Museum* nearby.

Medina in Tunis

Contact Address
Office National du Tourisme Tunisien, 1 avenue Mohamed V, 1001
Tel: (1) 341 077. Fax: (1) 341 997.
E-mail: info@tourismtunisia.com
Web site: www.tourismtunisia.com

Location
Tunis city centre.

Transportation
Air: Tunis-Carthage International Airport.

Opening Times
Not applicable.

Admission Fees
Not applicable.

Visitors Annually
Not available.

Special Needs
Wheelchair accessible.

Description
The *medina*, or old quarter, of *Tunis* was built during the seventh century AD. From the twelfth to the sixteenth centuries, Tunis was considered one of the greatest and wealthiest cities of the Islamic world and its medina is testimony to its former grandeur. Among the more frequented attractions are the ninth-century *Zitouna Mosque*, the perfume makers' *souq*, and Tunis's first Ottoman-style mosque.

Yemen

Old City of Sana'a

Contact Address
General Authority of Tourism, PO Box 129, Sana'a
Tel: (1) 252 319. Fax: (1) 252 316.
Web site: www.yenet.com/tourism

Location
Sana'a city centre.

Transportation
Air: Sana'a International Airport.

Opening Times
Not applicable.

Admission Fees
Not applicable.

Visitors Annually
Not available.

Description
Surrounded by ancient walls, the *Old City of Sana'a* is the largest preserved old city in the Arab world. Made up of friezes and towering minarets, it is a wonderland of over 40 mosques and houses that date back more than 400 years. One of the most popular attractions is the 1000-year-old *Bab al-Yemen Market*, famed for its spice market. Other attractions include the *Great Mosque of Sana'a*, one of the oldest in the Muslim world, the *Liberty Gate* and the *National Museum*.

Zambia

Victoria Falls – see also Zimbabwe

Contact Address
Zambia National Tourist Board, PO Box 30017, Lusaka
Tel: (1) 229 087. Fax: (1) 225 174.
E-mail: zntb@zamnet.zm
Web site: www.africa-insites.com/zambia

 Historical    Man-made   Amusement

Africa & the Middle East – **Zambia/Zimbabwe**

Location
11 km (seven miles) southwest of Livingstone, forming a natural border between Zimbabwe and Zambia.

Transportation
Air: Lusaka International Airport, Harare International Airport.

Opening Times
Daily 0700-1800.

Admission Fees
US$3.

Visitors Annually
15,000.

Special Needs
Wheelchair accessible.

Description
Revealed to the west by the famous explorer Dr David Livingstone, *Victoria Falls* is one of Africa's best-known natural wonders and one of the world's most impressive waterfalls. The falls are formed as the calm two-kilometre-wide (1.2 miles) *Zambezi River* spills out of a flat basalt lip and plunges into the gorge below. At its highest, Victoria Falls drops over a distance of 108m (345ft). As much as 546,000,000 cubic metres (713,725,490 cubic yards) per minute plummet over the edge at the height of the flood season. Viewing the falls from the Zambia side means that visitors can follow a path that goes right up to the falling water.

Zimbabwe

Great Zimbabwe

Contact Address
PO Box CY286, Causeway, Harare, Zimbabwe
Tel: (4) 752 570. Fax: (4) 758 828.
E-mail: mktg@ztazim.org
Web site: www.tourismzimbabwe.co.zw

Location
292km (181 miles) south of Harare.

Transportation
Air: Harare International Airport. Car: road south from Masvingo.

Opening Times
Daily 0800-1630.

Admission Fees
Z$50.

Visitors Annually
Not available.

Special Needs
Wheelchair accessible.

> Please see the map at the front of each section for the location of attractions.

Cultural Natural  Religious

Description
Great Zimbabwe was a large iron-age settlement that existed from the thirteenth to the fifteenth centuries and lent its name to modern-day Zimbabwe. The *Great Enclosure*, with a perimeter wall of 250m (820ft) and height of 11m (36ft), is the largest single ancient structure south of the Sahara Desert. For many years, the origin of Great Zimbabwe and its inhabitants were the subject of much debate; claims were made for various different groups of white colonisers. However, archaeologists have proved that it is an authentic indigenous African site, developed by a civilisation advanced enough to trade with people as distant as China.

Victoria Falls – see also Zambia

Contact Address
PO Box CY286, Causeway, Harare, Zimbabwe
Tel: (4) 752 570. Fax: (4) 758 828.
E-mail: mktg@ztazim.org
Web site: www.tourismzimbabwe.co.zw

Location
878km (546 miles) west of Harare, forming a natural border between Zimbabwe and Zambia.

Transportation
Air: Lusaka International Airport, Harare International Airport. Car: main road from Hwange.

Opening Times
Daily 0800-1700.

Admission Fees
US$3.

Visitors Annually
Not available.

Description
Discovered by the famous explorer Dr David Livingstone, *Victoria Falls* is one of Africa's best-known natural wonders and one of the world's most impressive waterfalls. The falls are formed as the calm two-kilometre-wide (1.2 miles) *Zambezi River* spills out of a flat basalt lip and plunges into the gorge below. At its highest, Victoria Falls drops over a distance of 108m (345ft). As much as 546,000,000 cubic metres (713,725,490 cubic yards) per minute plummet over the edge at the height of the flood season.

Wanted

– Your Suggestions –

All comments are welcome, whether concerning attractions featured in this edition or suggestions as to any which might be included in future ones.

Please contact:

The Editor, *Columbus Guide to World Tourist Attractions*, Columbus Travel Guides,
Jordan House, 47 Brunswick Place, London N1 6EB.
Tel: +44 (0)20 7608 6622. Fax: +44 (0)20 7608 6569.
Email: kmeere@columbus-group.co.uk

 Historical  Man-made   Amusement

section four
asia & australasia

The numbers alongside the attractions below correspond to their locations on the maps overleaf, and not to the page numbers on which information on the attractions appear. For more detailed locations of these attractions consult the World Travel Atlas.

1 Kakadu National Park
2 Sydney Opera House
3 Uluru-Kata Tjuta National Park
4 Angkor Wat
5 Forbidden City
6 Great Wall of China
7 Summer Palace
8 Terracotta Army
9 Three Gorges of the Yangtze River
10 Victoria Peak
11 Ellora Temple Caves
12 Ghats at Varanasi
13 Indian Museum
14 Kaziranga National Park
15 Khajuraho
16 Palace of the Winds
17 Red Fort
18 Taj Mahal
19 Prambanan Temples
20 Meiji Shrine
21 Mount Fuji
22 Sanjusangen-do Temple
23 Sensoji Temple
24 Batu Caves
25 Petronas Towers
26 Fiordland National Park
27 Tongariro National Park
28 Banau Rice Terraces
29 Raffles Hotel
30 Sigiriya
31 Temple of the Tooth
32 Phang Nga Bay
33 Royal Barges National Museum
34 Royal Grand Palace
35 Potala Palace

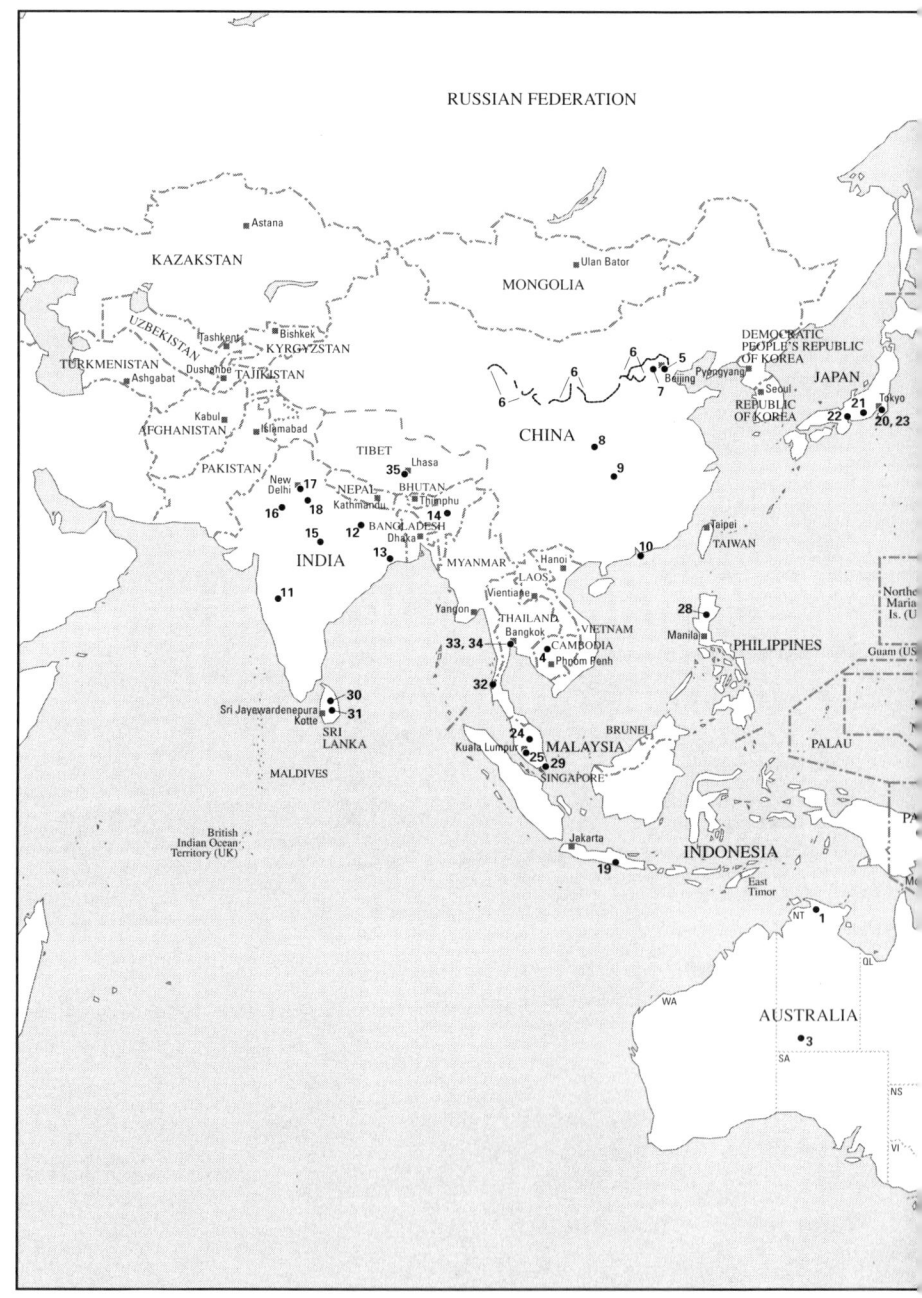

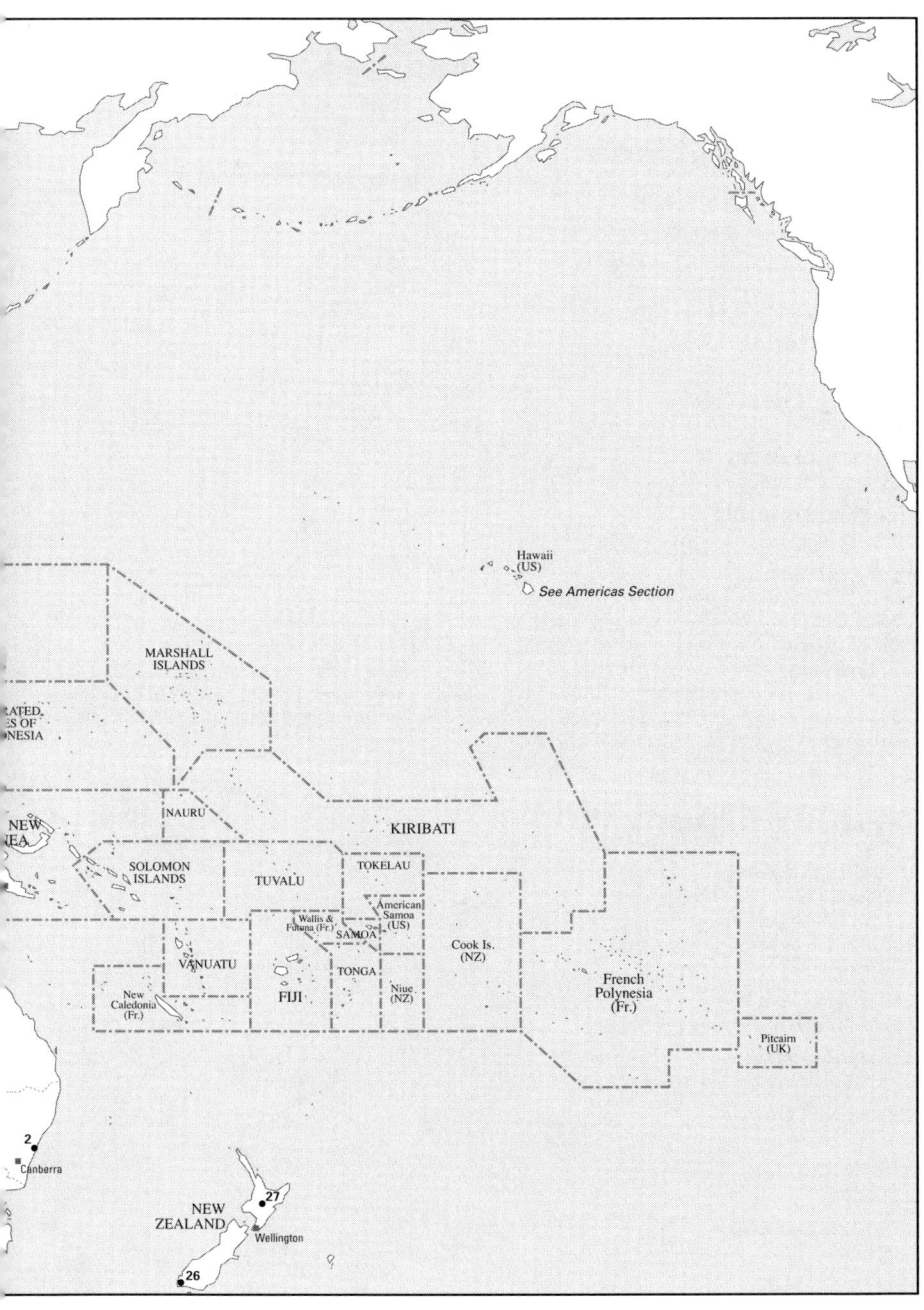

Asia & Australasia – **Australia**

Australia

Kakadu National Park

Contact Address
Kakadu National Park, Jabiru, NT 0886
Tel: (08) 89 81 43 00. Fax: (08) 89 81 43 76.

Location
250km (155 miles) east of Darwin.

Transportation
Air: Darwin International Airport. Car: Arnhern Highway.

Opening Times
Daily 24 hours.

Admission Fees
A$15.

Visitors Annually
Not available.

Description
Located in Australia's tropical Northern Territory, *Kakadu National Park* is one of the few UNESCO World Heritage Sites to be listed for both natural and cultural reasons. Many believe the park has been continuously inhabited for up to 40,000 years, and cave paintings and other archaeological sites, such as the famous *Ubirr and Nourlangie Rocks*, testify to the Aboriginal history of the region. Kakadu is also home to 900 species of plant, 300 types of birds, 50 native mammals and 75 reptiles, including the giant and very dangerous saltwater crocodile.

Sydney Opera House

Contact Address
PO Box R239, Royal Exchange NSW 1225
Tel: (2) 92 50 72 50.
E-mail: tservice@soh.nsw.gov.au
Web site: www.soh.nsw.gov.au

Location
Bennelong Point, Sydney Harbour.

Transportation
Air: Sydney Airport. Rail: Circular Quay.

Opening Times
Daily 0830-2400.

Admission Fees
A$14.80.

Visitors Annually
4,400,000.

Special Needs
Wheelchair accessible.

 Natural

Description
Opened in 1973, the *Sydney Opera House* is the most recognisable symbol of both the city of Sydney and the country of Australia. The building is best known for its billowing white roof that resembles a ship at full sail, but it is also one of the busiest performing arts centres in the world, housing a large complex of theatres and halls. Its design, by Danish architect Jørn Utzon, is still considered revolutionary. *Sydney Harbour Bridge*, located nearby, is another stunning visual attraction adding to the popularity of Sydney Harbour.

Uluru-Kata Tjuta National Park

Contact Address
Uluru-Kata Tjuta National Park, NT 0872
Tel: (08) 89 52 58 00. Fax: (08) 89 53 02 95.

Location
1489km (931 miles) south of Darwin.

Transportation
Air: Darwin International Airport.

Opening Times
Daily 24 hours.

Admission Fees
A$10.

Visitors Annually
650,000.

Special Needs
Wheelchair accessible.

Description
Uluru-Kata Tjuta National Park is home to one of Australia's most popular tourist attractions and best-known national symbols: *Uluru*. Formerly known as *Ayers Rock*, Uluru is a 3.6km-long (2.2-mile), 348m-high (1142ft) smooth chunk of sandstone that rises abruptly and unexpectedly out of the sandy scrubland. Aside from its natural magnificence, the rock is of deep significance to the local Aboriginal people who believe it was formed during the creation period. The nearby Kata Tjuta, meaning 'many heads', is a series of massive rock domes and a system of gorges and valleys. The park is owned and co-managed by local Aboriginal people.

Cambodia

Angkor Wat

Contact Address
Ministry of Tourism, Boulevard Preah Monivong, Corner Rue 232, Phnom Penh
Tel: (23) 362 085. Fax: (23) 426 364.

Location
Southeast corner of city of Angkor, six kilometres (four miles) from Siem Reap.

Transportation
Air: Pochentong Airport. Car: Route 6.

 Historical   *Man-made*   *Amusement*

Asia & Australasia – **Cambodia/China**

Opening Times
Daily 0500-1900.

Admission Fees
US$20 (one day), US$40 (two days), US$60 (one week).

Visitors Annually
Not available.

Description
Angkor Wat, located in *Angkor*, the capital of the ancient Khmer Empire, is one of the greatest and most spectacular Hindu religious sites in the world. Built in the twelfth century AD, the central complex features an elaborate, unmortared 66m (215ft) central tower surrounded by four smaller towers. Stretching around the outside of the temple complex is an 800m-long (2625ft) bas-relief, the longest in the world, best known for the scene of the *Churning of the Ocean of Milk*.

China

Forbidden City

Contact Address
China National Tourism Administration (CNTA), 9A Jianguomennei Avenue, Beijing 100740
Tel: (10) 65 20 11 14. Fax: (10) 65 12 28 51.
Web site: www.cnta.com

Location
North of Tiananmen Square, Beijing city centre.

Transportation
Air: Beijing Capital International Airport. Subway: Qianmen.

Opening Times
Daily 0830-1630.

Admission Fees
RMB50.

Visitors Annually
Not available.

Description
Built in the early fifteenth century during the Ming dynasty, the *Forbidden City* served as the home for 24 of China's Ming and Qing emperors. The palace drew its name from the fact that vast sections of it were off limits to virtually all save the emperor himself. In China, the site is officially known as the *Former Imperial Palace* or *Gugong*. Its 9000 rooms, filled with paintings, pottery and bronzes, are redolent of China's imperial past, an era of concubines, palace eunuchs and rigid power structure. Among the Forbidden City's more notable landmarks are the *Meridian Gate*, the *Hall of Supreme Harmony* and the *Imperial Garden*.

 Flight Times? Climate? Theme Parks? Time Zones? Museums? UNESCO Heritage Sites? Railways? Ski Resorts? Game Parks?
— for all this, and more besides, consult the *World Travel Atlas*.

 Cultural   Natural    Religious

Asia & Australasia – **China**

Great Wall of China

Contact Address
China National Tourism Administration (CNTA), 9A Jianguomennei Avenue, Beijing 100740
Tel: (10) 65 20 11 14. Fax: (10) 65 12 28 51.
Web site: www.cnta.com

Location
Running along the southern edge of the Mongolian plain, from Gansu province to Hebei province.

Transportation
Air: Beijing Capital International Airport. Bus: 5 or 44 to Deshengmen. Rail: from Beijing Main Station to various towns along the route.

Opening Times
Daily 0600-2130 (certain sections).

Admission Fees
Not applicable.

Visitors Annually
Not available.

Description
One of the only man-made structures visible from space, the *Great Wall of China* is the greatest symbol of China's history and grandeur. Begun in the third century BC, the Great Wall connected a number of earlier walls to create a defence against nomads invading from the north. Although the wall ultimately failed in this regard, it was effective in bringing stability and continuity to Chinese culture. Much of the wall that exists today was rebuilt between the fourteenth and eighteenth centuries by the Ming dynasty. The wall has an average height of 7.6m (25ft) and is between 4.6m (15ft) and 9.1m (30ft) at the base.

Summer Palace

Contact Address
China National Tourism Administration (CNTA), 9A Jianguomennei Avenue, Beijing 100740
Tel: (10) 65 20 11 14. Fax: (10) 65 12 28 51.
Web site: www.cnta.com

Location
Ten kilometres (six miles) west of Beijing city centre.

Transportation
Air: Beijing Capital International Airport. Rail: Beijing Station.

Opening Times
Daily 0600-1800.

Admission Fees
RMB90.

Visitors Annually
Not available.

Please see the map at the front of each section for the location of attractions.

 Historical    *Man-made*   *Amusement*

Description
Considered one of the finest classical gardens in China, the *Summer Palace* was first built in 1153 and functioned as an imperial palace for short stays away from the capital. It was rebuilt in 1888 by the Empress Dowager Ci Xi, who spent large amounts of money, from a fund intended for building a Chinese navy, on bringing the garden to its present state of glory. At 290 hectares (717 acres), the gardens consist of a large lake with halls, towers, galleries, pavilions and bridges dotting the surrounding hilly landscape.

Terracotta Army

Contact Address
China National Tourism Administration (CNTA), 9A Jianguomennei Avenue, Beijing 100740
Tel: (10) 65 20 11 14. Fax: (10) 65 12 28 51.
Web site: www.cnta.com

Location
35km (22 miles) east of Xi'an.

Transportation
Air: Beijing Capital International Airport. Coach: services from Xi Balu.

Opening Times
Daily 0930-1700.

Admission Fees
RMB80.

Visitors Annually
Not available.

Description
The *Terracotta Army* is an enormous collection of Chinese warriors made out of hardened clay. The army was created in second century BC by the emperor Shih Huang-Ti, the first emperor of a unified China, and was entombed with him on his death. It was discovered in 1974 during an attempt to dig a well, and since then three separate chambers have revealed over 10,000 figures. The clay figures are all individual, and are made to represent actual members of the imperial army. Some are armed with real weapons, standing in battle formation next to real wooden chariots.

Three Gorges of the Yangtze River

Contact Address
China National Tourism Administration (CNTA), 9A Jianguomennei Avenue, Beijing 100740
Tel: (10) 65 20 11 14. Fax: (10) 65 12 28 51.
Web site: www.cnta.com

Location
Stretches from Baidi City, Sichuan Province to Yichang City, Hubei Province.

Transportation
Air: Beijing Capital International Airport, Shanghai International Airport.

Opening Times
Not applicable.

Admission Fees
None.

 Cultural   *Natural*   *Religious*

*Asia & Australasia – **China/India***

Visitors Annually
Not available.

Description
The *Three Gorges of the Yangtze River* are a system of breathtaking gorges on China's longest river. The *Qü-tang Gorge*, the shortest of the three gorges, is best known for its steep precipices that form an enormous gateway over the river. At 45km (28 miles), the *Wu Gorge* is the longest gorge, and is home to the famous 12 peaks of *Mount Wushan*. The *Xiling Gorge* is known for its hidden reefs, perilous cliffs and tumbling rapids, as well as the orange groves and tea plantations on its shores. The Yangtze River's watershed covers about 20% of China's total land and is home to over 350 million people.

Victoria Peak

Contact Address
Hong Kong Tourist Association, 9-11th Floor, Citicorp Centre, 18 Whitefield Road, North Point, Hong Kong
Tel: (852) 25 08 12 34. Fax: (852) 28 06 03 03.
E-mail: info@hkta.org
Web site: www.hkta.org

Location
Hong Kong city centre.

Transportation
Air: Hong Kong International Airport. Rail: Peak Tram from Garden Road.

Opening Times
Not applicable.

Admission Fees
Not applicable.

Visitors Annually
Not available.

Description
At 547m (1795ft) above sea level, *Victoria Peak* is the most conspicuous landmark in Hong Kong. The peak was rarely visited until 1888, the year the *Peak Tramway* was opened, and its popularity has climbed steadily ever since. Today, the peak is home to Hong Kong's wealthiest executives and bankers who favour its rarefied, natural surroundings. Visitors can enjoy unparalleled views over Hong Kong, as well as Macau and mainland China on clear days. The area's natural beauty offers forests of bamboo and fern, stunted Chinese pines and sightings of birds, such as magpies, goshawks and kites.

India

Ellora Temple Caves

Contact Address
Government of India Tourist Office, Krishna Villas, Station Road, Aurangabad, Maharastra 431005
Tel: (02) 408 1217.

 Historical *Man-made* *Amusement*

Asia & Australasia – **India**

Location
30km (19 miles) northwest of Aurangabad.

Transportation
Air: Mumbai Chhaprati Shivaji International Airport. Rail: Aurangabad Station.

Opening Times
Tues-Sun 0900-1700.

Admission Fees
Rs50.

Visitors Annually
Not available.

Description
The *Ellora Temple Caves* consist of 34 separate religious shrines carved into the actual rock of a basaltic hill and containing a wealth of sculptural and architectural treasures. Carved between 200 and 1000AD, the caves represent three separate faiths: Hinduism, Buddhism and Jainism. The sixteen *Buddhist caves* are the oldest in the group and consist of graceful angles, intricate detail and a 4.6m (15ft) statue of a preaching buddha. In terms of stylistic ambition, the *Hindu caves* outdo their neighbours – one cave alone, the *Temple of Kailasa*, covers twice the area of the Parthenon in Athens and took 100 years to complete. The *Jain caves* illustrate the non-violent, ascetic beliefs of this religion, depicting scenes of pastoral beauty and images such as lotus flowers.

Ghats at Varanasi

Contact Address
Government of India Tourist Office, 15B The Mall, Cantt, Varanasi, Uttar Pradesh
Tel: (05) 424 3744.

Location
Varanasi city centre.

Transportation
Air: Delhi Indira Gandhi International Airport. Rail: Cant Station. Car: NH2, NH7 and NH29.

Opening Times
Not applicable.

Admission Fees
Not applicable.

Visitors Annually
Not available.

Special Needs
Restricted wheelchair access.

Description
Varanasi, one of the oldest and holiest cities in India, is home to the most famous *ghats* in India. These *ghats* (steps leading down to the river) allow worshippers to bathe in the holy River Ganges and then worship at the many temples lining the bank. Big crowds flock every morning to partake in this ancient ritual, with large numbers of tourists flocking to observe.

 Cardboarding? Harmattan? Chondla? Midnight Sun Coast? Gîte? Dude Ranch? Consolidation? Zorbing? Code Sharing? – for all this, and more besides, consult the *World Travel Dictionary.*

Cultural   *Natural*   *Religious*

*Asia & Australasia – **India***

Indian Museum

Contact Address
27 Jawaharlal Nehru Road, Calcutta 700016
Tel: (33) 249 9902 *or* 249 9979 *or* 249 8948. Fax: (33) 249 5699.
Web site: www.indianmuseum-calcutta.org

Location
Calcutta city centre.

Transportation
Air: Calcutta Netaji Subhas Chandra Bose International Airport.

Opening Times
Tues-Sun 1000-1700 (Mar-Nov), 1000-1630 (Dec-Feb).

Admission Fees
Rs150.

Visitors Annually
Not available.

Description
Established in 1878, Calcutta's *Indian Museum* is the largest and best museum in the country. Housed in a magnificent Italian-style building, the museum is divided into six different sections: archaeology, art, anthropology, geology, zoology and industry. The art section contains a picture gallery, with Persian- and Indian-style drawings and paintings, other artefacts and textiles, including silk-woven Tibetan temple banners. Other sections of the museum contain diverse treasures, such as an Egyptian mummy, the skeleton of a whale, rare statues and a collection of meteorites.

Kaziranga National Park

Contact Address
PO Bokaghat, District Jorhat, Assam 785612
Web site: www.india.indiagov.org/tourism/wildlife/kazirang.htm

Location
22km (14 miles) from Bokaghat, northern India.

Transportation
Air: Delhi Indira Gandhi International Airport, Jorhat Airport. Rail: Jorhat Station.
Car: National Highway 37.

Opening Times
Daily dawn-dusk (Nov-Mar).

Admission Fees
Varies depending on tour taken.

Visitors Annually
Not available.

Restrictions
Access controlled and limited; supervised tours only. Closed during monsoon season.

Description
Kaziranga National Park was set aside as a reserve in 1908 and became a national park in 1974. It is made up of 688 sq kilometres (266 sq miles) of breathtaking land, containing rainforests, mighty rivers, sprawling grasslands and herds of wild elephant. It is best known

for its thriving population – the largest in the world – of one-horned rhino. The rhino's natural enemy, the tiger, is also found in abundance, along with many other typical species of Indian wildlife, including king cobras, monitor lizards, leopards, swamp deer, Hoolok gibbon and a variety of bird life.

Khajuraho

Contact Address
Regional Office, Madhya Pradesh State Tourism Development Corporation Ltd, Chandela Cultural Centre, Khajuraho
Tel: (768) 644 051. Fax: (768) 642 330.
Web site: www.indiatouristoffice.co.uk/west/khajuraho.htm

Location
590km (367 miles) southeast of Delhi.

Transportation
Air: Delhi Indira Gandhi International Airport. Rail: Harpalpur Station, Mahoba Station. Coach: services from Satna, Harpalpur, Jhansi and Mahoba.

Opening Times
Daily dawn-dusk.

Admission Fees
Rs5; free Fridays.

Visitors Annually
260,000.

Description
The famous erotic temples of *Khajuraho* form one of the most popular tourist attractions in India. Built between 950 and 1050AD by the kings of the Chandela, the site originally possessed 85 temples, of which 20 are still reasonably preserved. Lost for centuries after the decline of the Chandela, Khajuraho was rediscovered in 1838 by a British army captain. The temples, of Hindu and Jain origin, are best known for the erotic friezes on their walls, which in fact only make up a fraction of the total ornamental carvings, depicting gods, goddesses and celestial maidens.

Palace of the Winds

Contact Address
Rajasthan Tourism, Department of Tourism, Arts and Culture, Government of Rajasthan, Government Hostel Campus, M I Road, Jaipur
Tel: (141) 376 362. Fax: (141) 376 362.
E-mail: mail@rajasthan-tourism.com
Web site: www.rajasthan-tourism.com

Location
Jaipur city centre.

Transportation
Air: Delhi Indira Gandhi International Airport. Car: Rajasthani Roadways from Delhi to Jaipur.

Opening Times
Daily 0900-1700.

Admission Fees
Rs4.

 Cultural *Natural* *Religious*

Visitors Annually
Not available.

Description
Built in 1799, the *Palace of the Winds*, or *Hawa Mahal* as it is known locally, is the most stunning sight in the city of Jaipur. The palace overlooks one of Jaipur's main streets and was originally constructed to offer ladies of the court a vantage point, behind stone-carved screens, from which to watch the activities taking place in the bazaar. For this purpose, it was designed with over 900 niches, the entire building shaped like the crown adorning Lord Krishna's head. Today, the Palace of the Winds offers superb views of the city.

Red Fort

Contact Address
Government of India Tourist Office (GITO), 88 Janpath, New Delhi 110 001
Tel: (011) 332 0005 *or* 332 0342. Fax: (011) 332 0109.
E-mail: newdelhi@tourisminindia.com
Web site: www.tourisminindia.com

Location
Delhi city centre.

Transportation
Air: Indira Gandhi International Airport.

Opening Times
Daily dawn-dusk.

Admission Fees
Rs0.50.

Visitors Annually
Not available.

Description
Completed in 1648, the *Red Fort*, or *Lal Quila*, is the largest of Old Delhi's monuments. Its red sandstone walls dominate Old Delhi's Muslim district, rising above a wide dry moat to a height of up to 33m (108ft), and are lined with turrets and bastions. Today, rather than repel enemy invaders, they keep out the noise of the surrounding city, and the serene gardens and pavilions within the fort hark back to the power and majesty of the Mughal emperors. The main entrance of the Red Fort opens onto a bazaar that was, at one time, home to the city's most skilled goldsmiths, carpet makers and jewellers. Further within lies the *Hall of Public Audiences*, where the emperor would listen to the complaints of the common people, and the *Royal Baths*, three large domed rooms with a fountain in the centre.

Taj Mahal

Contact Address
Government of India Tourist Office, 191 The Mall, Agra 282001
Tel: (562) 363 959. Fax: (562) 363 377.
E-mail: goitoargr.nde.vsnl.net.in
Web site: www.tourisminindia.com

Location
Agra, 199km (123 miles) from Delhi.

Transportation
Air: Indira Gandhi International Airport. Rail: Agra Cantt. Car: NH2.

 Historical  *Man-made* *Amusement*

Asia & Australasia – **India/Indonesia**

Opening Times
Tues-Sun 0600-1900.

Admission Fees
Rs105.

Visitors Annually
1,000,000.

Description
The *Taj Mahal* has been described as the most extravagant monument ever built in the name of love. It is also India's most famous and emblematic tourist attraction. Renowned for its tree-lined reflective pond leading up to the fabulous domed roof, few know that the Taj Mahal is, in fact, a mausoleum not a mosque. Completed in 1653, it was built by the Emperor Shah Jahan to commemorate the memory of his second wife, Mumtaz Mahal. Revered for its grace and detailed beauty, the Taj Mahal is considered to be the high point of Indo-Persian architecture.

Indonesia

Prambanan Temples

Contact Address
Yogyakarta Tourist Information Centre, Maioboro 16, Yogyakarta
Tel: (27) 458 6809.

Location
15km (10.6 miles) east of Yogyakarta, Island of Java, Indian Ocean.

Transportation
Air: Soekarno-Hatta Airport. Coach: services from Yogyakarta.

Opening Times
Daily 0600-1800.

Admission Fees
Rp5000.

Visitors Annually
Not available.

Description
The *Prambanan Temples* form the largest temple complex on the Indonesian island of Java. Constructed around 900AD, the compound was deserted soon after it was completed. The temples were restored, however, in 1953 and now form one of the world's great Hindu shrines. There are 224 temples in total, but the site is dominated by the imposing figures of the three main temples: the *Brahma Temple*, the *Vishnu Temple* and the *Shiva Temple*, which is the largest at 47m (154ft) tall.

 Health? Currency? Passport Requirements? Contact Addresses? Airports? Public Holidays? Accommodation? Festivals? Nightlife? Climate? Duty Free? Visas? Excursions? Journey Times? Sport? – for all this, and more besides, consult the *World Travel Guide*.

 Cultural   Natural    Religious

Japan

Meiji Shrine

Contact Address
1-1 Kamizonocho, Yoyogi, Shibuya-ku, Tokyo
Tel: (03) 33 79 55 11.

Location
Tokyo city centre.

Transportation
Air: New Tokyo International Airport. Rail: Harajku Station. Subway: Meijijingumae Station.

Opening Times
Daily 0540-1720 (spring, autumn), 0400-1700 (summer), 0600-1700 (winter).

Admission Fees
Free (shrine); Y200 (Treasure Museum).

Visitors Annually
Not available.

Special Needs
Wheelchair accessible.

Description
Tokyo's *Meiji Shrine* is one of the holiest and most visited temples in the country. This pure Shinto shrine is dedicated to the Emperor Meiji, the monarch credited with opening Japan up to the outside world. The large gates to the shrine are made of Japanese Cypress and are said to be over 1700 years old. The *Treasure Museum* behind the shrine houses photos and personal belongings of the emperor and empress. The *Iris Garden* at the shrine is considered to be one of the best in Japan.

Mount Fuji

Contact Address
Japan National Tourist Organisation (JNTO), Overseas Promotion Department, 2-10-1, Yuraku-cho, Tokyo 100-0006
Tel: (3) 32 16 19 02. Fax: (3) 32 16 18 46.
E-mail: jnto@jnto.go.jp
Web site: www.jnto.go.jp

Location
100km (62 miles) southeast of Tokyo.

Transportation
Air: New Tokyo International Airport. Rail: Shinjuku (Tokyo) to Kawaguchi-ko.
Coach: services from Shinjuku to Kawaguchi-cho.

Opening Times
Not applicable.

Admission Fees
Not applicable.

Visitors Annually
200,000 (climbers to the summit).

 Historical   Man-made   Amusement

Asia & Australasia – Japan

Restrictions
Climbing in the winter months is strictly for experienced mountaineers.

Description
The perfectly symmetrical, 3776m (12,389ft) volcanic cone known as *Mount Fuji*, or *Fuji-san* to the Japanese, is one of the most famous volcanoes in the world. Of extreme historical and religious importance to the Japanese, the mountain is also one of the nation's greatest national emblems. Although it has erupted 16 times since 781AD, the mountain is safe and popular for climbing. Most excursions take place in July and August, although it can be climbed at any time of year. The top offers overnight huts, a volcanic crater and unparalleled views over the surrounding Japanese landscape.

Sanjusangen-do Temple

Contact Address
Tourist Section, Kyoto City Government, Kyoto Kaikan, Okazaki, Sayo-ku, Kyoto
Tel: (075) 752 0215.

Location
Kyoto city centre.

Transportation
Air: Nagoya International Airport. Rail: Kyoto Station. Bus: 205 or 208 to Sanjusangen-do.

Opening Times
Daily 0800-1700 (Mar-Oct), 0800-1600 (Nov-Mar).

Admission Fees
Y400.

Visitors Annually
Not available.

Description
Completed in 1266, the *Sanjusangen-do Temple* is a faithful copy of an original that was built in 1164 but burned down in 1249. The temple is a national treasure, best known for its wooden image of the *Thousand-Armed Kannon* (the Buddhist Goddess of Mercy), a masterpiece of the Kamakura period, which stands surrounded by 1000 smaller statues of the same goddess. A long, narrow building, its name refers to the 33 bays (*sanjusan*) that exist between its many pillars.

Sensoji Temple

Contact Address
2-3-1 Asakusa, Taito-ku, Tokyo 111-0032
Tel: (03) 38 42 01 81. Fax: (03) 38 45 69 33.

Location
Tokyo city centre.

Transportation
Air: New Tokyo International Airport. Subway: Asakusa.

Opening Times
Daily 0600-1700 (summer), 0630-1700 (winter).

Admission Fees
Free.

 Cultural *Natural*  *Religious*

Asia & Australasia – **Japan/Malaysia**

Visitors Annually
Not available.

Description
Founded in 628AD to enshrine a gold statuette of the Thousand Armed Kannon (the Goddess of Mercy), the *Sensoji Temple*, Tokyo's most revered temple, has attracted visitors and pilgrims for over a thousand years. The temple and its five-storey pagoda are concrete reconstructions, but the temple precincts are nevertheless always bustling with worshippers. A huge incense burner at the front of the temple is said to have curative healing powers. The *Kaminarimon* (Thunder Gate) is famous for its enormous red paper lantern and guardian statues.

Malaysia

Batu Caves

Contact Address
Malaysia Tourist Office, 17th, 24th-27th & 30th Floors, Menara Dato' Onn, Putra World Trade Centre, 45 Jalan Tun Ismail, 50480 Kuala Lumpur
Tel: (03) 293 5188. Fax: (03) 293 5884.
E-mail: tourism@tourism.gov.my
Web site: www.tourism.gov.my

Location
13km (eight miles) north of Kuala Lumpur.

Transportation
Air: Kuala Lumpur International Airport. Car: Ipoh Road. Coach: Pudu Raya Bus Terminal.

Visitors Annually
100,000.

Restrictions
Access to the *Dark Cave* is restricted – permission must be sought from the Malaysian Nature Society.

Description
Since their discovery just over 100 years ago, the *Batu Caves* have consistently attracted visitors. There are three main caves and numerous smaller ones; but the best known is the *Temple Cave*. Accessible only by a climb of 272 steps, the Temple Cave is a large cavern with a vaulted 100m-high (328ft) ceiling. Below it is the *Dark Cave*, a vast network of untouched caverns inhabited by several endemic species of animals. The Batu Caves are also an important Hindu shrine, attracting as many as 80,000 devotees during the holy festival of Thaipusam.

Petronas Towers

Contact Address
Malaysia Tourist Office, 17th, 24th-27th & 30th Floors, Menara Dato' Onn, Putra World Trade Centre, 45 Jalan Tun Ismail, 50480 Kuala Lumpur
Tel: (03) 293 5188. Fax: (03) 293 5884.
E-mail: tourism@tourism.gov.my
Web site: www.tourism.gov.my

Location
Kuala Lumpur city centre.

 Historical   *Man-made*    *Amusement*

*Asia & Australasia – **Malaysia/New Zealand***

Transportation
Air: Kuala Lumpur International Airport.

Opening Times
Mon-Sat 1000-1600.

Admission Fees
Free.

Visitors Annually
Not available.

Description
At a height of 452m (1483ft), the 88-storey *Petronas Towers* took the crown of tallest building in the world upon completion in 1997. The building consists of two similarly shaped towers joined by a 58m (192ft) *Skybridge* at the 41st and 42nd floors. The design is based on geometric principles typical of Islamic architecture, with each floor plan based on an eight-point star. The historically referential design and sheer size are symbolic of Malaysia's emerging international importance.

New Zealand

Fiordland National Park

Contact Address
Visitor Centre, PO Box 29, Te Anau
Phone: (3) 249 7924. Fax: (3) 249 7613.
E-mail: fiordlandvc@doc.govt.nz

Location
Southwest corner of South Island.

Transportation
Air: Christchurch International Airport. Car: Highway 94.

Opening Times
Not applicable.

Admission Fees
Free.

Visitors Annually
Not available.

Special Needs
Certain areas wheelchair accessible.

Description
At nearly 1.2 million hectares (4,600 sq miles), *Fiordland National Park* is New Zealand's largest national park – a breathtaking stretch of coastal landscape that typifies the country's natural splendour. It is a land of ice, beech forests, mountains and waterfalls tumbling into the ocean below. One of the park's most famous regions is *Milford Sound*, whose glacier-carved coastline attracts sightseers and cruise ships. The park is also immensely popular for outdoor activities, such as hiking, sea kayaking, diving, cycling, golf, fishing and sailing.

Please see the map at the front of each section
for the location of attractions.

 Cultural  Natural   Religious

Asia & Australasia – **New Zealand/Philippines**

Tongariro National Park

Contact Address
Tongariro/Taupo Conservation Board, c/o Department of Conservation, Turangi
Tel: (7) 386 8607. Fax: (7) 386 7086.

Location
Just south of Lake Taupo, centre of North Island.

Transportation
Air: Wellington International Airport.

Opening Times
Not applicable.

Admission Fees
Free.

Visitors Annually
1,000,000.

Special Needs
Certain areas wheelchair accessible.

Description
Originally a gift to Queen Victoria by a Maori chief, *Tongariro National Park* was the first national park in New Zealand and is the fourth oldest in the world. Since its inception, the park has grown to a size of nearly 80,000 hectares (309 sq miles). Of religious and cultural importance to the Maoris, the core of the park centres around three active volcanoes, *Tongariro, Ruapehu* and *Ngauruhoe*. The park resembles a 'lunar landscape', that has been carved by flowing lava, sitting alongside forests and tussock land. Visitors can enjoy skiing on an active volcano and hiking through alpine herb fields, beside waterfalls and emerald-coloured lakes, and up to lookout points. The *Tongariro Crossing*, considered one of the best one-day walks in the country, receives 70,000 hikers alone each summer.

Philippines

Banau Rice Terraces

Contact Address
Tourism Office, Cordillera Administrative Region, Department of Tourism, DOT Complex, Government Pack Road, 2600 Baguio City
Tel: (74) 442 6708. Fax: (74) 442 8848.
E-mail: dotcar@mozcom.com
Web site: www.tourism.gov.ph

Location
Banaue, Ifugao Province, North Luzon.

 Cardboarding? Harmattan? Chondla? Midnight Sun Coast? Gîte? Dude Ranch? Consolidation? Zorbing? Code Sharing? – for all this, and more besides, consult the *World Travel Dictionary*.

 Historical    Man-made   Amusement

Asia & Australasia – **Philippines/Singapore**

Transportation
Air: Manila Ninoy Aquino International Airport.

Opening Times
Not applicable.

Admission Fees
Not applicable.

Visitors Annually
50,000.

Description
Nestled deep in the heartlands of the Cordilleras and rising to an altitude of 1525m (5000ft) are the *Banau Rice Terraces*, dubbed the eighth wonder of the world. Centuries ago, the terraces were carved out of mountain ranges by the Ifugaos, the oldest mountain tribe in the area, using only the most primitive tools. Measured from end to end, the terraces would stretch a total length of 22,400km (13,919 miles), enough to encircle half the globe.

Singapore

Raffles Hotel

Contact Address
1 Beach Road, Singapore 189673
Tel: (65) 337 1886. Fax: (65) 339 7650.
E-mail: raffles@pacific.net.sg
Web site: www.raffles.com

Location
Singapore city centre.

Transportation
Air: Singapore Changi Airport. Rail: MRT City Hall Station.

Opening Times
Not applicable.

Admission Fees
Not applicable.

Visitors Annually
Not available.

Description
Built in 1887, *Raffles Hotel* is one of the world's last remaining grand hotels of the East. Somerset Maugham, Rudyard Kipling, Joseph Conrad and Charlie Chaplin made it a favourite retreat, and its recent 160-million-Singapore-dollar facelift has ensured that the hotel retains the unique charm of the colonial era. Tourists flock for afternoon tea in the *Tiffin Room* and a Singapore Sling in the *Long Bar*. The new arcade houses 70 boutiques, as well as restaurants, a museum and the Victorian-style playhouse, *Jubilee Hall*.

 Health? Currency? Passport Requirements? Contact Addresses? Airports? Public Holidays? Accommodation? Festivals? Nightlife? Climate? Duty Free? Visas? Excursions? Journey Times? Sport? – for all this, and more besides, consult the *World Travel Guide*.

Sri Lanka

Sigiriya

Contact Address
Sri Lanka Tourist Board, PO Box 1504, Colombo 3
Tel: (1) 437 059 *or* 437 060 *or* 427 055. Fax: (1) 437 953.
E-mail: ctb_dm@sri.lanka.net
Web site: www.lanka.net/ctb

Location
169km (105 miles) from Colombo.

Transportation
Air: Colombo Bandaranayake International Airport. Coach: services from Dambulla.

Opening Times
Daily 0800-1800.

Admission Fees
US$15.

Visitors Annually
Not available.

Description
Taking its name from *giriya* ('jaws and throat') and *sinha* ('lion'), *Sigiriya* is a site in central Sri Lanka that contains the ruins of an ancient fortress and city. It stands on a remarkably steep large rock, known as *Lion Mountain*, that rises 180m (600ft) above the surrounding plain. Built in 477AD, Sigiriya was constructed as a safeguard against enemy attack, visitors being forced then, as now, to enter through the jaws of a massive monumental lion. The site itself features water gardens, renowned fifth-century rock paintings, trees and pathways. It is considered one of the best-preserved first-millennium city centres in Asia.

Temple of the Tooth

Contact Address
Sri Lanka Tourist Board, PO Box 1504, Colombo 3
Tel: (1) 437 059 *or* 437 060 *or* 427 055. Fax: (1) 437 953.
E-mail: ctb_dm@sri.lanka.net
Web site: www.lanka.net/ctb

Location
Kandy city centre.

Transportation
Air: Colombo Bandaranayake International Airport.

Opening Times
Daily 0800-1900.

Admission Fees
US$12.

Visitors Annually
Not available.

*Asia & Australasia – **Sri Lanka/Thailand***

Restrictions
Visitors are required to dress modestly and behave appropriately.

Description
Located in Kandy, an ancient religious centre for Buddhism, the octagonal, golden-roofed *Temple of the Tooth*, or *Dalada Maligawa*, built between 1687 and 1707, is a stunning sacred temple that is said to hold the left upper canine of the Lord Buddha himself. As the story goes, the tooth was taken from the Buddha as he lay on his funeral pyre and smuggled to Sri Lanka in a princess' hair, where it survived numerous attempts at capture and destruction. The relic attracts white-clad pilgrims bearing lotus blossoms and frangipani for religious ceremonies that take place each day. The temple is joined to a tower, built in 1803, that was originally used as a prison but now houses a collection of palm-leaf manuscripts.

Thailand

Phang Nga Bay

Contact Address
TAT Southern Office Region, 73-75 Phuket Road, Mphoe Muang, Phuket 8300
Tel: (76) 211 036. Fax: (76) 213 582.
E-mail: tathtg@phuket.ksc.co.th

Location
75km (47 miles) northeast of Phuket.

Transportation
Air: Phuket International Airport. Car: Highway 402 (Tepkassatri Road).

Opening Times
Not applicable.

Admission Fees
Not applicable.

Visitors Annually
Not available.

Description
Phang Nga Bay is one of the world's scenic wonders. It covers 400 sq kilometres (154 sq miles) and consists of verdant limestone islands, honeycombed with caves and aquatic grottoes, some of which reach 300m (984ft) high. Few of the islands are inhabited, apart from the occasional fishing village. The most famous of the islands are *James Bond Island* and *Koh Pannyi*. The former featured in the James Bond movie *The Man with the Golden Gun*. The latter is a village built on stilts over the water, where tourists can find many craft shops and places to eat.

Royal Barges National Museum

Contact Address
Tourism Authority of Thailand, Le Concorde Building, 202 Ratchadapisek Road, Bangkok 10310
Tel: (2) 694 1222. Fax: (2) 694 1326.
E-mail: info1@tat.or.th (information section) *or* 1155@tat.or.th (Tourist Service Centre).
Web site: www.tat.or.th *or* www.tourismthailand.org

Cultural *Natural* *Religious*

Asia & Australasia – **Thailand**

Location
Khlong Bangkok Noi, off the Chao Phraya River, near Phra Pin Klao Bridge, Bangkok.

Transportation
Air: Bangkok International Airport.

Opening Times
Daily 0830-1630.

Admission Fees
B10.

Visitors Annually
Not available.

Description
The *Royal Barges National Museum* houses several royal barges, which formerly served as war vessels and were subsequently used on royal and state occasions. The earliest evidence of the use of royal processions in these decorative barges dates back to 1357. One of the most well known of the barges is the *Suphanahong*, which was used by the king when celebrating a Buddhist ceremony known as the *Kathin* ceremony. Travelling along the river in this barge the king traditionally offered robes to monks during the months of October and November. The barges are incredibly intricate in design, reflecting Thai religious beliefs and local history.

Royal Grand Palace

Contact Address
Tourism Authority of Thailand, Le Concorde Building, 202 Ratchadapisek Road, Bangkok 10310
Tel: (2) 694 1222. Fax: (2) 694 1326.
E-mail: info1@tat.or.th (information section) *or* 1155@tat.or.th (Tourist Service Centre).
Web site: www.tat.or.th *or* www.tourismthailand.org

Location
Na Phra Lan Road, Bangkok.

Transportation
Air: Bangkok International Airport. Rail: Hualamphong Railway Station.

Opening Times
Daily 0830-1130 and 1300-1530.

Admission Fees
B125.

Visitors Annually
Not available.

Restrictions
Modest dress must be worn.

Description
The *Royal Grand Palace* is made up of a vast complex of intricate buildings, including the *Wat Mahathat* (the palace temple). Construction of the palace began in 1782 and was completed in time for the coronation of King Rama I. The palace lies at the heart of the old town and covers an area of 160,000 sq metres (1,720,430 sq feet). The palace compound is surrounded by a moat and contains two sections, the royal residence and the Buddhist temple. The Buddhist figure at the heart of the temple is carved from a single piece of jade and is the holiest and most revered religious object in Thailand.

Tibet

Potala Palace

Contact Address
Tibet Tourism Administration, Yualin Road, Lhasa, Tibet 85001
Tel: (891) 633 5472. Fax: (891) 683 4632.

Location
Marpo Ri Hill, Lhasa.

Transportation
Air: Shanghai Airport, Beijing Airport.

Visitors Annually
Not available.

Restrictions
Visitors may experience health problems due to the high altitude.

Description
The *Potala Palace* is the largest monumental structure in Tibet. It stands 130m (427ft) above the Lhasa Valley and was built in the seventh century as a retreat for the local lord, Songsten Gampo, and his bride Princess Wen Cheng. At 13 storeys, and standing on top of a 3700m (12,139ft) cliff, it is the world's highest palace. The palace complex is made up of two sections, the *Red Palace* and the *White Palace*. The upper Red Palace includes the living quarters and tombs of most of the Dalai Lamas, as well as many temples containing a myriad of gilded statues of Buddha. The White Palace below it housed a printing press, more temples and the administrative offices of the Tibetan government.

Wanted

– *Your Suggestions* –

All comments are welcome, whether concerning attractions featured in this edition or suggestions as to any which might be included in future ones.

Please contact:

The Editor,
Columbus Guide to World Tourist Attractions,
Columbus Travel Guides,
Jordan House,
47 Brunswick Place,
London N1 6EB,
United Kingdom.
Tel: +44 (0)20 7608 6565.
Fax: +44 (0)20 7608 6593.
E-mail: kmeere@columbus-group.co.uk

section five
appendices

Festivals

Travel Associations

International Dialling Codes

Festivals

ALPHABETICAL LISTING BY COUNTRY

This section provides a listing of some of the world's top festivals and carnivals. They are listed alphabetically by country and they include: date, location, description of the event and a contact telephone number or e-mail. All dates refer to when the events take place during 2000.

Australia

✦ SYDNEY GAY AND LESBIAN MARDI GRAS
February 2000
Sydney, Australia

Description
The *Mardi Gras* dates back to 1978, when a gay rights march took place in Sydney, attracting over 1000 participants. The revelers were told by the police that the march was banned and there was a riot, in which 53 people were arrested. That marks the very first *Gay and Lesbian Mardi Gras*. Today the event is said to be the world's biggest gay and lesbian celebration, attracting over 22,000 party-goers, with film crews from around the world covering the event. The event includes parades, floats, parties and music around the city of Sydney.

Contact
Sydney Gay and Lesbian Mardi Gras
Tel: 612 9557 4332

Belgium

✦ ROCK WERCHTER 2000
June 20 2000 – July 2 2000
Werchter, Belgium

Description
A three-day rock festival that attracts thousands of people from across Europe. Features top rock bands such as Oasis, Travis, Paul Weller and Macy Gray. The festival was originally named the Torhout/Werchter Festival.

Contact
Tel: 0900-80800 (for tickets).

Brazil

✦ RIO CARNIVAL (MARDI GRAS)
March 4 2000 – March 8 2000
Rio de Janeiro, Brazil

Description
This festival is one of the biggest in the world, attracting thousands of tourists and locals to participate in this incredibly lively carnival. Its date varies from year to year, usually ranging from late February to early March. It starts officially on a Saturday and goes through to the following Wednesday (*quarta-feira de cinzas* – Ash Wednesday). There are many events taking place all round Rio, including street parades, carnival balls and the samba school parade.

Contact
EMBRATUR – Instituto Brasileiro de Turismo
Tel: 21 509 6017

Canada

✦ CARIBANA FESTIVAL
July 2000 – Aug 2000
Toronto, Ontario, Canada

Description
Caribana is one of North America's largest cultural festival and it takes place in various venues around Toronto. It turns Toronto into a Caribbean paradise, with dancing and a lake front parade.

Contact
Tourism Toronto
Tel: 416 203 2600

France

✦ BASTILLE DAY
July 13 2000 – July 14 2000
Paris, France

Description
Quartorze Juillet (the fourteenth of July) commemorates the French Revolution of 1789. The event is celebrated throughout France, with parades, street dances and fireworks. The focus of the celebrations is in Paris, where, on the eve of Bastille Day, there are public balls (the most famous being one sponsored by the Communist Party on the Ile St. Louis).

✦ CANNES FILM FESTIVAL
May 10th 2000 – May 21st 2000
Cannes, France

Description
This is said to be one of the world's most important film festivals. It is now in its 53rd year and there is ample opportunity for star gazing as well as for checking out the latest films.

Contact
French Association of the International Film Festival
Tel: 33 1 45 616 600

Germany

✦ LOVE PARADE
July 8 2000
Berlin, Germany

Description
This parade attracts a mainly young crowd from across Europe and worldwide. It is essentially the world's biggest outdoor rave. It is dedicated to tolerance and a lust for life.

Contact
German National Tourist Office
Tel: (020) 7317 0908

Appendices – **Festivals**

✦ OKTOBERFEST
September 16 2000 – October 3 2000
Munich, Germany

Description
This festival is said to be the biggest public festival in the world. Known to locals as 'Wien', it is now in its 166th year. Each year the festival attracts some six million visitors, who drink around five million litres of beer and consume over 200,000 pairs of pork sausages, mainly in beer tents. The festival also has fun fairs, processions and a concert with brass bands.

Contact
The Munich Tourist Board
E-mail: tourismus@muenchen.btl.de

✦ PASSION PLAY
May 22 2000 – October 8 2000
Oberammergau, Bavaria, Germany

Description
Taking place once every ten years, these religious plays date back to the 1600s and attract tourists and devotees from around the world.

Contact
Tel: 49 88 229 2310

Ireland

✦ ST PATRICK'S DAY CELEBRATIONS
March 17 2000
Ireland

Description
This annual saint's day celebration is celebrated the world over, with parades, drinking and dancing. In Ireland almost all businesses, with the exception of restaurants and pubs, close on March 17th. As it is a religious holiday, many people attend mass, where it is traditional to offer prayers for missionaries all over the world. However, it is also a day of great celebrations. Saint Patrick is said to have driven snakes from Ireland and according to legend was buried in AD 493 in the same grave as Saint Bridget and Saint Columba at Downpatrick, County Down.

Contact
The Irish Tourist Board, London
Tel: (020) 7518 0800

Jamaica

✦ JAMAICA CARNIVAL
January 2 2000 – April 30 2000
Jamaica, Caribbean

Description
This massive carnival was started in 1989 by Byron Lee (a local musician), as a means of bringing together the whole of Jamaica. The first carnival took place in 1990 and although there had been annual festivals before this, this was the first major event, freely available to a huge audience. During carnival week, participators can party from dusk until dawn.

Contact
Jamaica Tourist Board
Tel: (020) 7224 0505

Mexico

✦ DIA DE LOS MEURTOS
November 1 2000
Nationwide, Mexico

Description
This is one of Mexico's most traditional holidays, dating back to prehispanic Mexico. It was believed that only in dying is a human being truly awake because the soul was set free. Death was not seen as mysterious or fearful, but part of life. When Christianity was introduced to Mexico in the 16th Century, religion and its symbols became part of the altars that are on show in Mexico today. November 1st (All Saints Day) is when the spirits of the children 'los angelitos' (the little angels) are expected to return. A special altar is made to commemorate their lives. People gather at the burial grounds, decorating and cleaning graves and picnicing with the dead.

Contact
Mexican Ministry of Tourism
Tel: (020) 7488 9392

Spain

✦ LA TOMATINA
August 30 2000
Bunyol, Valencia, Spain

Description
This event, which began as a prank between friends in 1945, takes place to honour Saint Louis Beltran, patron saint of Bunyol. A great tomato battle takes place that uses up more than 125,000 kg of tomatoes – no one is safe!

Contact
Spanish Tourist Office
Tel: (020) 7486 8077

✦ SAN FERMIN AND RUNNING OF THE BULLS
July 7 2000 – July 14 2000
Pamplona, Navarra, Spain

Description
The bull-running takes place as part of the San Fermin Festival. The event receives international coverage and is held every morning at eight o'clock between July 7 and July 14. Young bulls are released from their pens and people (usually young men) run in front of the bulls to lead them into the bull ring. It usually lasts about three minutes. There is also a 24-hour fiesta on the streets, with lots of wine and music, a folk festival, music, theatre, religious ceremonies and parties.

Contact
San Fermin Festival
Web site: http://www.sanfermin.com

Appendices – **Festivals**

Trinidad and Tobago

✦ CARNIVAL
February 2000
Trinidad and Tobago, Caribbean

Description
The major event in Trinidad is the *Carnival*, renowned throughout the Caribbean and the rest of the world. The festivities climax at the beginning of Lent, on the two days immediately preceding Ash Wednesday, although the run-up to Carnival starts immediately after Christmas when the Calypso tents open and the Calypsonians perform their latest compositions and arrangements. During Carnival normal life grinds to a halt and the whole of Trinidad and Tobago is absorbed in the festivities. A week before the Carnival proper, *Panorama* is staged. This is the Grand Steel Drum (pan) tournament; all the big steel bands parade their skills around the Savannah, the large park in the north of Port of Spain. The Panorama preliminaries and local finals in Tobago are worth visiting, as are the pan yards as the bands practise for the big event.

Contact
Tourism and Industry Development Corporation of Trinidad and Tobago (TIDCO)
Tel: 624 2953

United Kingdom

✦ CHELSEA FLOWER SHOW
May 15 2000 – May 16 2000
Chelsea, London, England

Description
The UK's top flower show has been running since 1913. The show is held in the grounds of the Royal Hospital, home to the Chelsea Pensioners, next to the River Thames. It is one of the biggest flower displays in the world and attracts visitors from around the globe.

Contact
The Royal Horticultural Society
Tel: (020) 7649 1885

✦ EDINBURGH FESTIVAL
Mid-August 2000 – early-September 2000
Edinburgh, Scotland

Description
Every year this world-renowned festival attracts around one million visitors to Edinburgh. It was first held in 1947 as a celebration of the end of the Second World War. It is made up of several mini-festivals, the main one being the International Festival, featuring music, dance and drama. Other events include: the Fringe Festival (more offbeat than the main festival); the Film Festival (an established part of the film industry's calendar); the Book and Jazz Festivals; and the Military Tattoo (one of the most popular events of the whole festival, attracting over 200,000 visitors). There is also a huge open air concert held in Princes Street Gardens which features a firework display which takes place on the last day of the festival.

Contact
Scottish Tourist Board
Tel: (0131) 332 2433

✦ TROOPING THE COLOUR – THE QUEEN'S BIRTHDAY PARADE
June 17 2000
London, England

Description
A troop of massed bands and troops from the Household Division parade to celebrate the Queen's birthday. Festivities start at 1100 with a colourful ceremony of music and pageantry.

Contact
British Tourist Authority
Tel: (020) 8563 3342

✦ NATIONAL EISTEDDFOD OF WALES
August 30 2000 – August 31 2000
Llanelli, Wales

Description
This is an annual celebration of the music and culture of Wales. It is unique throughout Europe and is the oldest and largest celebration in Wales, dating back to the twelfth century. Each year it is held in a different town in Wales. It annually attracts over 170,000 visitors and includes 6000 competitors.

Contact
National Eisteddfod Headquarters
Tel: 01222 763 777

✦ NOTTING HILL CARNIVAL
August 26 2000 – August 28 2000
Notting Hill, London, England

Description
This is Europe's largest street festival, celebrating all things Caribbean. It features two days of parades, a vast array of sound systems, stages and partying. It is always held on the last bank holiday in August.

Contact
Carnival Office
Tel: (020) 8964 0544

United States of America

✦ MARDI GRAS
February 25 2000 – March 7 2000
New Orleans, Louisiana, USA

Description
The Mardi Gras carnival first took place in 1827 in New Orleans. The celebration includes elaborately decorated floats, marching bands, parades, parties and lots of live music. The day itself, Mardi Gras (or Fat Tuesday) fell on Tuesday March 7 this year.

Contact
Louisiana Office of Tourism
Tel: 225 342 8100

Appendices – **Travel Associations**

Travel Associations

This section provides contact details for a selection of travel trade organisations. The brief descriptions have, in the main, been provided by the associations themselves.

ABTA

✦ ASSOCIATION OF BRITISH TRAVEL AGENTS
68-71 Newman Street
London W1P 4AH
Tel: (020) 7637 2444
Fax: (020) 7637 0713
E-mail: abta@abta.co.uk
Web site: http://www.abtanet.com
ABTA is a self-regulatory body that aims to improve conditions and maintain high standards throughout the travel industry. It promotes the interests of its members and protects consumers.

ABTOF

✦ ASSOCIATION OF BRITISH TOUR OPERATORS IN FRANCE
PO Box 54
Ross-on-Wye HR9 5YQ
Tel: 01989 769140
Fax: 01989 769066
E-mail: abtof@aol.com
Web site: www.holidayfrance.org.uk
ABTOF promotes travel to France and represents the interests of its member companies.

ACTA

✦ ALLIANCE OF CANADIAN TRAVEL ASSOCIATIONS
Suite 201
1729 Bank Street
Ottawa
Ontario
Canada K1V 7Z5
Tel: 613 521 0474
Fax: 613 521 0805
E-mail: acta.ntl@sympatico.ca
Web site: http://www.acta.net
ACTA's mission is to represent the interests of its members, primarily retail and wholesale to the public, to governments, suppliers and other bodies to further develop high professional standards among members, and to support and assist them in maximising their economic objectives.

 Flight Times? Climate? Theme Parks? Time Zones? Museums? UNESCO Heritage Sites? Railways? Ski Resorts? Game Parks? – for all this, and more besides, consult the *World Travel Atlas*.

Appendices – **Travel Associations**

AFTA

✦ AUSTRALIAN FEDERATION OF TRAVEL AGENTS
AFTA
3rd Floor
309 Pitt Street
Sydney
NWS 2000
Australia
Tel: 02 92 64 32 99
Fax: 02 92 64 10 85
Web site: http://www.afta.com.au
AFTA aims to be truly representative of travel agents in Australia and to promote travel and tourism and enhance the professionalism and profitability of its members through effective representation in industry and government affairs, education and training by identifying and satisfying the needs of the travelling public.

ANTOR

✦ ASSOCIATION OF NATIONAL TOURIST OFFICE REPRESENTATIVES
ANTOR
211 Picadilly
London W1V 9LD
Tel: (020) 7917 9536
Fax: (020) 7917 9537
E-mail: antor@tourist-offices.org.uk
Web site: http://www.tourist-offices.org.uk
ANTOR promotes travel and tourism worldwide, to the trade and the public, and represents member tourist organisations.

ASTA

✦ AMERICAN SOCIETY OF TRAVEL AGENTS
ASTA World Headquarters
Suite 200
1101 King Street
Alexandria
Virginia 22314
USA
Tel: 703 739 2782
Fax: 703 684 8319
E-mail: asta@astanet.com
Web site: http://www.astanet.com
ASTA enhances the professionalism and profitability of members worldwide through effective representation in industry and government affairs, education and training, and by identifying and meeting the needs of the travelling public.

Health? Currency? Passport Requirements? Contact Addresses? Airports? Public Holidays? Accommodation? Festivals? Nightlife? – for all this, and more besides, consult the *World Travel Guide*.

Appendices – **Travel Associations**

BTA

✦ BRITISH TOURIST AUTHORITY
Thames Tower
Black's Road
London W6 9EL
Tel: (020) 8846 9000
E-mail: bbarton@bta.org.uk
Web site: http://visitbritain.com

The BTA promotes tourism to Britain and ensures that the national and regional tourist boards respond effectively to the needs of the Government, the industry and the public.

ITT

✦ INSTITUTE OF TRAVEL AND TOURISM
113 Victoria Street
St Albans
Hertfordshire AL1 3TJ
Tel: 01727 854 395
Fax: 01727 847 415
E-mail: itt@dial.pipex.com

ITT develops the professionalism of its members within the industry by acknowledging the importance of education and training at all levels. The institute also arranges regular meetings that allow a forum for discussion for its members.

WATA

✦ WORLD ASSOCIATION OF TRAVEL AGENCIES
The Secretary General
WATA
14 rue Ferrier
1202 Geneva 1
Switzerland
Tel: 22 731 4760
Fax: 22 732 8161
E-mail: wata@wata.net
Web site: http://www.wata.net

This non-profit making organisation helps locally respected agencies to attain the highest levels of professionalism in their industry. It has over 200 members worldwide.

International Dialling Codes

The following codes only relate to those countries listed in the book.

Argentina	54	Kenya	254
Australia	61	Malaysia	60
Austria	43	Malta	356
Belgium	32	Mexico	52
Bolivia	591	Morocco	212
Botswana	267	Netherlands	31
Brazil	55	New Zealand	64
Cambodia	855	Norway	47
Canada	1	Panama	507
Chile	56	Paraguay	595
China	86	Peru	51
China: Hong Kong	852	Philippines	63
Costa Rica	506	Poland	48
Cuba	53	Portugal	351
Czech Republic	420	Russian Federation	*7
Denmark	45	Singapore	65
Ecuador	593	South Africa	27
Egypt	20	Spain	34
France	33	Sri Lanka	94
Germany	49	Sweden	46
Greece	30	Switzerland	41
Guatemala	502	Tanzania	255
Hungary	36	Thailand	66
Iceland	354	Tibet	86
India	91	Tunisia	216
Indonesia	62	Turkey	90
Ireland	353	United Kingdom	44
Israel	972	United States of America	1
Italy	39	Venezuela	58
Jamaica	1 876	Yemen	967
Japan	81	Zambia	260
Jordan	962	Zimbabwe	263

* The 0 of the Moscow code should not be omitted when dialling.

section six
index

1. Alphabetical

2. By Category

1. Alphabetical

Abu Simbel, 106
Acropolis, 69
Alcatraz Island, 21
Algonquin Provincial Park, 8
Alhambra, 91
Angel Falls, 37
Angkor Wat, 127
Anne Frank House, 83
Arc de Triomphe, 58
Arenal Volcano, 12
Auschwitz, 87
Banau Rice Terraces, 141
Banff National Park, 8
Batu Caves, 139
Bayeux Tapestry, 58
Big Ben, 48
Blackpool Pleasure Beach, 49
Blarney Castle, 74
Blue Mosque, 98
Brandenburg Gate, 65
British Airways London Eye, 49
British Museum, 50
Bryggen, 86
Buda Castle Palace, 71
Budapest Central Synagogue, 71
Caernarfon Castle, 101
Cambridge University, 50
Canterbury Cathedral, 51
Cape Point, 114
Carthage, 118
Castle of St George, 88
Cave of Lascaux , 59
Central Park, 22
Charles Bridge, 45
Chartres Cathedral, 59
Château de Chenonceau, 60
Château de Versailles, 60
Chichén Itzá, 15

Cité des Sciences et de l'Industrie, 61
Cliffs of Moher, 74
CN Tower, 9
Cologne Cathedral, 66
Colosseum, 76
Copper Canyon, 16
Death Valley, 22
Delphi, 69
Disneyland Paris, 61
Doge's Palace, 77
Drottningholm Palace, 96
Dunn's River Falls, 15
Easter Island, 11
Edinburgh Castle, 91
Egyptian Museum, 107
Eiffel Tower, 62
Ellora Temple Caves, 131
Empire State Building, 23
Englischer Garten, 66
Ephesus, 99
Fiordland National Park, 140
Fisherman's Bastion, 72
Flanders Fields, 44
Florence Duomo, 77
Forbidden City, 128
Freedom Trail, 23
Galapagos Islands, 14
Geysir, 73
Ghats at Varanasi, 132
Giant Ferris Wheel, 42
Giants Causeway, 85
Glendalough, 75
Golden Gate Bridge, 24
Graceland, 25
Grand Canyon, 25
Great Wall of China, 129
Great Zimbabwe Ruins, 120

Index – **Alphabetical**

Guggenheim Museum Bilbao, 92
Hadrian's Wall, 52
Hagar Qim, 82
Hardanger Fjord, 86
Hawaii Volcanoes National Park, 26
Hofburg Palace, 42
Hollywood Walk of Fame, 26
Hoover Dam, 27
Iguaçú Falls (Arg.), 4
Iguaçú Falls (Bra.), 6
Iguaçú Falls (Par.), 19
Independence National Historical Park, 28
Indian Museum, 133
Jet d'Eau, 97
Jungfraujoch, 98
Kakadu National Park, 126
Kaziranga National Park, 133
Kennedy Space Center, 28
Keukenhof Gardens, 83
Khajuraho, 134
Kilimanjaro National Park, 116
Knossos, 70
Kremlin, 89
Kruger National Park, 114
Kunsthistorisches Museum, 43
La Sagrada Familia, 93
Lake Titicaca, 5
Lake Titicaca, 20
Las Vegas Strip, 29
Legoland, 46
Lincoln Memorial, 30
Little Mermaid, 47
Los Glaciares National Park, 4
Maasai Mara Game Reserve, 111
Machu Picchu, 20
Manneken-Pis, 45
Masada, 109
Medina in Fez, 113
Medina in Tunis, 118
Meiji Shrine, 137
Metropolitan Museum of Art, 30
Millennium Dome, 52
Monasterio de San Lorenzo de El Escorial, 93
Monte Alban, 16
Monteverde Cloud Forest, 12
Moremi Wildlife Reserve, 106
Mount Fuji, 137
Mount Kenya National Park, 112
Mount Rushmore National Memorial, 31
Musée du Louvre, 63
Musée d'Orsay, 63
Museum of National Antiquities, 96
Nahuel Huapi National Park, 5
National Air and Space Museum, 32
National Archaeological Museum of Athens, 70
National Gallery, 53
National Museum of Anthropology, 17
Neuschwanstein Castle, 67
Niagara Falls (USA), 32
Niagara Falls (Can.), 10
Notre Dame Cathedral, 64
Old City of Sana'a, 119
Old Havana, 13
Old Quebec, 10
Oxford University, 53
Palace of the Winds, 134
Palenque, 17
Panama Canal, 19
Pantheon, 78
Pergamon Museum, 67
Perlan, 73
Petra, 111
Petronas Towers, 139
Phang Nga Bay, 144
Pompeii, 78
Pont du Gard, 64
Pont St-Bénézet, 65
Ponte Vecchio, 79
Potala Palace, 146
Prado Museum, 94
Prague Castle, 46
Prambanan Temples, 136
Pyramids and Sphinx, 107
Raffles Hotel , 142

Index – **Alphabetical**

Red Fort, 135
Reichstag, 68
Rijksmuseum, 84
Robben Island, 115
Rock and Roll Hall of Fame, 33
Roman Aqueduct at Segovia, 94
Roman Baths and Pump Room, 54
Roman Forum, 79
Royal Barges National
 Museum, 144
Royal Grand Palace, 145
St Basil's Cathedral, 90
St Paul's Cathedral, 55
St Peter's Basilica, 80
St Sophia, 99
Sanjusangen-do Temple, 138
Santiago de Compostela
 Cathedral, 95
Schönbrunn Palace, 43
Sensoji Temple, 138
Serengeti National Park, 117
Seville Cathedral, 95
Sigiriya, 143
Sistine Chapel, 80
State Hermitage Museum, 90
Statue of Christ the Redeemer, 6
Statue of Liberty, 33
Stonehenge, 55
Sugar Loaf Mountain, 7
Summer Palace, 129
Sydney Opera House, 126
Table Mountain, 116
Taj Mahal, 135
Temple Mount, 109
Temple of Karnak, 108
Temple of the Tooth, 143
Teotihuacán, 18
Terracotta Army, 130
Three Gorges of the Yangtze
 River, 130
Tikal, 14
Tivoli Gardens, 47
Tongariro National Park, 141
Topkapi Palace, 100
Tour Hassan, 113

Tower of Belém, 89
Tower of London, 56
Tower of Pisa, 81
Trinity College Dublin, 75
Troy, 100
Uffizi Gallery, 81
Uluru-Kata Tjuta National Park, 127
Universal Studios Florida, 34
Valley of the Kings, 108
Van Gogh Museum, 84
Victoria Falls (Zam.), 119
Victoria Falls (Zim.), 121
Victoria Peak, 131
Walt Disney World, 35
Wawel Royal Castle, 87
Western Wall, 110
Westminster Abbey, 56
White House, 35
Yellowstone National Park, 36
York Minster, 57
Yosemite National Park, 36

2. By Category

Amusement

Las Vegas Strip, 29
Universal Studios Florida, 34
Walt Disney World, 35
Giant Ferris Wheel, 42
Legoland, 46
Tivoli Gardens, 47
Blackpool Pleasure Beach, 49
British Airways London Eye, 49
Millennium Dome, 52
Disneyland Paris, 61

Cultural

National Museum of Anthropology, 17
Alcatraz Island, 21
Central Park, 22
Graceland, 25
Hollywood Walk of Fame, 26
Kennedy Space Center, 28
Metropolitan Museum of Art, 30
Rock and Roll Hall of Fame, 33
White House, 35
Kunsthistorisches Museum, 43
Manneken-Pis, 45
Little Mermaid, 47
Tivoli Gardens, 47
British Museum, 50
Cambridge University, 50
National Gallery, 53
Oxford University, 53
Cité des Sciences et de l'Industrie, 61
Musée du Louvre, 63
Musée d'Orsay, 63
Englischer Garten, 66
Pergamon Museum, 67
National Archaeological Museum of Athens, 70
Trinity College Dublin, 75
Uffizi Gallery, 81
Keukenhof Gardens, 83
Rijksmuseum, 84
Van Gogh Museum, 84
Kremlin, 89
State Hermitage Museum, 90
Guggenheim Museum Bilbao, 92
Prado Museum, 94
Museum of National Antiquities, 96
Egyptian Museum, 107
Sydney Opera House, 126
Indian Museum, 133
Raffles Hotel, 142
Royal Barges National Museum, 144

Historical

Old Quebec, 10
Old Havana, 13
Tikal, 14
Chichén Itzá, 15
Monte Alban, 16
Palenque, 17
Teotihuacán, 18
Machu Picchu, 20
Alcatraz Island, 21
Freedom Trail, 23
Independence National Historical Park, 28
Kennedy Space Center, 28
Lincoln Memorial, 30
Mount Rushmore National Memorial, 31

Index – **By Category**

National Air and Space Museum, 32
Statue of Liberty, 33
White House, 35
Hofburg Palace, 42
Schönbrunn Palace, 43
Flanders Fields, 44
Charles Bridge, 45
Prague Castle, 46
Big Ben, 48
British Museum, 50
Cambridge University, 50
Hadrian's Wall, 52
Oxford University, 53
Roman Baths and Pump Room, 54
Stonehenge, 55
Tower of London, 56
Arc de Triomphe, 58
Bayeux Tapestry, 58
Cave of Lascaux , 59
Château de Chenonceau, 60
Château de Versailles, 60
Pont du Gard, 64
Pont St-Bénézet, 65
Brandenburg Gate, 65
Neuschwanstein Castle, 67
Reichstag, 68
Acropolis, 69
Delphi, 69
Knossos, 70
National Archaeological Museum of Athens, 70
Buda Castle Palace, 71
Fisherman's Bastion, 72
Blarney Castle, 74
Trinity College Dublin, 75
Colosseum, 76
Doge's Palace, 77
Pompeii, 78
Ponte Vecchio, 79
Roman Forum, 79
Tower of Pisa, 81
Hagar Qim, 82
Anne Frank House, 83
Bryggen, 86
Auschwitz, 87
Wawel Royal Castle, 87
Castle of St George, 88
Tower of Belém, 89
Kremlin, 89
Edinburgh Castle, 91
Alhambra, 91
Monasterio de San Lorenzo de El Escorial, 93
Roman Aqueduct at Segovia, 94
Drottningholm Palace, 96
Ephesus, 99
Topkapi Palace, 100
Troy, 100
Caernarfon Castle, 101
Abu Simbel, 106
Egyptian Museum, 107
Pyramids and Sphinx, 107
Temple of Karnak, 108
Valley of the Kings, 108
Masada, 109
Petra, 111
Medina in Fez, 113
Robben Island, 115
Carthage, 118
Medina in Tunis, 118
Old City of Sana'a, 119
Great Zimbabwe Ruins, 120
Forbidden City, 128
Great Wall of China, 129
Summer Palace, 129
Terracotta Army, 130
Indian Museum, 133
Palace of the Winds, 134
Red Fort, 135
Sigiriya, 143
Royal Barges National Museum, 144
Royal Grand Palace, 145
Potala Palace, 146

Man-made

Statue of Christ the Redeemer, 6
CN Tower, 9

Index – By Category

Easter Island, 11
Tikal, 14
Chichén Itzá, 15
Monte Alban, 16
Palenque, 17
Teotihuacán, 18
Panama Canal, 19
Machu Picchu, 20
Empire State Building, 23
Golden Gate Bridge, 24
Hoover Dam, 27
Mount Rushmore National Memorial, 31
Statue of Liberty, 33
Millennium Dome, 52
Eiffel Tower, 62
Pont du Gard, 64
Perlan, 73
La Sagrada Familia, 93
Jet d'Eau, 97
Abu Simbel, 106
Pyramids and Sphinx, 107
Sydney Opera House, 126
Great Wall of China, 129
Terracotta Army, 130
Taj Mahal, 135
Petronas Towers, 139
Banau Rice Terraces, 141

Natural

Iguaçú Falls (Arg.), 4
Los Glaciares National Park, 4
Nahuel Huapi National Park, 5
Lake Titicaca, 5
Iguaçú Falls (Bra.), 6
Sugar Loaf Mountain, 7
Algonquin Provincial Park, 8
Banff National Park, 8
Niagara Falls (Can.), 10
Arenal Volcano, 12
Monteverde Cloud Forest, 12
Galapagos Islands, 14
Dunn's River Falls, 15
Copper Canyon, 16
Iguaçú Falls (Par.), 19
Lake Titicaca, 20
Death Valley, 22
Grand Canyon, 25
Hawaii Volcanoes National Park, 26
Niagara Falls (USA), 32
Yellowstone National Park, 36
Yosemite National Park, 36
Angel Falls, 37
Geysir, 73
Cliffs of Moher, 74
Glendalough, 75
Giants Causeway, 85
Hardanger Fjord, 86
Jungfraujoch, 98
Moremi Wildlife Reserve, 106
Maasai Mara Game Reserve, 111
Mount Kenya National Park, 112
Cape Point, 114
Kruger National Park, 114
Table Mountain, 116
Kilimanjaro National Park, 116
Serengeti National Park, 117
Victoria Falls (Zam.), 119
Victoria Falls (Zim.), 121
Kakadu National Park, 126
Uluru-Kata Tjuta National Park, 127
Three Gorges of the Yangtze River, 130
Victoria Peak, 131
Kaziranga National Park, 133
Mount Fuji, 137
Batu Caves, 139
Fiordland National Park, 140
Tongariro National Park, 141
Phang Nga Bay, 144

Religious

Statue of Christ the Redeemer, 6
Canterbury Cathedral, 51
St Paul's Cathedral, 55
Westminster Abbey, 56
York Minster, 57
Chartres Cathedral, 59

165

Index – **By Category**

Notre Dame Cathedral, 64
Cologne Cathedral, 66
Budapest Central Synagogue, 71
Glendalough, 75
Florence Duomo, 77
Pantheon, 78
Sistine Chapel, 80
St Peter's Basilica, 80
St Basil's Cathedral, 90
La Sagrada Familia, 93
Monasterio de San Lorenzo de El Escorial, 93
Santiago de Compostela Cathedral, 95
Seville Cathedral, 95
Blue Mosque, 98
St Sophia, 99
Temple Mount, 109
Western Wall, 110
Tour Hassan, 113
Angkor Wat, 127
Ellora Temple Caves, 131
Ghats at Varanasi, 132
Khajuraho, 134
Prambanan Temples, 136
Meiji Shrine, 137
Sanjusangen-do Temple, 138
Sensoji Temple, 138
Batu Caves, 139
Temple of the Tooth, 143

Notes

Notes

DEVIL I NEED

THE SEQUEL TO CAPTURED LIGHT

BOOK TWO IN THE KING OF ICE & STEEL TRILOGY

RAYA MORRIS EDWARDS

DEVIL I NEED
By Raya Morris Edwards

Copyright © 2022 Morris Edwards Publishing

All rights reserved. No part of this publication may be reproduced, stored, or transmitted without prior permission of the publisher of this book.

This is a work of fiction. Names, characters, places, and incidents either are the product of the author's imagination or are used fictitiously. Any resemblance to actual or fictional persons, living or dead, events, or locales is entirely coincidental.

FIRST EDITION

Author's Note

This book picks up about a year after the epilogue in Captured Light. While there is a conclusive ending (no cliffhangers!) this book *must* be read after reading Captured Light or it will not make sense.

Trigger Warning & Content Tags

Discussion & brief descriptions of abuse and trauma
Violence, including murder
Trying to conceive and pregnancy
Body issues & eating disorders/recovery are mentioned throughout.
Care was taken that ED content is not instructional or graphic.

Explicit depictions of PIV, oral, and anal sex acts
Breeding kink
CNC
Light spanking
Praise & degradation

This book is for all my readers who love Lucien the most.

CHAPTER ONE

OLIVIA

I couldn't sleep without Lucien.

The bed went from being a haven to being a wasteland when he was away. I went through my nightly ritual of steaming my face, rubbing thick creams into my skin, and tying up my hair so it would be wavy in the morning.

Then I slipped on my silk mask and tossed and turned all night.

When he was home, Lucien slept like the dead, completely still and barely breathing. Sometimes when I woke I had to roll over to check he was still in bed. But I needed the weight of his arm across my side and his protective embrace, even if his presence was like a ghost.

My body felt small without his and I had nightmares when he wasn't there to keep them at bay.

Tonight was worse than usual. I sat up, finally giving up on sleep. Maybe I could get some work done and fall asleep in the big chair in the living room. Marco's nanny was spending the night so she would hear him if he woke.

I tied my silk dressing gown over my slip, pushed my slippers on, and padded from the room. The nightlights were on and they provided a little trail of light all the way from my bedroom to the nursery. I cracked the door open and peered in.

Marco lay in his daybed, his favorite fluffy blanket wrapped around his small body. He was snoring quietly beneath the flickering light of the little lamp I kept in the window.

My chest warmed as I backed up and closed the door. Downstairs the grandfather clock chimed four. I retrieved my phone and my laptop from the bedroom and padded down the huge, dark hallway. I missed the Esposito Mansion, but Lucien preferred our new home. We'd both put a lot of work into it and it was nice to finally have a house set up exactly how I pleased.

But I did sometimes miss the room we'd shared during our first year of marriage while I was pregnant with Marco.

Shaking off my melancholy, I climbed the huge, split staircase and turned down the winding hallway to the kitchen. The light flickered once and warmed to a soft, golden glow. On the table sat three large bouquets of white roses from Lucien.

He always sent me flowers, or rather he had his secretary arrange for them to be sent. But it was the thought that counted and it always thrilled me when I opened the door to another bunch of roses and a note from my husband that said:

I love you.

That was all he ever wrote, but I understood what those words meant to him. He wasn't the most expressive man, emotions being his archenemy. Being able to vocalize those three little words to me had been a monumental moment in his life.

I didn't mind. I'd learned to see his love in the things he did, in the protective brush of his hand on my back, and even in the spired ice of his eyes.

Smiling, I ran my fingertips over the crystal vases. My manicured fingernails and the heavy, diamond ring on my finger clinking against the glass. There was part of me that wished I wasn't so swayed by material things, that wished my chest didn't fill with excitement every time Lucien dangled something shiny in front of me.

It was too late for that. I was utterly, hopelessly spoiled by him and I loved it.

And it wasn't like he didn't make me work for it.

My body warmed as I poured myself a cup of chamomile tea. Just before he'd left, we'd gotten up at four in the morning, before any of the servants had arrived. And I'd made him breakfast while he ran his hands over my back, up under my skirt, and his mouth left little trails of wetness down my throat. He was insatiable and I loved it.

He'd eaten me out slowly as soon as breakfast was done. Kneeling on the kitchen floor, my leg up over his shoulder. His mouth working between my legs slowly, licking my pussy until I had to bite my tongue to keep from crying out.

He kept me on the edge until my hips were working against his mouth and then he bent me over the counter and fucked me until I cried out, pulsing around his cock.

My hips shuddered at my memory and warmth stirred in the deepest part of me.

The part that only he was able to satisfy.

Shaking off the memory, I flipped open my laptop and opened my task manager to see what Leah, the co-president of my charity, had put on the agenda.

About three years after our marriage, I told Lucien I wanted to do something outside the house. I was growing isolated from the world, locked up in the new Esposito mansion.

He'd asked me what I wanted and I'd thought about it for a while and told him I wanted to start a charity. He'd been sitting in bed wearing the sluttiest pair of reading glasses, a stack of paperwork in his lap. His icy eyes shot to mine and his brow twitched.

"Isn't that hypocritical?" he said. "You're married to a criminal."

I shrugged from the bathroom door. "Iris does work with a charitable foundation and Duran is part of the outfit. How is it any different?"

He shrugged. "Who does your little heart want to help then?"

"Well, I was thinking that there are probably a lot of people who are in the same situation that you and I were growing up, but they don't have any financial options," I said. "Maybe I could start a foundation that raises money for victims of domestic abuse who have no resources to get them out. To help them into better situations."

He cocked his head, remaining quiet.

"Is...do you think that's not a good idea?" I asked hesitantly.

He took off his reading glasses and beckoned me. I drew close and he lifted me into his lap easily, his hard, lean hands resting on my hips.

"I think you're a better person than I," he said. "And if that's what you want, that's what you'll have."

He was true to his word. Less than six months later, we cut the ribbon on the Esposito Foundation and I got to work, overjoyed at finally having a job for the first time in my life. I was the co-president of the company, along with Leah, who had a background in business and philanthropy. She managed the more complicated, technical side of things and I managed the fundraising and social aspects.

I spent three days a week in the office and four days at home with Marco. About once a month there was a benefit to attend, or a party I had to appear at to represent the foundation.

What I hadn't expected was the public's response to my new venture. Everyone suspected what Lucien was, they were just too scared to say it aloud, and our pairing made a sensational headline.

Millionaire mafia businessman and his wife open a charity for victims of childhood abuse. It sounded too strange to be true and suddenly our faces were on the cover of tabloids. Suddenly I had to think through how I looked and what I wore when I went out because someone might take a picture of me and sell it.

The most intimidating thing was being thrust into the city's high society. I was surprised to find that people liked me, that they wanted me to attend events as Olivia Esposito, instead of just Lucien's wife. They were interested in my story and what I had planned for the foundation in the future.

"You're charming the city," Lucien remarked, as we got ready for a gala one night. "And you're improving my image immensely."

"You're welcome," I said, spinning in my Dior dress.

"They love you," he said. "You look good on a magazine cover, baby."

Now, sitting hunched over my computer at four in the morning, I didn't feel glamorous. I felt tired and worn out from work, from attending social events, from trying to raise my son around those things all while performing my social and personal duties for my husband.

Maybe I was working too hard.

Eyes burning, I finished my emails and closed the laptop and went to heat up my tea. It was almost five so I had a few hours before Marco would want breakfast. Deciding I would try to sleep in the chair for a little while, I grabbed my tea and padded out into the hall.

My heart leapt and I froze.

The door had just opened to reveal Lucien, wearing the woolen overcoat he'd gotten in Russia, and carrying a briefcase. His face was cut with shadows, but his eyes still glittered from beneath lowered brows. As cold as the wind and snow swirling around him.

I set aside my cup, practically dropping it on the hall table, and ran to him.

He caught me in his arms, lifting me so I could wrap my legs around his waist. He smelled so good, clean like soap and a little like he'd just had a cigarette. The cold clung to the scratchy fabric of his coat, but beneath it, his body was warm. Every ridge of his stomach and pecs beneath his shirt was so comforting and familiar. I swallowed the lump in my throat and nestled my head against his hard chest.

He carried me into the hall and shut the door quietly. I unlatched my legs and slid down his body, my bare feet stinging as they hit the cold floor. I'd kicked off my slippers somewhere in the dark hall, but I didn't care. His tattooed hand slipped up, closing in my hair, and drew my head back. When his mouth contacted mine, I felt my whole body go limp.

He tasted so good it made me weak. When he drew back, his glacial eyes raked over me. Devoid of emotion and hard like ice. But I didn't care that I rarely saw warmth in him—I understood how he chose to show his emotions now. Those distant eyes were mine and I loved them for every shard of ice.

"Bed," he said hoarsely.

"Lucien, don't you want something to eat?" I whispered.

"No, I want you. In our bed."

His mouth twitched as he let me go and shrugged out of his heavy coat. Then he picked me up before I could protest and carried me up the winding hall, up the stairs, and to our bedroom. Without missing a beat, he deposited me onto the bed and stripped his clothes down to his boxer briefs.

My heart pattered. No matter how many times my husband fucked me, I never got used to it. I never tired of seeing him undress and reveal his tattooed, scarred body. And I definitely never tired of the heavy-lidded, lust filled expression in his hazel eyes as he backed me up and pushed me down onto the bed.

"Lucien," I whispered.

His big, lean hands pushed my dressing gown open and slid beneath my slip, palming my breast. Kneading it hard until I winced. He eased his grip and bent his head, taking my nipple into his mouth. A shock moved through my body from his scorching touch and it went all the way to my soles of my feet and curled my toes.

There was nowhere I would rather be than right here with him.

He slid down between my thighs, pushing aside the front of his boxer briefs. Then he spat into his cupped hand and slid his fingers over my pussy to wet me. I closed my eyes, biting my lip, waiting for that sweet burn.

It would hurt because he was big and he hadn't been inside me for a month, but that pain was everything I'd longed for every night since he'd been away. He knew what I wanted, he knew I craved the torturous pressure of his cock inside me without preparation.

The familiar head of his cock nudged against my sex. His jaw tightened, the corded muscles of his forearms on either side of me tensed, and he slid his heavy length into me in a smooth motion. Forcing me to take all of it at once. I arced my lower back and lifted my hips to make room.

"Jesus *fucking* Christ," he breathed, his head falling back.

I whimpered, biting my lower lip.

"Hush, you can take it," he breathed. "This was all I could fucking think about for a month. Listening to you take it all."

His mouth hovered over mine, nipping once at my lower lip. His hips moved, seating himself deeper and deeper until I swore I felt him in every part of my being.

He rode me with short strokes to break me in and I sighed quietly as my muscles began to loosen.

I wanted to drown in him.

He fucked me slowly, our bodies entwined so tightly I wasn't sure where I ended and he begun. His forearm slid beneath my upper back and his other hand gripped my hip as he drove into me with methodical strokes. Taking my body so completely that when he finally emptied himself into me, I was left breathless.

He pulled from me, leaving me weak and desperate. I lay in a haze and watched him slide down my body and take my clit into his mouth. The familiar curl of his tongue sent heat surging through my hips as he licked it with short strokes until an orgasm burst to the surface. Forcing out the gasping cry I could never seem to bite back. My fingers tangled in his dark hair as I fell through space, ebbing and pulsing under his touch.

Lucien lifted his head and ran a hand over his mouth.

"Good girl," he said.

I laughed, wiping my sweaty bangs from my forehead. He moved back up my body, flipped on his back, and pulled me to straddle his hips. I ran my palms up over the smooth, ridged muscles of this stomach. Marked with tattoos to cover all the scars on his skin. His cold eyes watched as I traced each curve of ink and bend of muscle.

"You should sleep," I said.

He shook his head. "I have things to do today before we leave."

I'd planned a weekend away, just the two of us, and it was all I'd thought about for days. It had been so long since Lucien and I got time to ourselves and I missed him. Little bits of his time before and after work weren't enough. I wanted to wake up with him slowly, to watch him have an espresso, to shower with him before getting breakfast together.

"What do you have to do?"

"Work."

He didn't like talking about his work when he was home, which I understood. I sighed and dismounted him and went to the bathroom to wash.

He appeared in the doorway in just his boxer briefs and leaned against the frame, arms crossed, watching as I turned on the hot water and began filling the tub.

"Care to take a bath with me?" I asked.

He cocked his head. "I just might have time for that."

That evening, we stood on the porch and watched as Cosimo and Lorenza drove away with Marco. Then there was a long silence and I closed my eyes as Lucien's warm palm slid down between my shoulder blades and rested on my lower back. He bent and kissed my temple.

"We've already had dinner," he said softly. "Let's get our things together and get to the hotel. I want to fuck my wife."

There was never any room for argument with him, although I wasn't inclined to tonight. He took my hand and led me back into the house, up the hall, and into our bedroom. I'd half expected him to push me down on the bed for a quickie, but he went to the closet and took down his suitcase. I had already packed my things, so I climbed onto the bed and sat cross-legged to watch him.

Every detail of him thrilled me with a familiar blend of fear, adoration, and desire. He was just as handsome and, thanks to an hour and a half in the gym every morning, he was beautifully muscled. There was a line of silver running through the top of his hair and a few specks of it around his ears. I found it incredibly sexy and I loved running my fingers through it while he pleasured me.

He paused, glancing up at me. The corner of his mouth twitched.

"What is it, baby?"

I shook my head. "Nothing. I just missed you."

He felt all the longing in that word and he circled the bed and bent, kissing me briefly.

"I'll make up for it tonight."

"I know you will."

I thought I saw the ghost of a smile on his face below his cold eyes. He turned and disappeared into the bathroom and I heard his footsteps halt. There was a long silence and then he appeared in the doorway, something in his hand. My stomach flipped as my eyes fell on the little, cardboard box.

"Did you stop taking your birth control?" he asked.

I swallowed. "Yes. You weren't here."

"I am now." His jaw twitched. "I came in you this morning."

Damn it, I'd been so turned on I'd totally forgotten I wasn't on the pill. I froze, my hand going to my mouth, trying to read his face. He didn't seem upset, but it was hard to tell what he was feeling.

"I'm sorry, Lucien," I said in a rush. "I'm so used to being on it, I just didn't think."

"That's not a small mistake, Olivia."

The silence was heavy between us. My heart thumped as I waited for him to react.

"Do you want me to get you pregnant?"

His voice was soft and his head was cocked, his watchful gaze on me. Even after all these years, I still struggled to read him, but I swore he looked more aroused than angry. There was a distinct, telltale flush between his collarbones.

"I just thought we could see what happened this weekend, but I didn't mean to spring it on you," I whispered. "I'm sorry, Lucien. Are you upset?"

He shook his head and beckoned me. Heart in my throat, I slipped down from the bed and padded to him and looked up into the cold face I loved more than anything.

God, even after six years of being his wife, he still knew how to send a shiver down my spine. His palm cradled my elbow and he pressed my hand to his groin. He was hard and deliciously hot beneath the front of his pants, twitching against my touch.

His heavy, dead eyes connected with mine.

"Can I fix this for you?" I asked.

He shook his head. "No, I'll fuck you at the hotel. If you want a baby, I'll give you one."

I couldn't hold back my smile. "You'd better finish packing your things while I get dressed then."

I felt his eyes on me as I pulled on a comfortable pair of jeans and a cashmere sweater. We'd already had dinner so I didn't need to dress up and I knew there was a chill to the air. When I turned to sit down and put my shoes on, he was still watching me, his lips parted.

His eyes were on my bare feet. Grazing over the brand new pedicure I'd had done earlier that day and the delicate gold chain around my ankle.

"Lucien," I said.

He blinked and the habitual frost crept back over his eyes. I thought I saw his brow curve as he turned away to finish packing.

"You know what you're doing to me," he said.

I didn't argue with that. I tied my sneakers and gathered my hair into a ponytail while he carried our suitcases out to the car. Then I bounced down the stairs, elated for the first time in a long time. I'd spent the last month with nothing on my mind except getting my husband back, taking him away from his work, and having him completely to myself for one glorious, long weekend.

Nothing was going to mess this up.

When he settled into the driver's side of the Tesla, he paused with his hand on my knee. He was looking at me impassively, studying me with those eyes I had no hope of reading.

As usual, I had no idea what he was thinking.

His throat bobbed and he reached out and gently took hold of the nape of my neck and bent to kiss my mouth. My nipples hardened instantly as the tip of his tongue brushed my mouth, slipping past my lips.

I'd forgotten how good he was at this and it all came back in a rush. My body tingled, my breasts ached against my bra, and there was a raw pulse between my legs. Our kiss deepened and I wished desperately that he would slide down the seat and take me here in the dark car in front of the house.

I needed him. I needed the heavy pressure of him, the little ache of pain as he bottomed out so deep inside my body.

More than that, I needed there to be only Lucien. I wanted there to be nothing in the world but our bodies between the sheets, my nose filled with his clean scent, my limbs wound around his, my mouth drenched with his taste.

I hadn't realized almost six years ago when I fell in love with him that I would just keep falling again and again, more deeply every time.

He pulled back and swallowed.

"I love you," he said.

His voice inflection didn't change and neither did his eyes. But I felt his words, somewhere under all the ice and steel armor.

"I love you too," I whispered.

"We'd better get to the hotel before I fuck you right here."

"I wouldn't turn that down."

The corner of his mouth twitched and I knew that was his version of a smile. And that was enough, it was so much more than enough. He pulled the Tesla out onto the road and settled his long body back in the seat and rested his lean hand on my knee.

He was left handed, but he no longer wore his wedding ring on his dominant hand after an incident in the city he wouldn't tell me about.

All I knew was it had gotten caught on something during a fight, stripped the skin from his first knuckle to his last. He hadn't told me when it happened, he just came home with stitches up and down his finger.

Now he wore the ring on his right hand, which I didn't mind. I liked that when we held hands in the car our rings touched.

I glanced over at his left hand on the wheel. There was a thick, silvery scar running down his finger that always sent a wave of anxiety through me. Lucien was a careful man, he never acted without thinking his next move through like a master chess player.

But he was also just a man and bullets and knives pierced his skin as easily as other men.

I wished he remembered that more often.

"You're quiet tonight," he said softly.

I sighed and pulled my knees up to sit cross-legged. "I'm just glad you're home and that we get to spend the weekend together."

His jaw worked, but he kept his eyes on the highway. We pulled off the second exit and headed into the city. The hotel was on the far side, a little out of the way, in a historic building. We had never stayed there before and by our standards, it was quaint, which sounded perfect to me. I wasn't sure how Lucien would feel about it however—he could be surprisingly particular where he stayed.

"Can you handle another baby right now?" he asked.

I chewed the inside of my mouth, thinking carefully. "I'll have to cut back at the foundation a little bit as I get further along. And I might need to hire more help. But I just don't feel like I want Marco to be an only child and I'd like his sibling to be close to his age."

"You'll have everything you need," he said. "Don't get me wrong, I want nothing more than to fuck you until you're pregnant, but I want to make sure this is what you want. I feel like we were reckless when we tried earlier in the year."

"I don't know if reckless is the right word."

"It was too much for you. We were right to put trying on hold."

"I think I'm ready to be pregnant again," I said slowly.

He flicked his eyes to me for a second as he took a left and headed back onto the highway going east.

"Have you had a full cycle since you stopped taking your birth control?" he asked.

I nodded. "I just finished my period."

We didn't speak again until we pulled up in front of the hotel and he leaned forward to look at the glowing sign. It was a large, square building made of white stone with three stories of blue shutters. It was just fancy enough there was a valet, but not enough that they would know us here.

That was what I wanted. I desperately wanted to just be a regular couple having a weekend away instead of the millionaire crime boss and his philanthropic wife.

Lucien parked and gathered our suitcases in one hand and wove his fingers through mine. We moved up the stairs and the doors slid open to reveal an elegantly decorated lobby. The carpet below our feet was a rich blue and there was a spiral staircase on the far end and a sleek, wooden front desk. The man standing behind it wore a crisp suit and a gold name tag.

"How much was this room?" Lucien asked.

"I didn't want anything fancy," I said firmly.

"It's...quaint."

"I like it."

"Whatever makes you happy, baby," he said, stepping up to the desk.

I slipped around in front of him. "Hi," I said brightly. "I have a room booked for the next four days under Olivia Esposito."

"Alright, let me see," the man said, smiling. He leaned closer to his computer and pushed his glasses up his nose, squinting hard. "It looks like there's a note here to upgrade you to the honeymoon suite, Mrs. Esposito."

I frowned. "Who is that from?"

"The owner of the hotel," the man said. "He was very insistent it be kept open for you. He said he knows you, Mr. Esposito."

"Really?" Lucien frowned, leaning on the counter. "What's his name?"

"Mr. Emerson-Green," the man said.

"Oh, of course, he's the...the second ward councilman's cousin," said Lucien airily. "Please let him know we're grateful for that, although I'd like to pay for the upgrade. His cousin, Bennett, is a good friend of mine."

"He won't hear of it, sir," the man said firmly.

I was doing my best not to scowl as the man handed Lucien the keys and they chatted back and forth. I'd planned this weekend away all on my own and had looked forward to being anonymous, but I should have known Lucien didn't have that luxury. Maybe next time I wouldn't be so stupid as to use my real name to book the room.

We stepped into the elevator and Lucien stood looking at me with a hint of amusement in his eyes.

"Don't pout," he said.

Without thinking, I rolled my eyes.

"Don't roll your eyes at me, Olivia."

There was a sudden edge to his voice. I knew how much that annoyed him and the fact that I did it anyway drove him crazy. It was one of the few ways I could get a rise out of him.

I lifted my chin and locked gazes with him. His brow twitched and his head cocked slowly. Then I rolled my eyes again, exaggerating the motion.

The suitcases fell and he was on me in a second, his lean body pressing against mine. His hard palm slid up my hip and under my sweatshirt, over my bare skin, and slipped out the neckline. His fingers wrapped gently around my throat and his mouth hovered over mine.

"You will be good for me this weekend," he said firmly. "Or I will put you over my knee and spank your lovely ass. Understood?"

"Is that a promise?"

His fingers tightened and his lids flickered.

"Don't bait me, Olivia. You know better."

My mouth was dry and my heart hammered against my ribs like the wings of a bird. The raw, hungry ache between my thighs roared to be satisfied. It was so hard to be good for him when he touched me like this when I was bad. But deep inside, there was a still a part of me that respected his strength and power too much to push him any further than rolling my eyes.

"Do you understand?" he murmured into my neck.

"Yes, sir."

The door pinged and he drew back, gathering our suitcases as if nothing had happened. His free hand slid around my lower back and he guided me gently into the hall and slid his fingers through mine.

Leading closer and closer to the room where we would finally be alone after months.

He unlocked the door and led me inside, letting it fall shut behind him. It wasn't a suite by our usual standards because it was all one room, but the bed was big and looked comfortable. It sat on a dark wood frame covered in a cloud of white sheets and pillows. There was a couch in the far corner, a desk, and a table with two chairs. On the opposite wall was a large, almost floor-to-ceiling mirror that offered a prime view of the bed.

I could see why it was the honeymoon suite.

Lucien laid the suitcases down and pulling out a black gift box. My heart fluttered. After all this time, there was something about the gifts he gave me that set my pulse racing. Perhaps because he was so cold, so impersonal, and it amazed me that he seemed to always be thinking of me even when we were apart.

"For you," he said, setting it on the bed. "Well...it's for me too."

I slipped out of my shoes and climbed up on the bed, kneeling and lifting the lid from the box. Nestled in the black tissue paper was a set of pink lace lingerie and a velvet box. My stomach clenched at the sight of the lingerie. It looked so small and skimpy—since having Marco, I didn't really wear that kind of thing in bed with Lucien.

I still hadn't come to terms with the way my body looked yet. It was on my schedule, I'd booked an appointment with my therapist.

But I kept putting it off.

"It's lovely," I said.

He lifted the smaller box and snapped the lid open. I gasped at the large, teardrop sapphire necklace inside.

"Lucien, how much was that?"

He took it out, the jewel glittering in his fingers.

"Priceless. Like you."

I sat still for him as he brushed aside my hair, kissed the nape of my neck, and draped the necklace around it. My spine tingled and my stomach flipped as the sapphire slid down between my breasts under my sweater.

He dragged his mouth up my neck to my ear, biting my earlobe and tugging gently with his teeth. I moaned and pushed my ass back against his groin, grinding a little against the hard ridge there.

"Put your pretty things on for me," he whispered.

I swallowed. "Lucien, I don't know."

He knew what I was trying to say. After the things my mother had said and done to me, I would never be able to think about my body normally. But at least I knew that now. At least I was able to identify the thoughts in my head as disordered.

Before, it had all blended together in a confusing mess of self-loathing and starvation and despair.

Lucien had been there through it all. He'd found me a good therapist, he'd watched me subtly every night to make sure I ate something. He'd held me while I cried the first time I looked at myself in the mirror after Marco's birth. And he'd watched me like a hawk as I slid back into the endless, bitter cycle of restriction in the weeks afterwards.

He'd picked me up off the floor and loved me enough to make me walk back into my therapist's office and slog through the entire recovery program for the second time.

He'd learned all the things to say and the things not to say. The red flags, the lies I told him. And he'd finally accepted that this was something I would always have to work on.

And now, years later, I was doing better than I ever had in my life.

"This is a small challenge," he said softly. "Let's do it together, baby."

He rose and gathered the lingerie in his hand, guiding me to the mirror. I held still, forcing the voice in my head that sounded just like my mother to be quiet.

This room had space only for Lucien and I.

He knelt before me and unfastened my jeans and worked them from my legs. Then he slipped my sweater from my body, leaving me in my cotton bra and panties.

"My God," he breathed.

CHAPTER TWO

LUCIEN

I'd missed her so much it was all I could do not to throw her down and fuck her until she was begging me to stop. But when I lifted my eyes to hers, there was so much vulnerability in them. She needed my gentle side right now and I could give her that. I could touch her until her layers peeled back and I found the perfect little slut she hid underneath.

The woman she showed to me alone.

I peeled her panties aside and the sweet, champagne scent of her pussy hit my senses as I bent to run my tongue over her clit. Her little gasp went right down my spine to my cock and it pressed painfully against my zipper. I pulled back and slid both my palms up her thighs and under her panties, tugging them down around her ankles.

Fuck me, those delicate, little ankles. She shifted her weight and lifted her foot so I could pull her panties free of her legs. She'd gone to the salon earlier, I could tell, because her toenails were done with white half moons that drove me crazy.

Supporting her with one hand, I lifted her foot and kissed under the arch. Her toes clenched and a shudder moved through her.

"Fuck, I've missed you so much, baby," I breathed.

"Do you want me to take care of you?"

Her dark eyes were wide, looking down at me. Her mouth was parted and her tongue was caught between her teeth.

"No, I want you to wear this lingerie for me."

She bit her lip as I rose and unhooked her bra. Her breasts were heavy and full, easily a cup bigger than they were when we'd met. Her nipples had changed and each breast was lined with delicate, white stretch marks.

There was a line of the same marks across her lower belly and I bent and kissed down to them. Running the tip of my tongue over each one.

She shuddered and I looked up at her standing over me. My God, she was devastating, more lovely than anything I'd ever laid my eyes on. Sometimes I wished I was a more eloquent man so I could truly express my feelings when I saw her naked like this.

But the words simply weren't there. I'd never had the chance to learn to process the things I felt into words.

That was a luxury afforded to other men.

Her eyes followed my hands as I lifted the lace panties and slid them up her thighs, settling them on her soft hips. I took up the bra and stood, turning her to face the mirror.

She studied her body and bit her lip, clearly disappointed.

"Careful what you say about her," I murmured into her neck.

She frowned. "Who?"

I slipped the bra around her and hooked it in the back. There was the prettiest bit of spillage over the top. She gave a little gasp when I cupped her left breast and stroked her cleavage with my thumb. Our eyes met in the mirror.

"Careful what you say about her. That's my wife."

She swallowed and her eyes dropped to the floor. I stroked down her hips and knelt behind her, biting her soft ass hard enough to make her yelp. She whirled, staring at me incredulously.

"You're a bit frisky," she scolded.

"Yes, I am," I said. "I have the most beautiful woman in the world in this room for the next four days."

I rose and bent to kiss her, but I could tell she was still upset. When I drew back, she wouldn't meet my eyes. Sighing internally, I took her chin and tilted it up.

She chewed her bottom lip and I gave her the time to sort through what she was feeling instead of forcing her to speak. Her feathery bangs hung in her eyes and I brushed them back, playing with the longer tendrils around her ear.

Her hair was so soft. Every bit of her was. When I came home to her at night and slid into bed beside her body, it always amazed me how soft she was. Every part of her was a silky bit of paradise that made her gasp and writhe when I played with it. And she smelled so fucking good, even when she was sweaty from the gym.

Especially then.

I was so obsessed with this woman it was hard to keep it concealed sometimes. The taste of her pussy and her mouth, the touch of her hands, the sounds she made when she shuddered with an orgasm.

And her fucking slender, little feet. My God, just looking at them made me want to throw her down and fuck her on the bed until we owed the hotel for a new one. Her manicured toenails, the anklebone beneath her delicate skin and blue veins, the arch that slid up into her heel.

"Lucien?" she asked.

I shook my head. "Yes."

"You just glazed over for a second," she said. "I was just saying that I'm okay."

I looked into the depths of her dark eyes and I wished I could break into her mind and put it to rights. But I'd learned a long time ago that I couldn't fight her demons for her as much as I wanted to. I could kill anyone who dared touch her physical body, but I couldn't save her from herself.

This time it was her turn to glaze over. I gently took her face in my hand.

"Come back, baby," I said. "I'd like to sleep with my wife."

I knew what she needed when my words didn't work. The little gasp that burst from her mouth ghosted over my neck as I lifted her and carried her to the bed, spilling her onto her back. I ran my palm up her smooth thighs to her hips and climbed atop her, slipping off my shoes.

"Can you be good for me tonight?" I whispered, kissing up her throat.

She nodded, the pain fading from her eyes.

I slipped my hand between her legs and traced over the lace of her panties. I could feel the heat of her cunt burning through to my skin. She shuddered as I stroked over the lace and the hot flesh beneath and her fingers came up and gripped my wrist.

"I want your fingers in me," she breathed.

I shook my head. "I'll touch you the way I want."

"Lucien, please."

I cocked my head. "I love it when you beg, but no."

She writhed with frustration and I slapped her thigh gently to remind her who she answered to and she fell quiet. Her fingers came up and gripped the railings in the headboard. Her knuckles were white and her breasts heaved.

"Would you like me to kiss your pretty cunt?" I asked.

"Yes, please," she moaned.

"You can beg for me better than that. Try again, baby."

She bit her lip and I saw her struggle not to scowl at me. She knew I'd make her pay if she didn't behave herself. I could tell she was weighing the ramifications of sassing me and deciding how sore she wanted her pussy to be tomorrow morning.

"Beg," I ordered.

"Lucien, please touch me," she whispered, her hips grinding against nothing. "I'm so wet and you haven't been home in so long."

I pressed my lips together. "You're disappointing me, baby."

Her eyes widened and it wasn't a game for her anymore. I saw her pride fall away and she was fully vulnerable, the way I liked her when we fucked.

Now it was personal. She'd felt my ice between her teeth and she didn't like it.

"Please, please," she breathed. "I'll do anything, Lucien, just lick my pussy. Please."

I observed her coolly. "Are you begging me or not?"

"I'm begging you." Her voice was fragile.

"That's my girl," I said softly, and slid my hand between her thighs.

She moaned and her head fell back, her eyes closed. Her lashes were soft and dark against her skin and her dusky mouth was parted. Transfixed, I slid my fingers beneath the edge of her panties and tugged them down her thighs.

The sight of her lovely pussy made my chest tighten and my cock throb painfully against my pants. I pushed her up on the pillows and settled in the only place where my mind was at peace—between my wife's thighs.

"Open all the way for me, baby," I murmured.

She obeyed hesitantly. Even after all this time, she still sometimes got shy when she spread herself for me. Perhaps it was all the years she'd been shamed for her body, perhaps because she'd grown up being told sex was the worst thing she could do. Whatever it was, she didn't need to worry. Every time those thighs fell apart, it was like the first time all over again.

She was a little wet around her pussy and her skin was bare from laser. I bent and ran my nose up her soft flesh, inhaling the sweet, musky scent of her pussy. Like tangy champagne. Fuck, I was so goddamn hard. If I didn't get inside this woman soon, I was going to come in my pants.

I bent my head and licked once over her sex, from top to bottom. Her hips stiffened and she moaned. Her fingers wove through my hair, her fist clenching. I warmed her slowly, taking my time with the soft curves of her pussy, and she panted and moaned with every touch. When she was swollen and her entrance glistened with arousal, I moved up to her clit.

Bending, I kissed it gently. "Is that what you wanted, baby?"

She released a shuddering breath. "Yes, but more."

"More?"

"Suck it, please," she begged.

I complied, taking her delicate bud in my mouth and applying light pressure. When we'd first started fucking, she liked being stroked with my fingers until she came. But time and the hormones in her body changing had made her more sensitive and now she preferred my mouth.

Perhaps it was just because we knew each other's bodies so well, but she came so fucking easy now. And some nights, if I really pushed her hard, she could orgasm one after the other until she went limp in my hands.

She gasped as I pulled her clit fully into my mouth and began sucking and licking in tandem. My two fingers slid into her easily and her slick, inner muscles gripped them hard. She was tensed, hot and coiled up around my fingers, and I knew it wouldn't take long. I found her G-spot and flicked it gently as I sucked and licked her clit. Driving her closer and closer to release.

Her stomach tensed and her fingers fisted in the sheets. A shudder moved down her body and she began panting, whining softly in her throat. Her stomach was tight, like a spring coiled for release. Then that sweet gasping cry burst from her mouth and her body shook hard. Arousal shot straight to my cock and I ground my hips against the bed, desperate for release.

Fuck me, I needed to get inside her now.

I pulled my mouth from her and stripped my clothes. Her eyes were wide, dark pools and her mouth was swollen from how she'd bitten it when she came.

Kneeling over her, I pulled her down beneath me and lifted her thigh, wrapping her leg around my waist. For a second, our eyes locked, and then I thrust to the hilt. Fuck me, my wife was hot and tight and so impossibly wet as she clamped down around my cock. Drawing me deep with rhythmic pulses.

This was home. This was the only place I found rest.

"Oh my God, you feel so good," she breathed.

I already knew I wasn't going to last. But it didn't matter because this was just the first of many rounds tonight. Bracing my knee against the bed and holding her leg open, I began pounding into her sweet cunt. And she just clung to me and took it like such a good girl as she whimpered into my chest.

Still fucking her hard, I bent to kiss her mouth. Letting my saliva drip down onto her tongue, edged with the taste of her pussy.

She moaned and her perfect breasts bounced with every thrust. Spellbound, I groaned softly, losing myself in the sensations of her body. Not bothering to hold back the heat moving down my spine and building in my hips, I slammed into her, my head back and eyes shut.

"Come inside me," she whispered.

My lids snapped open. She was panting and her eyes were glazed with desire. In that moment, I remembered we'd agreed that I would try to get her pregnant again. The realization hit me with a wave of arousal that had me right on the edge, leaking inside her.

"Is this what you want?" I asked. "Do you want me to fuck your little cunt until you're pregnant?"

She moaned, nodding hard.

"I'll breed this pussy for you, baby," I panted. "Just beg me for it like a good whore."

Her eyes locked with mine and her hand curled on my bicep. "I want your cum inside me," she breathed. "Please."

I'd intended on making her beg longer, but it was too late. I buried myself inside her, pushing in until I bottomed out, and emptied every drop of cum I had in my body into her pussy.

She moaned with satisfaction and her head fell back as I wrung myself dry with short, quick thrusts. It took a minute to come back down to earth and realize my ears were ringing as I released the breath caught in my lungs.

CHAPTER THREE

OLIVIA

I lay beneath him for a half second, my legs locked around his waist, keeping him deep inside. Our breaths slowed. He stirred and pulled back, brushing my bangs back from my face.

He kissed me softly, his tongue grazing mine. When he drew back, there was nothing in his eyes, but after six years together, I didn't expect warmth or vulnerability.

Even in our most intimate moments, he was still a firmly closed door.

He pulled from my body, still hard, and rolled onto his back and sat up. His clothes were on the floor and I watched as he put on his boxer briefs and took a pack of cigarettes from his pocket. He didn't smoke very often, but he did enjoy it after sex. I never said anything about it because I knew how hard he'd worked to cut back.

He crossed the room and pushed open the window, letting in a rush of cool air. Slick from him and thoroughly satisfied, I slid beneath the plush comforter and rolled onto my side to watch him. He leaned on the windowsill and flicked the lighter, inhaling deeply. His lids flickered and the tension in his shoulders eased.

There was a softness to his mouth, a sensual curve, and it was the only oasis of emotion in his face. I studied it as he put the cigarette to his lips and let the smoke waft from between them.

"What do you want?"

"What?" I sat upright, pulling the covers around my shoulders.

"Boy or girl?"

"Oh…I don't know," I said slowly. "I guess either is fine. What do you want?"

"Boy," he said.

"You already have a boy."

He shook his head reflectively. "I don't think I'd be a very good father for a girl. Even Cosimo admitted he doesn't know what the fuck to do when it comes to raising his daughter. And he's a lot less of a cunt than me."

"He's doing a good job," she said. "But you would too."

He put the cigarette back to his lips. I studied him in silence, my gaze following the curve of his body. He'd gotten more tattoos over the last few years and both his arms had been made into full sleeves. The skeleton wings on his chest were updated with larger roses and dark thorns. The skull above his penis had gotten an upgrade and was now three times larger and wrapped in a snake.

Sometimes it would throw me off to look up when he had his cock buried in my throat and see a skull with gaping, dark eyes inches from my face. But the way he held my head when I gave him a blowjob was so gentle it made everything worth it.

I lived and died by the rare moments of gentleness in him.

He finished his cigarette and stabbed it out, pushing down the window. "I'll run a bath for you."

I nodded and he disappeared into the bathroom. In a few moments I heard the water turn on and I climbed out of bed and padded into the bathroom. I still wore the lace bra and this time when I slipped it off, my body looked perfectly fine.

That was how this worked. Sometimes when I saw myself, I liked my body, but sometimes all it took was a glance and I wanted to cry.

Thank God for a brief respite from my thoughts. Thank God he was back.

I watched as Lucien bent over the sink and splashed his face with cold water. The muscles in his biceps rippled beneath the tattoos and I remembered the first time he'd let me explore his body. How I'd run my touch over the ink on his skin and felt the scars beneath it. The ones he hid from the world, the ones I felt in the darkness when I ran my fingers over his body as he took me between the sheets.

The scars he never discussed.

I slid into the hot water and let it cover my head. Enveloping me in a single moment of soundless peace. Then I burst, gasping from the water to find Lucien watching me from the edge of the tub.

"Was I too rough?" he asked.

I shook my head.

"Good."

"Why? Did you think you were?"

He considered the question carefully. "Every time I fuck you, I think I should be gentler. Then my dick gets hard again and I can't think straight."

I leaned on the edge of the tub and he bent, kissing my wet forehead.

"I love the way you fuck me, Lucien," I said.

He made a low noise of satisfaction in his throat and stood, going to the door and leaning against the frame.

"How is the foundation?"

"It's good," I said. "After this weekend, I have a lot of work to get done. There's a big fundraiser at the Grand Imperium Hotel and I have to be there. A lot of our big donors are going."

"I'm proud of you," he said.

I was quiet, my throat tightening. It meant a lot that Lucien was proud of me. He was hard on everyone, although no one more than himself, and he expected complete loyalty and perfect work. He never complimented me unless he meant it so I knew he was telling the truth, that he really was proud of the work my foundation did.

"Are you hungry?" he asked.

I shook my head and he narrowed his gaze.

"Okay," I relented. "I'd have a small snack."

"I'm ordering room service. I know I ate earlier, but I worked up an appetite trying to satisfy my wife," he said.

"I'll have a soup and sandwich if they have it," I said. "And maybe ask for a bottle of champagne."

He took care of ordering the food and champagne and then he showered while I finished up in the bath. By the time the food arrived, we were curled up in the bed, Lucien in his boxer briefs and me in my silk slip.

I turned on the news and rested against his side, watching him eat his steak and potatoes while I sipped on my soup. The elections in the city always caused a stir at least a year before they happened. I'd always found it boring until I started the foundation and now I watched the city politics carefully.

There were two news anchors having a discussion about possible contenders for the city commissioner seat. I turned up the sound and poured two glasses of champagne.

"...with Bennett Emerson-Green so popular in his current position, I think he's a natural pick," the woman said.

Lucien shook his head. "Emerson-Green won't leave his seat."

"Why?' I asked curiously.

"He's too invested in the second ward."

I nodded, turning back to the TV. Lucien opened a paper box on the corner of the tray and revealed a slice of cheesecake. He handed me a fork and put the box in front of me.

"Eat that, baby."

"Lucien—"

His flat gaze bored into me. "Eat it or I'll eat your ass."

I blushed. That wasn't exactly a threat to me, but I realized I would get nowhere with him when he was belligerent like this, so I took a bite. It was amazing and I forced my attention back to the TV so I could eat the rest without overthinking.

"You know who I think is a good fit?" the male anchor said. "Lucien Esposito."

I tensed and Lucien's eyes flicked to the screen.

"Really?"

"Think about it. He's got the whole package. Money, connections, a stunning wife who everyone loves. Maybe more than him. He'd be a natural."

"What about his connections to…more unsavory organizations?"

"In this city, he'd probably be fine."

The female anchor shrugged, still on the fence. "I mean...he is pretty."

They both started laughing and I clicked the remote, uncomfortable with my family being discussed on live TV. Lucien reached across and took my champagne, emptying it.

"Are you jealous because she said I was pretty?"

"No. I just don't want to hear other people talk about us," I said, getting up to refill both our glasses. "You're not interested in the commissioner seat, are you?"

He shook his head. "I don't see the point in it."

He moved the tray aside and I crawled onto the bed, a glass in each hand, and straddled his lap. It felt so good, so right, to be here with him. He took a sip of his champagne and bent forward, kissing my mouth. Coaxing my lips apart so he could taste my tongue briefly before pulling back.

"What will you do next then?" I asked.

He shrugged. "Work hard, make money. Get my wife pregnant. Take care of my son. Rinse and repeat."

I brushed my thumb over his jaw, relishing in the scratchy feel of his skin. He always had a bit of stubble by the end of the day and I liked the way it felt, especially on the inside of my thighs. His stare bored into me. The hazel ice in his eyes remained firmly in place, although the curve of his mouth was soft.

"Are you bored?" I asked.

"No," he said quickly.

"Lucien."

"Olivia."

I huffed and he'd bent to kiss between my breasts.

"You could never bore me," he said.

"I didn't ask if I bored you, I just asked if you were bored."

He shrugged and shook his head and I knew it wasn't any use trying to get an honest answer. Maybe I didn't need one. Lucien had a quick mind that worked best when faced with an impossible challenge. I knew all that restless, power-hungry energy would need somewhere to release before too long.

He lifted his glass and clinked it gently against mine.

"What are we toasting to?" I asked.

"I'm toasting myself," he said. "To having the sexiest woman in the world half naked in my lap. Little does she know, she's going to get a little tipsy with me and we'll do some fucking filthy things to each other in this bed tonight."

CHAPTER FOUR

LUCIEN

I usually slept like the dead when I was with my wife, especially after two hours of vigorously fucking each other, but tonight I lay awake. Olivia was curled up beneath the white comforter, three more blankets draped over her body. She couldn't sleep unless she'd built a pillow fort around herself and piled it with blankets. When I put my hand on her leg, she was approximately the temperature of the inside of a furnace.

It was almost two when my phone lit up and I rolled over, swiping the screen. There was a text from Peregrine, my diplomat.

Interesting segment about you running for commissioner on the news tonight. Any truth to it?

My temple throbbed and I got up and went to the bathroom to take some Tylenol. Olivia always preemptively took it when she drank, so the bottle was open on the sink. I swallowed two white pills and drained the rest of the water from my glass. As I set it aside, I caught my reflection's eye.

I'd never been sure how to feel about the way I looked. Objectively, I knew I was attractive. But that wasn't what I saw when I looked in the mirror. Instead, I saw a body that used tattoos like bandages to cover up things I never wanted to think about again. A body that had been through too much.

But lately, I saw something else.

A husband, a father, a brother, a friend. Someone who was loved, despite years of isolation and violence.

It was all thanks to the woman who slept in the other room. Olivia was the first person to look right at my ugliness, my penchant for violence, and my restless need to conquer, and accept it.

There was a time before her when everything felt dull, when I put my dick into women I didn't know or like and fell asleep drunk early in the morning. When I woke up and hated the prospect of having to push through the day.

When the only thing that motivated me was hatred and revenge.

Things were different now. They were so fucking good I had to shake myself just in case I was dreaming. Now I had Olivia and the world felt like it moved a hundred miles a minute in high definition. It was all I could do to stop and try to soak her in, to notice the things that made me so obsessed with her, to give her everything she wanted just to see her smile.

There was evidence of her everywhere even though we'd only been here a night. Dark hairs on the sink, skimpy lace panties on the floor, a cotton bra hanging on the doorknob, makeup piled in a pink bag, bottles lined up along the tub. I felt a rare smile jerk the corner of my mouth as I took it all in.

I didn't care that she made messes, even though I was meticulously clean. I loved that everywhere she went, she left her mark. I was entranced by the scent of her on my pillows, the sound of her footsteps on the floor, the way her voice went husky when she woke up in the morning.

I was fucking obsessed and falling harder every day.

Swiping my phone, I called Peregrine. He would be up until at least three due to chronic insomnia and a teething toddler. He answered instantly.

"You still up?"

"Obviously."

"Me too," he said wearily. "Cecilia threw up before bed so I'm sleeping in the guestroom with her so Lia can rest."

"That's how it goes," I said distractedly. "Listen, can you just ask around about the city commissioner issue and figure out why my name was brought up?"

"I can tell you why right now," Peregrine said.

"Olivia?"

"Olivia."

"If you don't want to get dragged into the tabloids, Lucien, don't let your young, hot wife start a charitable foundation and parade it around high society. It's as simple as that."

I sighed, keeping my voice down. "Well, please keep an ear out and let me know if I'm brought up in any city related meetings. I don't fucking like being the topic of discussion on television for any reason. It pisses me off."

"Stop making waves then," Peregrine said. "Or at least, stop your wife from making them."

I hesitated, glancing up at myself. "Do they talk about Olivia in those meetings?"

"Sometimes?"

"What do they say?"

Peregrine hesitated and when he spoke there was a note of reluctance in his tone. "You married an attractive, much younger woman who likes to dress herself for the part. What do you think they're going to say about her?"

The ugliest part of me reared its head when I got jealous over my wife. It had taken me a long time to temper it back and it was made all the harder by the way Olivia chose to dress. I rarely said anything about it because it was her body, but I saw how men looked at her. I watched them like a hawk as they turned when she walked by, raking their gazes over her body in those tight, little dresses.

Fuck.

I met my own gaze in the mirror and there was a glitter there that reminded me I needed to keep a handle on my jealousy.

"Is that all they say?" I asked. "Just that they want to fuck her?"

"They don't all say that, the younger men are a little more respectful," Peregrine said. "But the general consensus is that she's hard to miss. She's likable, she's got kind of an old fashioned charm and sweetness that people are drawn to, but then she's also got spunk when she's pushed."

I knew what he was talking about and I also knew that was Olivia's anxiety manifesting as a quiet shyness. Of course I would never reveal that to anyone—her secrets were mine to keep. The spunk, however, was pure Olivia, the person she could have been if she hadn't been so beaten down by life.

"Keep me updated on this," I said. "I don't like that she's a topic of conversation."

"It was bound to happen," he said. "But I understand why you're feeling that way."

"I'm not jealous," I said coolly.

"Of course not."

I hung up the phone and set it aside, turning off the light. When I returned to bed, Olivia was still fast asleep in her nest of blankets. I rolled onto my side and reached out to brush her bangs from her forehead. She shifted and let out a little moan and rolled onto her back. The blanket slid, revealing the top of her breast.

She'd given me permission to fuck her while she slept, but I rarely did. It wasn't really my thing. I preferred having her awake so I could watch her moan and writhe under me. So I could feel her legs wrap around me and her lovely, little ankles cross against my lower back, keeping me deep inside her.

Instead, I ignored my jealous erection and worked my way under her pile of blankets so I could pull her into my chest. There was an ugly part of me that wished I could keep her locked up, away from men that looked at her and people who might harm her.

But I knew I could never do that to her, she'd been beaten down so much already.

No, Olivia was too bright, too beautiful, too full of potential to be hidden. She was a diamond and she deserved to be seen, to be admired by the world.

CHAPTER FIVE

OLIVIA

When I opened my eyes, he was already awake and dressed in one of his charcoal gray suits. The sunlight glinted through the windows, catching the little flecks of gray around his ears. I stretched luxuriously in the plush, hotel bed. My entire body felt limp and completely relaxed, snuggled beneath the covers. I eyed him as he ran a hand over his dark hair, slicking it back. Maybe I could entice him back into bed for a quickie before breakfast.

I tossed back the covers and moved past him, pausing long enough to run my palm over his groin and cup him through his pants. His hips jerked and I thought I saw the ghost of a smile pass over his mouth as he gave me a little tap on the ass.

"Behave yourself, Olivia," he said sternly. "Breakfast first."

I loved any attention from him, but nothing was better than when he was a little playful. It was a rare occurrence to get a shred of warmth from my cold husband and I basked in it like the clouds had parted and let the sun through. He trailed his hand up my back and gently gripped the nape of my neck, turning my face up so he could kiss my mouth.

"Be a good girl and put something pretty on," he said. "Preferably with easy access."

"Lucien!"

His mouth twitched and he turned away to retrieve his watch from the dresser. I showered quickly, did my makeup, and slipped on a simple sweater dress and heels. When I returned from the bathroom, Lucien's eyes skimmed over me with a faint hint of approval.

"Are you ready?"

I nodded. He opened the door and ushered me through with a light hand to my lower back. In the hall, I waited as he locked the door and pushed the key into his pocket. Then he took my hand and led me downstairs.

In the dining room, the curtains were up and pale sunshine shone through the glass. A thick, glittering frost lay over the grass. I gave a little shiver as we took our seats at a table by the cool window. Lucien's eyes locked on me, never missing a thing.

"Shall I get you a coat from the room?"

I shook my head. "I'm alright."

He rose, taking off his jacket, and placed it over my shoulders. The warm, clean scent of him filled my senses and my legs went weak.

There was a flicker of something in his eyes as he sat down again. He could tell I was aroused again and he liked it.

We had hot coffee and fresh, buttered scones, sausage, eggs, and nut bread. Normally Lucien would have eaten an egg white omelette, but he knew I was feeling fragile around my food. So we didn't watch what we ate, we just enjoyed it, grateful for the time we had together.

In the middle of our meal, the manager walked up to us and extended his hand to Lucien. He was a tall, willowy man that I thought perhaps I'd seen at a party before, but I wasn't sure. Lucien recognized him instantly and rose to his feet to shake his hand.

"Mr. James Emerson-Green," he said. "Thank you for your hospitality."

"It's my pleasure, I hope everything has been perfect," the man said, smiling pleasantly. "Thank you for choosing to stay with us, Mrs. Esposito. We're thrilled to have you."

"You have such a beautiful hotel, sir," I said.

Mr. Emerson-Green waved a hand. "We do our best. Is there anything else I can get for you, ma'am? More coffee?"

I shook my head. "Breakfast was perfect, we're very happy with everything."

He inclined his head and Lucien bent forward, speaking quietly. I didn't hear what he said, but the man's brows rose and he nodded.

"Would you excuse us for a moment?" Lucien said. "I just had a quick question for Mr. Emerson-Green."

Deep down, I was annoyed. This always happened, even when Lucien promised he wouldn't work. It was the reason I'd tried to book a hotel so far on the other end of town in hopes we wouldn't run into anyone who knew him.

But I wasn't about to make a scene. After a few incidents at the beginning of our marriage, Lucien and I had made a promise to keep certain things private.

Fighting and fucking were to be done strictly behind closed doors.

"Of course, it's no problem," I said, smiling.

Lucien and Mr. Emerson-Green disappeared into the kitchens. I sighed, slumping back in my seat, and gazed out the window. Cars moved by on the road beyond the treeline. There was a woman in a fur coat with a small dog that kept trying to bite passersby. I watched it with fleeting interest.

"Olivia."

I whirled as a tall figure sank into Lucien's seat. My whole body seized and my heart began hammering so fast I couldn't breathe. It had been six years of freedom, six years of trying to recover, six years of trying to put my broken pieces together. But it was all gone in an instant as I looked into my father's eyes.

"What...what are you doing here?" I whispered.

His dark eyes pierced into me and suddenly I was a teenager again. Dry-mouthed and full of the worst kind of panicky fear. Waiting with a pit in my stomach as he decided if he was going to scream, hit me, or drag me to my room by the hair.

My stomach roiled and I fought the urge to lean over and empty it all over the table.

"We stay here often," my father said. "The better question is, what are you and your fucking traitorous husband doing here?"

"I...um...please don't," I stuttered. "You need to go."

My ears rang. How did he look even more evil than I remembered? The eyes boring into me reminded me of a hawk, waiting and watching until I caved. Relishing my fear. Anticipating the spoils of my breakdown.

"Your husband ruined me," he said. "And I saw you over here and thought I should give you a warning. I've gotten back all that money we lost when he fired me and I'm coming back to the city. So your husband had better watch his fucking back."

I gaped at him, shivering.

"I'm taking everything from him," he said softly. "And you won't say a word because if you do, I'll come after your son."

Rage moved through me like wildfire and I gripped the side of the table. Leaning in.

"You don't have any power over my family," I said, my voice shaking.

"I am running for mayor this coming election," he said coolly. "I have the full support of the incumbent mayor and some powerful city officials. Do you know what platform I'll run on? Cleaning the mafia out of this city. Turns out, I have a lot of insider information."

My mouth was dry and my stomach was a painful pit. Was he telling the truth? Was Lucien's position really in danger? And if it was, did that mean Marco wasn't safe? We sat there, staring at each other and a slow, cold smile broke over his face. I shook my head, unable to find words.

He'd thoroughly shaken me—his mission was accomplished. My father tapped the table once and stood, but before he could move, something slammed into him. Shoving him face-first into the table and jerking his arms back to crush him down onto the tabletop.

Plates fell to the ground, shattering. Cold coffee soaked the front of my dress and dripped down my face. I sputtered, wiping it away to see Lucien had my father bent over the table, his hands locked behind his back. My father was panting, his eyes burning dark with rage.

Lucien was beyond angry. The lines of his face were hard and deadly, any rare bit of softness replaced by a man I barely knew. A man who terrified me. I shrank back against my chair, heart pounding in my throat.

"What the fuck are you doing here?" Lucien hissed. "You don't talk to my wife, you fucking cunt. You don't so much as look at her."

My husband was angry and the sight shook me more than seeing my father. Lucien had an iron grip on his emotions and I hadn't seen him like this since he'd killed Romano. My head roared and my hands shook as I pushed back my chair and stood, soaked from head to toe.

I stared across the table at my husband and my whole body went cold.

It was in moments like these that I wondered if I had married the hero or the villain. Lucien could be so gentle with me and so caring with Marco. But then I saw him like this, with his jaw locked and his eyes nothing but cruel ice, and it scared me.

It reminded me that he was capable of terrible things.

I pivoted, every eye on me, and fled out of the dining room. My eyes burned and tears slid through my lashes. In the lobby, the woman behind the front desk stepped forward like she wanted to help, but I shook my head and kept walking as fast as I could. When the elevator slid shut, I slumped against the wall and released a shuddering breath.

The weekend had started out so well and now it was ruined. I couldn't get the image of Lucien holding my father down, his dead eyes like miles of frozen wasteland. Why couldn't we just have a nice breakfast without violence?

Why couldn't we have anything without violence?

I already knew the answer to that. I'd married a man who made his money with the blood on his hands.

Defeated, I wrapped my arms around myself as the door opened and ran down the hall to our room. My hands dug through my purse, but came up with nothing.

Fuck, Lucien had the key.

I slumped back against the wall and slid to the floor. My throat was tight with tears. I was supposed to be over this, I was supposed to be brave now. But looking into my father's vicious eyes had thrown me right back to the beginning.

Back to when I was terrified and helpless.

I heard my husband's footsteps and I lifted my head. He strode down the hall with his eyes empty, his face blank, and his jaw set. I kept my gaze lowered, following his shoes until they paused just before me.

"I'm taking you home."

I shook my head. "I'm not leaving."

"Olivia, do not question me."

I jumped to my feet, bunching my fists, ready to argue. Before I could speak, Lucien's arm shot out and circled my waist. Drawing me against his lean body. His gaze was endlessly cold and it chilled me to my core.

"I am your husband," he said flatly. "If I have to drag you kicking and screaming home, I will. I will keep you safe."

I had learned I could push Lucien and he would bend for me, but to a certain point. And right now, he had reached that point.

Miserably, I helped him pack our things and he carried the suitcases down to the car. I waited, holding his hand and staring down at the ground, while he insisted on overpaying for breakfast and the room to make up for the mess. When we finally drove away from the hotel, I was ready to be home.

CHAPTER SIX

LUCIEN

Back at the house, I broke my promise not to work this weekend and went directly to my office as soon as we got inside. Olivia stomped upstairs, refusing to look at me, and slammed the bedroom door. Part of me wanted to go after her, but the other part of me knew I needed to find out why her father was resurfacing after all this time.

I shut my office door and called Cosimo, my right hand and my wife's brother. He picked up immediately.

"I thought you were on vacation," he said.

"I was," I said, pacing back and forth. "But I was just at breakfast with Olivia and your father was there."

There was a short pause.

"Really? I haven't seen him in three years."

There was an edge to Cosimo's voice. He and his wife, Lorenza, had attempted briefly to work things through with Rosario Barone, but after a few years, they gave up and cut ties. There was too much bad blood, too many years of abuse, to fix.

"He said something to Olivia," I said.

"What did he say to her?"

"I don't know, she's crying upstairs," I said. "I brought her home right away because I have a fucking bad feeling about this."

I heard a door slam in the background and Cosimo's footsteps clattered. Another door shut and I knew he was in his office. Papers rustled and his laptop pinged.

"Alright, let me get on this," he said. "Do you want this done discreetly or can I bring in anyone else?"

I thought it over and decided I could trust my diplomat, Peregrine Calo. He knew everyone worth knowing in the city and no politician so much as sneezed without him hearing about it.

"Peregrine," I said. "Get him asking around. I want to make sure this isn't something more than a chance encounter."

"Understood," Cosimo said. "I'll circle back tomorrow."

"Thank you."

"Oh, and Lucien," Cosimo said, his voice tightening. "My father is a giant, evil cunt so if Olivia is a little....tender today, do me a favor and give her some space."

"Noted," I said coolly, hanging up the phone.

I moved through the enormous, empty house and tested our bedroom door to see if she'd locked it. It swung open and I slipped inside, looking around. The bathroom light was on and the door was ajar. Water ran in the tub and there was a faint scent of cherry blossoms in the air. I followed it into the bathroom to find her slumped in the tub with bubbles around her hunched form.

I turned the water off and she looked up, the bubbles coming up to her chin. My God, she was such a pretty thing it was hard not to get aroused, even in moments like this. I lifted her chin between my finger and thumb. Her dark eyes fixed on me, a little swollen.

"I'm sorry," I said.

Her lip trembled. "You scare me sometimes."

"I thought you were upset by seeing your father."

"I was. But I was more scared by seeing you like that." She swallowed. "You can be so violent sometimes."

"I know, baby."

There was a long silence and I hoped she wasn't expecting me to apologize for what I'd done. Because she would be waiting a long time.

I reserved the right to be who I was, to protect my wife without reservation. I leaned forward, kissed her forehead, and went to the bar area in the far corner of our room. I poured her a glass of her favorite red wine and brought it to her in the bath.

"It's a little early to start drinking," she said.

"I know," I said. "But you don't have anywhere to be. I'm handling the issue with your father. All you need to do is relax."

Her lids flickered and she brought the wine to her lips. Taking a slow sip.

"What are you going to do?"

I crouched by the edge of the tub, turning her so I could wash her hair. She practically purred as I massaged her scalp and shoulders with thick, cherry blossom scented lather.

"You didn't answer me," she said softly.

"I don't know yet," I said. "I need time to look into it and make a decision."

"Can...can you include me on that decision?"

I considered it for a moment as I rinsed her hair. My work was brutal sometimes and it required the ability to turn a blind eye to my own cruelty. She'd accepted what I did and who I was, so long as I kept the ugliness at work, and I agreed that was best. But this was a different situation because it involved her father and her private trauma.

"I'll think on it," I said.

She turned around, resting her arms on the edge of the tub. "That's almost a yes, at least when it comes from you."

"I'm glad you're grateful for it," I said dryly.

She pushed out her lower lip and I took her chin in my hand and bent to kiss her. When I pulled away, she turned to cover her mouth and yawn.

"Am I boring you?"

"I think I need coffee," she said. "Or maybe just more wine. I'm fine with drinking the rest of the day with you. It sounds nice."

"Dry off and we'll go down to the kitchen and get you some more wine," I said.

She complied and pulled on a pair of satin pajamas that barely covered her ass with straps that kept sliding off her shoulders. My groin stirred as I walked behind her down the enormous, dark hallway.

It blew my mind that she hated the softness in her hips and thighs, even though I knew that her problem didn't connect to reality. It had taken me a while to understand that just telling her I loved her body made her smile, but it didn't fix the fact that she had trauma from years of abuse.

I wished she could see what I saw. I wished she could see the sway of her ass, the way it jiggled when I slapped it. I wished she knew how good it felt when she wrapped those thighs around me in bed, enveloping me in the warmth I craved. I wished she knew how I loved how heavy and soft her breasts were now, how they felt so fucking good in my mouth.

But, like everything else, it wasn't that simple.

In the kitchen, I lifted her onto the counter. "Would you like a sandwich?"

She nodded. "Can you make a sandwich?"

I raised an eyebrow and went to take the ingredients from the fridge. "Yes, baby, I can make a sandwich. Just because I don't cook doesn't mean I'm totally helpless."

She laughed. "I don't care that you can't cook."

"It's not like you have to make food if you don't want to."

"That's true."

I made her a turkey and cheese sandwich and toasted it lightly to melt it. She watched, her brows lifted, and I could tell she was impressed. I might not be able to cook actual meals, but I'd been a teenager before and I knew how to make an excellent sandwich.

I brought it to her and she locked eyes with me as she bit into it. Fuck, seeing her eat and enjoy it made my dick twitch.

"It's good," she said through her mouthful. "Really good."

I watched her for a long time, tracing her thigh with my fingertips. I rarely got time off work and it felt so fucking good to be here in our kitchen together. With nothing to do but each other.

I kissed the side of her neck. "Want to get a little drunk?"

She swallowed, setting aside the crust. The heels of her hands braced against the counter and she leaned back. I felt her ankle brush my thigh and her foot trailed up to my waist. My lower stomach clenched and blood began pumping toward my groin. Eyes on me, she slipped her toes up my bare stomach and dragged them down the line of my lower abs.

My breath constricted and my cock went painfully hard. Tenting my sweatpants. Her soft mouth parted and her nipples tightened through her silk shirt. I glanced down between my arms. Her toes curled, those fucking half moons on her nails so perfect, and slid beneath my waistband.

"Fuck," I breathed, leaning into her neck. My mouth open and hot against her skin.

I felt the top of her foot, soft and arched, slide down the side of my hard cock. Trailing along the length of it to the underside. Rubbing back and forth in the most amazing rhythm that had me leaking precum in my pants.

Then she drew her foot back, leaving me panting.

"What the fuck?"

She smiled sweetly. "I thought you were getting wine."

Her eyes widened as my hand wrapped around her throat.

"You can't just tease me like that and leave me hanging," I said.

Her lashes fluttered and she pushed her lip out. Fuck, here I was again, all wrapped around her finger and helpless to do anything but kiss her mouth and bite that supple lower lip. I released her and adjusted myself, tucking my softening cock beneath my waistband.

"What kind of wine do you want?"

"Dealer's choice."

I kissed her mouth and dragged my teeth down her throat and bit her shoulder. Just to remind her who she belonged to. She whimpered and her fists pressed uselessly against my chest for a moment before I released her. There was a little flush up her throat and I could see a vein pulse in her neck.

I drew back and left her like that and went downstairs to the wine cellar. Just as I pulled the heavy door back, my phone rang and Cosimo's name lit up the screen.

CHAPTER SEVEN

OLIVIA

When Lucien returned, something was different. I wasn't sure what because it was so hard to read him, but I could just tell something was off. The ice around his edges was a little harder and sharper.

My toes curled involuntarily and I shrank back. He didn't look at me as he opened the bottle of wine and poured a glass for me. He swirled it once and brought it to his lips, tasting it.

Watching him brought me back to the day he'd taken me to his house for the first time and we'd stopped for coffee. I remembered staring at him, spellbound, while he took a sip, noticing the way his jaw tensed and his lips pulled back for the barest second. I'd thought it was oddly sexy and I still did.

"Do you like it?" I asked.

He nodded once.

"Do you still want to get drunk?"

He shook his head.

"Alright...so what do you want?"

He moved toward me, all those beautiful tattoos rippling over his body, and caged me against the counter with his arms. His lips parted as he dragged his eyes slowly, like two cold fingers over my skin, until they looked directly into mine.

"Do you know that game we play sometimes that helps get you out of your head? The one where I fucking degrade you?"

I nodded, my mouth suddenly dry. I did know that game.

"Let's play it," he said.

Heat flared deep in my pussy and spread like liquid fire down my thighs. His mouth parted and he leaned in and his tongue slid over my lips, slipping between them. I moaned and my nipples went hard as I sucked on the tip of his tongue. He pushed the rest in and began fucking my mouth slowly with it.

When he drew back, I was panting and he was stone faced.

"Do you want to be my little slut?" he said coolly.

The frightening side of him was back. The shiver that moved down my spine hit the deepest parts of me and set my hair on end. I never got used to how he could go from being my husband to something so subtly terrifying in a second.

I nodded. My heart thudded in my ears and a secret, shameful thrill started in my stomach.

"I need to hear you say it aloud." His voice was husky.

"I want it," I whispered.

He kissed my mouth and lifted me off the counter. "Then run along and get ready. I'll be up."

I downed the rest of my wine, hoping for some courage. My heart fluttered and as I climbed the steps and I chided myself for still getting butterflies in my chest. He was my husband and I trusted him more than anyone, even myself. I knew he could read my body well enough that even if I was rendered wordless, he could tell when my limit was reached.

And yet...he could be so cruel when we played like this.

Upstairs, I closed the bathroom door and stripped. My fingers slid over the stretch marks on my stomach to the soft flesh between my thighs. I inhaled sharply as my hand brushed my swollen pussy, already soaked by the prospect of what he might do to me. Delicious shivers rippled deep inside as I slid my fingers through my soaked folds. Back and forth the way he surely would.

I remembered he was waiting for me and if I was late, there would be hell to pay. I slipped on a black lace teddy that I knew he liked and put on a little makeup. Just enough mascara that it would run down my face. I knew that it got him so hard when I looked up at him while he fucked my mouth, my makeup running down my cheeks.

I paused, my hand hovering over the bathroom door. I felt small and naked despite still being clothed. Gathering my courage, I pulled open the door and stepped out.

He sat on the end of the bed, still dressed only in his sweatpants. When he lifted his head and fixed his eyes on me, I saw nothing but that empty wasteland. Forever locked beneath ice and snow. He pushed himself upright and got to his feet, but didn't come any closer. I thought I saw his jaw twitch.

"You haven't been very good, baby," he said, cocking his head.

My heart thudded.

"I...I thought I was."

He pushed his hands in his pockets and advanced on me. There was a tightness in his body that hadn't been there before. He paused directly before me and looked down and I looked up at him. Waiting for him to break and tell me what was wrong.

"I'm not angry," he said softly.

It would have been better if he was. At least then I would know where we stood.

He circled me slowly. Once, twice, three times. Then he stopped behind me and his hands came up and gathered my hair in a loose grip. He began gently stroking it through his fingers, pulling it into his fist only to let it slide back around my shoulders.

"Why didn't you tell me your father is running for mayor?"

I froze. He kept stroking my hair and a tingle moved up my spine.

"Because I can tell when you're lying," he said. "And I'd bet anything he told you exactly what he was doing. So, why did you choose to keep that from me?"

"I just...didn't know how to say it," I whispered. "And he told me he would hurt Marco if I told you."

He spun me around and his empty eyes narrowed. In the low light, he was the devil himself. If the devil was the coldest, most dispassionate man in the world.

I shuddered as the tip of his finger touched between my collarbones and slid down over my lace teddy. He cupped my pussy gently, taking care not to touch my clit.

"Who am I?" he said.

I faltered, unsure what response he wanted. My clit pulsed in the warmth of his palm.

"Who am I to you?"

"My husband," I whispered.

"Good girl. That means you are truthful with me, that you come to me first. But you know that, baby, so why did you disobey me?"

I squirmed, unsure how to answer. I knew deep down I should have told him what my father said right away, but I was too bruised by what had happened earlier to speak it out loud. Internally, I wanted nothing more than to go back to bed and hope tomorrow was better.

But Lucien would never allow that. Once he got his teeth in me, he never let go until he'd gotten what he wanted.

And I reveled in it even while it tortured me.

"I don't know," I whispered.

His hands slid up my back and rested on either side of my neck. Warm and rough and familiar. Then his right hand moved up and gently gripped my throat, holding me in place. I kept still, knowing all he wanted from me right now was total obedience.

"You will not keep things from me," he said.

His voice was soft and it might have sounded kind if there wasn't such a deadly undercurrent to it. I swallowed, searching his face, wishing I could see beyond the stone wall of his eyes.

"Yes, sir."

"You're not a good girl."

I bit back a gasp, pain flaring in my chest. Once before, in the throes of anger, he'd taken away the coveted title of good girl. But since then he'd done nothing less than tell me the things I loved hearing. I swallowed and lifted my chin, keeping my eyes on the floor.

"Do you want to earn back your title as my good girl?"

There was a casual, cold curiosity in his voice.

"Yes, sir," I said hoarsely.

"Go sit in that chair," he said, pointing to the leather seat across from the bed.

I obeyed, pressing my legs together and locking my ankles. His eyes dropped to my feet, but I kept my gaze down because I knew it was no use trying to figure out what he felt.

My chest tightened and I swallowed the lump in the back of my throat.

"I'm not angry," he said softly. "I'm just disappointed."

That was so much worse. Lucien expected a lot from the people in his life, never as much as from himself, but I did my best to make him proud of me. And usually it was easy. I was his weak spot, I knew that, and he praised me and treated me like a queen. But occasionally, I fell short of his expectations.

"What can I do to fix it?" I asked.

"Look at me."

I obeyed.

"I'm going to fuck you, baby."

"I understand."

"Tell me your safe word."

I wet my lips. "Red."

He leaned back, bracing himself on the heels of his hands. The light glinted off his tattoos. Off the top of the skull above his cock. I could make out the outline of him beneath his sweatpants, halfway hard. Fuck, he was so big and thick it almost scared me. My pussy pulsed softly and a shiver moved down my spine and culminated in heat between my thighs.

"Open your legs," he commanded.

I shivered and obeyed, spreading my thighs.

"Unfasten the lace over your cunt," he said.

His voice was hard. He leaned forward and braced his elbows on his knees, watching me from beneath his brows. Like an animal observing its prey.

"Go on, baby," he said softly. "Show me what belongs to me. Show me what I've fucked more times than I can count."

My fingers shook with anticipation as I unclasped the lace between my legs and bared my sex to him. His lips parted and his tongue flicked out for a second. His head cocked and I saw the hunger in every inch of him, like a flash of lightning. Then he composed himself again.

He rose slowly, unfurling the length of his hard, muscled torso. My whole body tingled, making me painfully aware of every inch of my skin. My legs were fully open, my knees cocked, and my soaked pussy spread for him. The armrests of the chair pressed into my thighs and the leather was cool on my flushed skin.

He stalked toward me and knelt. Keeping his eyes on mine, he dropped his head between my thighs. Then he paused, his mouth less than an inch from my pussy. His hot breath burned like fire.

"Do you deserve to be touched, baby?"

"Please, Lucien," I begged.

The delicate skin of my sex pulsed, tingling so close to his touch. He considered it for a moment, studying the lines and curves of my pussy. Then he parted his lips and let his saliva drip down onto my clit, sending a delicious shudder through the deepest parts of me.

He returned to the bed and sat back down. Disappointment flooded my chest and it took everything I had to bite back my words of protest.

"You have to work for my touch tonight," he said.

My chest was a confusing mess of disappointment, but the feeling was drowned out by the burning ache between my legs. His saliva dripped down my pussy, but I didn't dare move until he gave me permission.

"Touch yourself," he demanded.

Shamefully aroused and soaked, I reached between my thighs. Even my own touch felt like heaven as I gathered his saliva and my wetness and swirled them over my clit. I'd gone from being saddened by his disappointment to aching for him, hoping he would punish me because I wanted nothing more than to be his dirty whore.

"Slow down," he ordered.

I slowed, dragging my finger through my soaked folds, and his mouth parted again. He was transfixed.

"Show me your clit."

He knew being exposed like this made me burn with shame and he didn't care because it was what he wanted. And what he wanted made me burn with desire, willing to do anything he demanded of me.

He wanted me submissive and pleasured.

Drawn into the depths of his cold, brought to my knees.

With one hand I spread myself open and with the other, I gently tugged back the hood of my clit. Revealing the dark pink nub nestled there. His chest tightened as his lungs constricted. I saw it in the hard ridges along his stomach and the V that led down to his pants. Down to the cock beneath his sweatpants, punishingly hard and waiting to be unleashed.

"You've got such a pretty clit," he breathed. "Now suck your finger and touch yourself like my needy whore."

I loved it more than anything else when he degraded me. Even when the words stung, they somehow made me feel so safe. So loved. Heat coiled as my finger circled my clit, pulling pleasure from the deepest parts of me and drawing it to the surface.

He rose and turned on the intake fan in the far corner of the room and lit a cigarette. In the dim light, I saw the cherry tip of it glimmer, moving closer and closer. Until he was a few feet from my chair.

"Is that what you like, baby?" he purred. "Being made to fucking degrade yourself?"

I paused, distracted by the look on his face.

"Don't fucking stop," he ordered. "I want you to make yourself come three times, so you had better keep working."

"Three times?"

"Yes. Oh, and address me as sir or I will fuck you until you regret every time you've ever questioned me."

I gulped, my orgasm so close to the surface. "Yes, sir."

His eyes glittered and he expelled a stream of smoke from his nose. "I know what you like, I know what makes you drip," he drawled. "I can talk you through three orgasms and you know it."

I opened my mouth to answer, but the only thing that came out was a little gasp as I came hard. My eyes clenched shut as my body pulsed and spiraled into nothingness. I shook again and again until the sensations began to soften and ebb away.

My eyes snapped open and connected with his.

"Next one, baby," he drawled. "You're such a needy slut. Keep touching yourself, I don't care how sensitive your clit is. You're a filthy whore and you can take it. You've taken a hell of a lot worse."

My eyes rolled back, part from the sensitivity of my finger on my clit and part from the words falling from his lips. My God, he knew how to work my body without even touching me, like I was a puppet on strings. Harsh whimpers pulled from my throat and I gripped the armrest with one hand and rubbed my clit in quick circles with my fingers.

"What do you think about when you fuck yourself when I'm not there?" he mused, pacing like an animal. He looked painfully hard beneath his pants. "Do you remember all the times I've taken you home from a dinner or a party and stripped all your expensive jewels and clothes off and fucked your ass?"

His lip curled and he took a drag from his cigarette. Smoke drifted from his mouth and wreathed his dark head.

"Does it make you wet that you're a queen covered with my money in public, but in our bedroom, you're nothing but a whore for me to get off in?"

My hips shook and my finger moved faster as my second orgasm burst to the surface in a hot rush. This time I reached over my head and gripped the back of the chair and rode my pleasure out against the heel of my hand. There was nothing but the stars in my eyes and my husband, standing there like a tattooed god, smoke drifting lazily from his nose and mouth.

"What are you?"

I gasped, my orgasm still wrecking my body.

"Fucking tell me," he ordered. "I want to hear it from you while you're coming on your hand."

"I—I'm your whore," I gasped.

A glitter started in his glacial eyes.

"Good girl."

He knelt before me and his tattooed hand, so familiar and comforting, wrapped around my neck. I stopped touching my clit and ran my wet fingers up his arm, but he shook his head.

"I didn't say you could stop playing with yourself," he said.

"I'm sorry," I whispered. "Sir."

A flicker of approval moved through his eyes and vanished. I swallowed, feeling my throat bob in his grip. He lifted me gently so I could slide my knees under my thighs and sit on my heels. Then he put a bit of pressure on the sides of my throat to keep me on my toes, but allowing enough space between his finger and thumb for me to breathe.

"I'll let you warm up again before you touch your clit," he whispered.

He held the cigarette back to keep the smoke from my face, leaning on his heels so he could stab it out in the tray by the bed.

"I don't know if I can have another," I breathed.

"Oh, yes, you can," he said. "Just start playing with it. Nice and slow. You'll be dripping down your thigh in no time."

He held me upright by the throat and watched as I stroked slow circles around my pussy, building my arousal up again. His chest heaved and a trickle of sweat sank down between his collarbones and etched down his tattooed abs to the waistband of his pants. I let my eyes flicker down to his groin and along the heavy length of his cock to the tip where his precum stained through the fabric.

I kept my eyes down, fixed to the ridge against his thigh. I knew his cock was just below the fabric, hard, and velvety soft. So eager to sink inside me and fill the empty place that longed for him. My fingers moved faster and he moaned softly, a barely perceptible sound that didn't reach his barren eyes.

"Are you going to come for me, little slut?"

My stomach tensed and I rubbed harder and faster, pushing the last bit of pleasure I had in my body to the surface. He saw my orgasm arrive like an approaching storm as my thighs tensed and shook and my muscles went tight beneath his hands. Then he seized my wrists and pulled them back just as I was about to tumble over the edge.

"Lucien," I gasped.

He bent, licking my fingers clean as I sat there, crushed with disappointment. He picked me up, wrapping my legs around his waist, and fell onto the bed. Pinning me beneath his hard, hot body.

"You've had enough orgasms, baby," he said. "I'm cutting you off."

I dug my nails into his chest, frustrated heat pulsing between my legs. He winced, but didn't move.

"You wanted me to come," I whimpered.

"I wanted you to come the first and second time. The third time was just so I could watch you beg for it."

Before I could speak, he pushed down the front of his pants and thrust into me. Burying his cock to the hilt. My spine bent at the intrusion and I cried out as he stretched the deepest parts of me. The soaked muscles inside me gripped him, fighting to accommodate his size.

His hand circled my throat and our eyes locked. Beyond the hazel of his irises was that wasteland of nothing but miles of frozen earth and sky. I shivered and it ran all the way down to where we joined together, our bodies fused with lust.

"Lucien," I whispered.

His mouth grazed mine.

"You can take it, baby," he said.

He shifted, his hand still around my neck, and lifted my hips. Adjusting them so he could slide the rest of the way in. I hadn't realized there was more to take and I gave a quiet moan as the head of his cock rested up against my cervix. Pushing up into my innermost point until I squirmed from the pressure.

Instead of thrusting, he began rocking in little, angled thrusts up against my cervix. Fireworks burst in the back of my brain and hot, pulsing lava spread through my body. With every shift I felt him so deep in me, edging me, coaxing me toward ruin. My pussy spasmed as his pubic bone ground against my clit, but before I could come, he eased back.

He kept me on the edge like this for several minutes. I moaned shamelessly, my legs tightening around his hips, trying to get him to thrust just once. But he was relentless as he teased and tortured me.

Then, his face merciless, he got on his knees, pulled me close so he could push his cock back into me. I felt my eyes widen, knowing what he was doing, knowing I was about to have the breath fucked out of me.

He pulled my ankles up and bent me in half under him so my knees rested over his shoulders. His hand gripped the headboard over me as he held me steady and began thrusting. Stone faced, a muscle in his jaw tense. I whimpered from the pressure of him bottoming out as he pounded deep. My eyes watered, smearing makeup down my cheeks.

"You don't fucking disobey me, baby," he breathed. "And you don't keep things from me."

"Yes, sir," I gasped.

"You're going to fucking take it like this because you're a dirty slut and you deserve to get fucked like one. Understood?"

"Y—yes," I whimpered.

He began thrusting with more sinuous movements that still pushed his cock so deep in me I felt it in the back of my throat.

"That's a good girl," he praised. "You know just how to take it and you take it so fucking well."

He sucked in a harsh breath and sat up and gathered my ankles in one tattooed hand. Jaw tight, he gripped them to his chest as he fucked up into me. I cried out and clung to the sheets, holding onto anything to keep me from breaking apart. My body was almost at its limit, but my mind and soul were locked away in that beautiful place he put me in.

The place where there was nothing but his hands and his body and the comfort of being his possession.

His fingertips skimmed my stomach and found my clit, working it relentlessly. My lower body writhed and I came, pleasure pounding through me in one of the strongest orgasms I'd ever had.

From far away I heard him groan as my pleasure pulsed to nothingness. He pushed into me until he couldn't get any deeper and began rocking up against my cervix.

He shuddered, poised on the edge of release, and I knew what he was doing. He'd done the same thing when we'd tried to get pregnant the first time.

"Fuck—I'm going to fuck you pregnant, baby," he said, his teeth gritted. "Going to use your little cunt until you're knocked up for me."

My eyes rolled back as he thrust hard, locking his hips, and emptied himself as deeply as he could. We gasped as one, our eyes locking. His hips thrust in short strokes, almost nudges, like he was pushing his cum further up. Then he released a quiet sigh and pulled from my pussy and fell onto his back.

I bit my swollen lower lip.

His body was satisfied, but had he forgiven me?

I rolled onto my side, touching the line between his pecs. He shifted up, pulling the sheet over his lap and held out his arm. Relief flooding me, I curled up against him and he stroked his lean fingers through my hair.

"Are you angry?"

"I was never angry with you. Just disappointed."

"Lucien—"

"I'm going to handle it, Olivia," he said firmly. "You can always come to me and tell me anything and I'll handle it. Understood?"

I opened my mouth to protest and closed it. This was my husband and there was nothing I could do to change him even if I wanted to. I swallowed back my questions.

He joined me in the shower, washing me and rubbing lotion into my body after I'd dried off. I closed my eyes, giving myself over to him. His aftercare always put me in the best mood. Into a space where he had no hard edges and his touch was that of a loving husband only.

Then he carried me to the bed and laid me down, sliding beneath the sheets and pulling me to him.

I fell asleep in the middle of the day, my back against his firm chest and his lean fingers locked loosely around my throat.

CHAPTER EIGHT

LUCIEN

It had been easy to kill my own father. Childishly easy. He'd never expected an attack from inside his own home so all I had to do was cut the security cameras and walk into his room while he slept. The biggest roadblock was cleaning up all blood soaked down my clothes and skin. And even that hadn't slowed me down.

I'd worn only shorts so there would be less evidence to destroy. After he was dead, propped up against the pillows with his head in his lap like a macabre present, I'd gone into his shower and stripped. Washing all that fucking blood down the drain.

Then I'd walked naked back up to my room with my shorts zipped into a bag. The next morning, while everyone was panicking, I went into the woods and burned the bag and the shorts.

And no one was ever the wiser.

Then I went back to the house and took his place as underboss.

Killing Romano had been a lot more fun. I'd enjoyed the chase he'd put on, running through the cold dark to the river. It had been so satisfying to feel that hot gush slip over my hands, spilling his blood until it soaked to my skin. Bringing him back to the house and throwing his body down onto the ground in front of everyone had been sweet victory.

I'd never regretted any of it because both those men had deserved it. And my next target deserved it too.

Oh, he deserved it just as much as the first two had.

I was a methodical planner, and once I'd zeroed in on my prey, I was satisfied with waiting. Killing recklessly was a weak move. I'd played enough chess to know that it was important to go through the entire game before taking out the king.

And I'd waited six years for this kill.

On our honeymoon, she'd confessed the things her father and mother had done to her. How she'd been starved and abused until she fit the mold of the perfect mafia wife for me. At the time, she'd acted like she wasn't broken by it, but I knew better now. I watched her carefully and I saw how her abuse had changed her and it lit a deep fire inside me.

He had beaten her more than once. It had taken me over a year to get her to admit to all the times he'd put his hands on her, but even if it had just been once, that was enough. He had hurt her and that was all that mattered.

And for what? Because she was small and couldn't defend herself. Because they'd wanted another boy and they'd gotten a girl. Because she was starved and beautiful and exhausted from being forced to be both.

Because she was an easy target and she didn't fight back.

That made me deeply angry, but I was used to living with rage. If I could have killed her parents the minute I became boss, I would have. But there were some lines even I couldn't cross and killing women was one of them. As much as I loathed her mother, I wouldn't put my hands on her despite how fucking evil she was.

Her father, however, was fair game.

Almost a month after our disastrous weekend away, I woke to find Olivia doing her makeup in the bathroom. I bit back a wave of annoyance that she was already dressed. We hadn't fucked in a few days and there was a distinct ache in my groin and a need for release in my balls. She looked up as I walked into the bathroom and flipped the toilet lid up to relieve myself.

"Gross, Lucien," she said, wrinkling her nose.

There was a playful note in her voice so I decided to focus on that instead of my bad mood. I flushed the toilet, tucked my dick under my waistband, and came up behind her. She leaned forward, her mouth open in concentration, and applied her lipstick. I glanced down at her ass, jutted out inches from my groin.

Hmm, maybe there was a chance.

I ran my palm down her side and gripped her hip, grinding my hardening dick against her pretty ass. Annoyance flickered in her dark gaze.

"I'm heading to the foundation," she said.

"No time for a quick fuck?"

She turned and I caged her against the sink, nuzzling her neck. Fuck, she'd put her perfume under her earlobes and she smelled extraordinary. Sweet and a little tart, like good champagne. Her body softened a minute amount as I nipped her ear, letting her feel my breath wash over her neck.

"Just take your panties down and bend over," I said. "I'll make it quick."

"I'm already dressed," she protested. "And I'm wearing my nice panties."

I bit her shoulder gently and she moaned, her head falling back. My hand slid down and pushed under her dress, dragging my fingers over the sensitive underside of her knee and down to her calf. Her throat bobbed as she swallowed, trying to concentrate on putting large, gold earrings in.

"Lucien," she snapped.

"You want it," I observed.

She took a breath and her palms pushed against my chest. I relented, taking a step back and resisting the urge to palm my cock through my sweatpants. Her nose scrunched as she scowled, turning to fix the hairs around her neck I'd messed up.

"Can't you just...you know?"

"Jerk off in the shower?"

"Well...yes," she said. "I'm just in a hurry to get some things done at the foundation today. I have a full day scheduled."

Biting back my disappointment, I kissed her and she clicked out of the room on her towering heels. Her lovely ass swaying and making my cock ache. Releasing a sigh, I turned on the shower and stepped into the hot water.

I put on my usual gray suit and went into the uptown office because it was nearer to the foundation headquarters. There was a stack of paperwork I needed to go through for our legitimate businesses overseas, nearly five dozen emails I needed to answer, and several meetings waiting for me the moment I arrived. I bit the bullet and waded through it, but there was an annoying half erection hidden beneath my desk the whole time.

My body was stiff when my last meeting before lunch finally ended and I could safely stand. Making sure the door was locked, I went back to my desk and swiped my phone. I had an encrypted app where I kept every picture and video Olivia had ever sent for moments like this.

Feeling oddly dirty, I flipped through the images. They flashed across my screen, shockingly graphic. Olivia's pussy, her tits covered in my cum, her body bent over the sink with her panties around her ankles. The very first picture she'd sent me of her pussy, a string of pearls threaded over her soaked folds.

I had never sent her a single picture of my dick, but suddenly I wanted to. I wanted to revel in the thought of her shocked face as it appeared on her phone while she was at her desk. For a moment, I hesitated with my fingers above my zipper, and then I pulled it down and unleashed my cock.

Achingly hard and leaking precum.

I sent her the picture and then jerked off into a tissue to an image of her tits. It took all of ten minutes for my phone to ring and Olivia's name appeared. Vaguely satisfied, I swiped up and hit the speaker button.

"You alright, baby?" I asked casually.

"Lucien Esposito," she whispered. "What has gotten into you?"

"What do you mean?"

I heard her sharp intake of breath. "You can't send photos of your dick to me while I'm in meetings."

"Should I wait till your meetings are done?"

"Lucien!"

"Olivia."

"This is unfair...I can see the veins running down your lower stomach," she moaned. "How are you forty-three and you still look like this?"

"I'm wounded. Forty-three is young."

"You knew exactly what you were doing taking it from that angle."

"Maybe you should come ride my cock at my desk," I suggested lightly. "Just pull that pretty skirt up and sink down on it...let it fill up all that emptiness inside you. I know you're so fucking empty for me, baby."

She gave a quiet gasp.

"Are you in your office?" I asked.

"Yes," she said. "I was going to eat lunch."

"Is your door locked?"

"Yes." The word was breathless, drenched in desire.

I shifted back, my cock already twitching against my zipper again. Through the window, the sky was blue and the city stretched out around my highrise. But there was nothing that held my attention more than knowing my wife was needy and wet in her office, just a few blocks from me.

"Stand up and bend over the desk and put your phone on speaker, baby," I ordered softly. "Take your panties down and touch your empty pussy."

There was a shuffle as she moved the things on her desk and then a soft gasp and she gave a quiet moan that turned into a whimper.

"Are you soaked for me?"

"I'm...so wet for you, Lucien," she gasped. "All I can think about is your cock and I...I need to come so badly."

"Good girl. Now put your other fingers in your mouth, your pointer and middle, and suck on them. Then lift your knee up and brace it on your desk and put your wet fingers into your pussy. Can you do that for me?"

"Yes, fuck, yes," she gasped.

"Move the phone closer," I ordered. "I want to hear how wet you are when you fuck yourself."

There was a short silence and then I heard it—the slippery sound of her fingers pushing in and out of her cunt. Fucking it the way my cock would if I were there. The front of my pants strained, but I was too focused on hearing my wife make herself come to deal with my dick right now.

"My God," she breathed. "You have the sexiest cock."

I felt my mouth twitch. "You're touching yourself to the picture I sent you."

"Is that bad?" she panted.

"Fuck no," I murmured. "Look at it, think about how it would feel sliding between your thighs. Pushing into you so slowly, filling your pretty, tight pussy up to the brim. Slamming into you...again and again."

"Oh God, oh God, don't stop talking," she begged.

"Think how it would feel coming inside you," I urged. "Soaking you deep inside with my cum. Maybe I'd fuck you a little more after I finish, just to make it all drip down your thighs...so I can wipe it clean and make you suck it off my fingers. You want that, baby?"

Her hand hit the desk and she gasped and then cried out. My cock throbbed and excitement simmered in my groin. Fuck, if getting turned down in the morning meant phone sex later, I was happy to be rejected.

"Oh my God," she whispered. "That was intense."

"Would you like to have lunch with me?" I asked.

Her clothes rustled and I heard her take tissues from the box. The image of her trying to clean up her thighs, trying to wipe away all that wetness from her sex, had me throbbing harder.

"Do you need to...you know?"

"Send me something," I said. "I'll take care of it again and pick you up in a few minutes. If you want to make it really fast, send me a picture of your perfect feet and I'll come in seconds."

She hung up and obliged. My dick was still sensitive from jerking off twice, but I still finished to the picture of her slender, arched feet and delicate ankles. Then I washed up and put on my jacket, sliding my shoulder holsters on beneath, and left the office.

The street bustled, already decorated for the holidays. I kept my head down to avoid having to stop and talk with anyone and ducked into the big, stone building where she worked. Inside, she'd already had the front lobby decked in lights and set up a silver Christmas tree in the corner.

Of course she had, Olivia loved any excuse for excess, especially holidays. If she could have, she'd have painted the entire world in glittering silver and gold and encrusted it in diamonds.

I heard her footsteps on the spiral staircase before I saw her heels come into view. She'd taken her hair down at some point during the morning and it fell over her shoulders in a dark waterfall, her feathery bangs framing her face. Her full mouth was a dusky burgundy that matched her pencil dress and heels.

Fuck, she was so lovely.

She descended the stairs and turned her face up so I could kiss her mouth.

"I hope you had a good morning, baby," I said.

"It was...full of surprises."

"We'll go to that place you like on Fifth Street and maybe we can have dessert in your office when we get back."

Her eyes widened and she glanced over her shoulder, but the lobby was empty save for the clerk behind the front desk in the corner. I bent and kissed my wife again, savoring her taste. When I drew back, her eyes were drunk.

"Where's your coat?" I asked.

She moved to the front desk and gathered it up and I helped her into the soft wool jacket. Then, hand in hand, we went out onto the cold street and headed toward the French café. We were almost at the door when I heard a camera click and I turned, my ire rising like a flame doused in gasoline.

There was a tabloid journalist standing at the street corner. I didn't have to deal with too much press, but as one of the city's wealthiest businessmen, there was always a chance my name could end up in the papers. After Olivia started her foundation, the interest in us as a couple had risen.

The story practically sold itself—millionaire devil and his beautiful, angel wife.

I bit back my annoyance and circled Olivia to shield her from the camera. Her brows drew together and she bit her lip, shrinking back against the door.

"Sir," the man shouted. "Sir, do you have anything to say about the mayoral race?"

I turned. "No. No comment."

"But, sir, your wife's father is the favorite candidate."

I turned, making sure to keep Olivia behind me, and fixed him with an icy stare. His face paled and he took a step back, nodding an apology. I remained where I was, Olivia's cold hand gripped in mine, until he had disappeared down the street.

"Lucien, I—"

"Don't worry about it, baby," I said, pulling open the door and guiding her inside with a hand on the small of her back. "I have it under control."

We ate lunch by the window and no one bothered us. Olivia was feeling anxious, I could tell by how much food she left on her plate. But I was glad to see that she managed to drink her entire latte and eat the grilled chicken out of her salad.

I fucking hated how wounded she was. I hated that because of the abuse she'd endured, my brave wife would always be a little bit broken no matter how many times I put her back together.

It made me want to skin her father alive.

After lunch, I walked her back to her office and we made out in the elevator and I ate her pussy on her desk. Then my phone rang and it was Peregrine, letting me know he'd just sat in on a city meeting and we needed to talk about Rosario Barone. I promised to meet him in the downtown office as soon as possible. When I hung up the phone, Olivia's dark eyes were wide and flickering with worry.

"You heard that?"

She nodded.

"I have to go take care of this," I said, bending to kiss her mouth.

She swallowed. "Be careful."

I kissed her one more time and walked back to my uptown office to retrieve the Tesla. The air was still and smelled like November, but clouds were gathering on the edges of the horizon. Like a storm was about to break.

When I pulled up on the edge of the street, Peregrine was already standing there talking on his phone.

"Is Cosimo here?" I called, getting out of the Tesla.

He looked up, putting his phone away. "Not yet."

"We can go on and start without him," I said. "I don't have a lot of time."

Peregrine turned and I followed him up the sidewalk to the downtown office. It was a large, historic building where we usually held our meetings because it didn't look like much and was generally left alone by the public. I paused at the end of the walkway as Cosimo's motorcycle roared up and parked. He swung his leg off and reached for his helmet.

At that minute, my entire body prickled. The world went deadly quiet and my senses roared to life. Color moved in high definition and time slowed. I felt the ripple in the air before I ever saw anything and I seized Peregrine by the back of the coat and threw him down and fell over his body.

The world broke. Shattered.

And in that moment, all I thought of was my wife and my son.

I wasn't sure if I was dead, but if this was hell, it was a lot less interesting than I'd imagined. The air was chalky white and spots popped in the thick smoke and a faint ringing sounded from somewhere very far away. I shifted, slowly becoming aware of Peregrine beneath me. His body was completely still.

Fuck, I wasn't dead. We'd been attacked.

I blinked hard and the world swam into focus. I could hear faintly from my left ear, but my right side was completely dead. My mouth tasted of blood and I rolled onto my back, climbing to my hands and knees. Peregrine lay on his stomach, his eyes shut. A small trickle of blood ran from his hairline and dripped onto the pavement. In the distance, a siren wailed.

Cosimo's face appeared, still wearing his motorcycle helmet. He was shouting, but I couldn't hear him. His gun was in his hand and he circled, trying to cover us. But I knew there was no one there. We'd been bombed, not shot at.

I spat on the pavement and spat again, crimson mixed with saliva spattered between my hands. Why couldn't I hear anything but a siren and a shrill ringing? I shook my head like a dog, trying to get some life into my right ear.

It remained quiet.

The world reeled and I fell forward, scraping my right cheekbone on the sidewalk. I was losing consciousness, I could feel the blackness creep into my vision, sucking me down. My aching arms and legs were lead, completely unmovable. Less than a foot away, Peregrine's bloody face was as still as death.

CHAPTER NINE

OLIVIA

I'd never seen Lucien so helpless before. He lay on his back, still sleeping, with tubes running from whirring, clicking machines to his body. He was naked beneath the hospital sheets and his tattooed chest rose and fell softly.

I sat with my head on his thigh, waiting and watching for when he woke.

He was going to be fine. The only thing the doctors weren't sure about was his right ear. It had faced the bomb blast and his eardrum was ruptured. That didn't mean it would never work, the doctor said, but he also couldn't promise it would recover fully. The best case scenario was tinnitus, so I hoped for that.

I rose as Peregrine's wife, Rosalia entered, her face pale and tight with stress. I held out my arm and she moved to my side, embracing me for a long time.

"How is Peregrine?"

"He's going to be fine. Just a few scratches."

"Thank God."

"He'd be dead if Lucien hadn't covered him."

"I know."

Her fists clenched. "I fucking hate this sometimes. And I know it's worse for you because Peregrine isn't a target the way Lucien is. But I just...fucking hate worrying if he's coming home or not."

I understood her words on a deep level. I spent my days caring for his son, waiting for him in the sanctuary of his house, hoping he would return unharmed at the end of the day.

"They consume us," she whispered.

I knew what she meant. The men we loved lived dangerous lives and there was no escaping what they were. It seeped into everything they did and it permeated every corner of our lives. There was no escape.

It was the price we paid for their love. But I never doubted it was worth it. Every moment with Lucien made all that fear and uncertainty fade.

There was no other love but his that could satisfy me and I was willing to pay the steep price for it.

Rosalia left to return to her husband and I slipped into bed beside Lucien, taking care not to jostle him. He was so warm and he smelled so good it made my heart ache. My chest felt tight as I closed my eyes and nestled my face against his warm skin.

I woke around three in the morning to find Lucien awake and scrolling through his phone. For a second, I didn't move. I just lay there against his side and studied his face in the blue glow of the screen. He released a quiet sigh, a sound I rarely heard from him, and set the phone aside.

"Are you alright?" I whispered.

I felt him turn. "You should be sleeping, baby. At home in our bed."

"I'm not leaving you."

His arm shifted and slid around my shoulders, pulling me closer. I felt his lips brush the top of my head and a lump rose in my throat. I hadn't cried when I'd gotten the call, or on the way to the hospital, or while I sat and watched the nurses wash the dust and blood from his body. But now all those suppressed feelings welled up in my chest like a wave.

I swallowed, gasping.

"There now, baby," he said, his deep voice soothing in the dark. "You've been so brave for me."

I still felt stupid for crying. He didn't cry—I doubted he was even capable of it. I turned so I could lie on my side and buried my face against his ribs, breathing in the scent of him. The hospital room was pitch black save for two little lights on his IV stand. One kept blinking steadily and it was driving me crazy.

"How do you feel?" I asked.

"Fine," he said. "I can probably go home tomorrow. Have you seen Peregrine?"

"He's alright," I said. "He was just knocked unconscious and got a few scratches and bruises."

"This is my fucking fault," Lucien said, his voice tinged with something I didn't recognize. A chill moved down my spine.

"You saved him, Lucien."

"No, I didn't act fast enough."

"I don't understand."

He sighed again and the sound was almost chilling. Like a gust of icy air through the pit of my stomach.

"It's obvious who was behind this and I knew what he was planning and I haven't acted. I've been waiting because it's a delicate situation. But I need to take care of it."

We both knew what that meant.

I chewed my lip, my stomach turning sour at the thought of my father. I wasn't stupid, I knew what Lucien was trying to say. I hated my father down to my core, but the thought of letting my husband take care of him the way he did with other men who caused problems was too much.

It was too evil, too monstrous.

My chest tightened. It was Lucien's prerogative to kill his father and his choice. I hadn't known him then so I was able to compartmentalize and pretend it was a different man who had drawn that razor wire across his father's throat. And Romano's murder was a diplomatic move, as well as vengeance for what he'd done to Lucien and I, so it was fair.

At least that was what I repeated to myself again and again when I was in bed with him. Lying beside a man who'd killed his father and put his head on his lap like it was some kind of sick joke. I'd read the news articles despite Iris begging me not to and I knew the grotesque details.

And yet, I loved that man. I had given birth to his son. I kissed him every morning, ate dinner with him at night, and fucked him before we slept tangled together in our bed.

But killing my father…that was a step too far.

I sat up and shifted to face him even though I couldn't see through the dark.

"You can't kill my father," I said, my voice cracking.

He was quiet.

"Lucien, do you hear me?"

"I heard you," he said.

"But you're not listening." Desperation rose in my chest and I blinked hard, trying to keep the tears back.

He was silent again. Swathed in darkness.

I got up, a twinge of horror in my stomach. "You will not kill any member of my family. I won't allow it. It's just too far...where does this all end?"

He moved and the little lamp beside the bed came on, bathing the left side of his face with a pale glow. His expression was unreadable and his cold eyes were barren. Methodically, and with terrifying lack of emotion, he began unhooking his IV. I backed up, sitting down abruptly in the chair in the corner, and wrapped my arms around my body.

He pulled on his sweatpants and took something from the pocket, wrapping it in his fist.

"Where are you going?" I whispered.

"To the balcony to have a smoke," he said.

"You can't smoke on hospital grounds."

"Alright, I'm going for a walk and a smoke then." There was frost on the edges of his words.

I jumped up as he turned the door handle and he paused, his jaw twitching.

"Are you listening to me?" I said, gathering my courage. "Do not kill my father. I shouldn't have to fucking say that, but I guess I do.

That's a line I'm not willing to cross with you, Lucien. Please. We won't come back from that."

There was a flash of heat in his eyes, but it quickly died.

"Excuse me?" he said softly.

The air in the room went glacial and my spine tingled all the way down to the soles of my feet. He was the ice king again, tall, terrifying, and locked somewhere in his bleak kingdom where I was never allowed.

"I mean it," I whispered.

He sauntered across the room and bent until he was eye level with me. I held his gaze even though every part of me wanted to break down crying, begging him for some show of warmth. His fingers closed gently on my jaw and he kissed me softly. When he drew back, there was a ghost of a smile on his mouth.

"There is nothing we can't come back from, baby," he said. "And I'll do whatever it takes to keep you safe. I'll kill whoever needs killing. My hands are already bloody. What will it hurt to make them a little more red?"

He turned and was gone, the hospital door swinging in his wake. I'd never set a boundary so clearly with him before and I hated his reaction. My stomach twisted and I curled up in the chair, my hand drifting to my stomach. We'd had a lot of sex in the last few weeks and I wasn't on birth control so there was always a chance I was pregnant.

In this moment, I hoped I wasn't. Until this was sorted out, I didn't need anything else to deal with. When we got home tomorrow, I was going to start back on the pill whether he liked it or not.

CHAPTER TEN

LUCIEN

I had most of my hearing back by the next morning, which was a minor miracle. I left Peregrine with Rosalia outside the hospital and took Olivia home. She was quiet for the entire ride, staring out the window at the snow falling gently over the city. As we pulled up outside the mansion, I parked the Tesla and turned to her, but she kept her face hidden. Her hair was tangled, pulled back in a sloppy braid.

"What's wrong?" I asked.

She shrugged.

"Olivia, I don't play the silent treatment," I said. "Open your mouth and tell me what's bothering you."

She whirled, her lashes wet. "How can you just ask me what's wrong? What do you think is wrong, Lucien? Maybe I'm upset because my awful father that I thought was finally gone from my life is now back and he blew up my husband and now my husband is planning on killing him."

"I don't see how the last part is upsetting," I said coolly. "He has it coming."

As soon as the words were out, I knew they were wrong.

There I went again, being a heartless bastard.

She wrenched open the door and jumped out, slamming it. I sighed and followed her, pursuing her up the snowy steps and into the front hallway. She shed her coat on the floor and ran up the stairs, disappearing around the corner.

She was acting like a child and I really didn't have the patience for it right now. I climbed the stairs, ignoring the shrill ringing in my right ear. There was a dull ache where some shrapnel had hit my shoulder and they'd dug it out and stitched the flesh back together. I pushed the discomfort away—I'd dealt with a hell of a lot worse.

I turned the knob to our bedroom door, but it was locked.

Fucking locked.

A ripple of anger moved through my chest and I wrestled it back down. No one, not even my wife, denied me access to any part of my home.

There were two solutions before me. I could step back and let her cool off so we could talk this over. Or I could break down this fucking door and bend her over the sink and spank her ass with my belt until she promised to be good. The second one was tantalizing, but I knew better than to utilize that method right now.

I settled on a happy medium.

"Olivia, open the door," I called.

Silence.

The door was antique and the lock was fragile. I braced my elbow against it, putting upward pressure on the knob to destabilize the latch, and struck it once. Wood splintered and the knob pulled free. The door swung open to reveal Olivia, standing in the bathroom entrance in her black, lacy undergarments. Her mouth fell open and her dark eyes flashed.

"You did not," she whispered.

Not speaking, I walked into the bathroom and shut the door. She backed up against the sink and her face paled as she watched me take my clothes off. Her eyes lingered on the bruises on my chest and the stitches on my shoulder. She'd seen worse on my body, but she still winced at the sight.

"I think we can settle our differences in bed before Marco gets back," I said.

Her mouth tightened and a crease appeared between her brows.

"All you fucking do is think with your dick," she snapped, rolling her eyes.

Oh, that pissed me off. Not just because she was being disrespectful and insolent, but because she knew how much it annoyed me when she rolled her eyes.

"Turn on the shower," I said shortly. "Get in."

Her dark eyes crackled with heat, but she obeyed, turning on the hot spray. I kept my gaze on her stoically as she stripped off her jewelry, still taking care to put her ring in its case, and got into the shower. Slamming the door. She knew she was in trouble and she was pissed about it.

I let her sulk behind the glass for a few minutes while I checked my phone to make sure Peregrine and Rosalia had made it home. Then I joined her in the shower, ignoring her harsh glare.

"Turn around," I said.

"You're—"

I spun her around, holding her back against me by the shoulders. Her breath hitched as my hard cock pressed against her ass. Already pulsing with need. I kept my desire in check and reached for her bottle of body wash.

She held still while I lathered our bodies. The shower filled with the crisp scent of soap and her soft moans as I caressed her legs and played with the soft curves of her ass and breasts. She wouldn't look at me, but her lower lip was so swollen and bitten by the time I was done with her that she didn't need to. I knew her body was a storm of rage and arousal, that she didn't know if she wanted to fight or fuck.

I turned off the shower and patted her down with a soft towel. She gave a little gasp as I lifted her and placed her on the sink.

"What are you doing?" she whispered.

I pulled on a pair of boxer briefs and ran a hand through my wet hair to slick it back. She glanced down at my cock, halfway hard beneath the fabric, and lifted a judgemental brow. It was one of the few things we differed on sexually—when I got angry, I wanted to fuck it out and she preferred to argue.

"There are only two things you do that really piss me off, baby," I said evenly. "One is trying to give me the silent treatment and the other is rolling your eyes."

She looked directly at me and I saw the gears in her head turning. Olivia wasn't a brat, usually she was obedient and loved pleasing me. But occasionally she got in a mood where she just couldn't help herself. And right now, she was in that mood. I cocked my head, narrowing my gaze. Warning her not to push me.

She jutted her chin. And rolled her fucking eyes again.

I spun her around and bent her over the sink. She gasped as my palm contacted her ass, the soft flesh shaking. I spanked her twice and she scowled, pushing her lower lip out. Goddamn, she was in a mood today.

"You're a fucking bad girl, baby," I growled.

She scowled and I turned her back around and gripped her throat, holding her gently in place. The glare she sent me from beneath her bangs was monumental. For a moment, neither of us spoke as our chests heaved, our almost naked bodies barely touching. I wanted my wife badly and I knew she wanted me too, but we were riding a dangerous train very fast toward a place we'd been once. A place I didn't want to go again.

"Olivia," I said quietly.

Her jaw worked.

"You're being a brat."

"Am I supposed to care?"

Fuck me, she had a mouth on her tonight. I slid my hand from her throat to her chin, running my thumb lightly over her lips.

"Do you need your mouth put to a better use than sassing me?"

Her lids flickered and she shook her head, her curls falling around her face. I ran my fingers through her hair and tightened them into a fist against her scalp. She gasped softly as I drew her head back and her gaze went hazy with arousal.

Holding her head, I put my index and middle fingers into her mouth. Her soft lips wrapped around my knuckles and my cock throbbed as I fucked her gently with my fingers. Caressing her hot, wet tongue and teasing the back of her throat until she gagged.

I waited for her to pull away, but she remained as she was, mouth open and eyes locked on me.

"See, you're a good girl," I praised, taking them out.

Her eyes glittered and her chest heaved. The anger seeped out of her slowly and her lashes fell.

"I don't know why I'm so angry, Lucien," she whispered. "I just...I'm just pissed at you. Maybe you should punish me."

I studied her, knowing I needed to be careful. "How would you like that to happen?"

She shrugged. "You can spank me if you'd like."

"No, baby, I'm not going to spank you."

For some reason, that was not the response she wanted. She frowned as if I'd insulted her and slipped out of my grasp and flounced into the bedroom. I followed her as she threw herself onto the bed, crossing her arms over her chest. Angry, mouthy Olivia was back as abruptly as she'd left. I paused, leaning in the bathroom doorway, and studied her, unsure how to proceed.

"Olivia," I said flatly.

She sensed the change in my demeanor and she sat up slowly, her eyes wary.

"I'll punish you and you'll take it and then we won't hear anymore of this fucking conversation. Understood?"

She swallowed as I moved toward her, grasping her by the ankle and dragging her down to the middle of the bed. She gasped as I pulled her to the edge of the bed so her head was hanging off the side. We rarely did this because she still struggled to deepthroat me, but I knew she could do it and if she really wanted to be a good girl, she would.

"You know your safe signal," I said, shoving down the front of my boxer briefs. "Tell me you understand?"

Her mouth trembled as I unleashed my cock, hard and dripping from the tip. I'd been desperate for her since she'd turned me down in the bathroom the day we'd had phone sex. It wouldn't take too long of fucking her perfect throat before I spilled everything into it.

"I understand," she whispered.

"Wet your lips."

She obeyed, her pink tongue darting out.

"Palms flat on the bed at your side, baby," I said gently. "You don't get to come. I don't want to see your fingers go between your thighs or I might reconsider spanking you."

She gave a sharp intake of breath, her eyes still stormy, but this time partly with desire.

I jerked my cock slowly over her face. "Maybe I won't spank your ass, maybe I'll make you hold your legs open while I spank your cunt."

She moaned, her eyes rolling back.

"Fuck, you're such a whore," I said. "Open your mouth."

She obeyed and I slid my length into her throat, pausing when I hit resistance. She tensed, gagging a little as I pushed her limits with short, gentle thrusts.

"Swallow for me," I breathed. "I'm fucking your throat, not your mouth."

She whimpered around my cock and obeyed. I felt her throat contract around the head, pulling it into her until my groin was up against her lips. I wrapped my hand around her neck so I could feel the muscles constrict as she struggled to take me. Then I drew back a little to let her breathe.

She lay there, her hair hanging like a dark waterfall, her body so beautifully curvy and naked on the silk sheets, and let me thrust into her throat. All the anger was gone in this moment, dissipated in the face of something so raw and intimate.

Her thighs twitched and her fingers clenched as she fought not to touch herself. I knew she must be soaked, her pretty pussy swollen and needy between her legs. But I had to deny her—she'd been such a bad girl and she needed to earn back the right to come.

Heat moved slowly down my spine and my dick went rock hard, filling her past her limits. Pleasure shot down my spine and I came, pumping into her throat in short strokes, biting back the heavy moan that rose in my chest. When I pulled from her, she swallowed even though I'd bypassed her mouth, and rolled onto her stomach.

Her eyes watered, little streaks of leftover makeup staining her cheeks. I ran my fingertips over her swollen lips as she struggled to catch her breath.

"Get down on your knees and clean me off, baby," I ordered.

She obeyed at once, her fingers digging into the fronts of my thighs. Her wet tongue dragged over my softening length. The last bit of cum slipped from me and she caught it in her mouth, her lids flickering.

"Show me," I said.

She put out her tongue and there was a faint, pale sheen across it.

"Swallow."

She obeyed and I stroked her head, savoring the sight of her on her knees.

"Good girl," I praised softly.

CHAPTER ELEVEN

OLIVIA

Lucien was my weakest point, even when I was angry with him. And being on my knees at his feet, his lean fingers stroking through my hair wasn't helping. Warmth simmered in my stomach and arousal pounded a steady drumbeat through my pussy. It got me so wet when he dominated me like this, even while it scared me a little, and I was a slick mess between my legs.

"Lucien," I whispered.

"What is it, baby?"

His voice was soft, but his eyes were so cold they sent a shiver down my spine. He stroked down my jaw, his thumb running back and forth across my bottom lip.

"May I come too?"

His mouth thinned and he shook his head. Anger resurfaced and I felt my brows scrunch together as my fists clenched against my sides.

"Fine, I'll do it myself," I said under my breath.

He reached down and lifted me to my feet and his hand encircled my throat.

"What was that?"

I tilted back my chin and met his gaze. After all, he was always telling me not to be afraid, to keep my head high and my shoulders back.

"I can do it myself," I said, shrugging.

"I will restrain your wrists."

"You wouldn't."

His mouth twitched and he released me, heading to the bathroom. When he returned, he was dressed in gray pants and a white button up, rolled to his elbows. The man who held my throat and guided me while he fucked it was gone, replaced by the ice king, dressed in the pale shades of his kingdom. My fingers clenched involuntarily as he drew closer.

"Olivia."

"Yes?"

"Lie down and open your legs."

There was no room for protest in his tone. Heart pounding, I sat on the edge of the bed and lowered myself onto my back. His lean fingers pressed my thighs apart and he knelt between them, bending his head. I could hear my blood pumping, I could feel the tension build in my sex until the pressure was almost painful.

"Fuck, you made a mess," he murmured.

His hot tongue slid out and ran down the inside of my thigh, all the way up to my pussy. He repeated the motion, again and again, until all the arousal was cleaned from my inner thighs and I was whimpering aloud. Then his fingers came up and parted my soaked folds, baring the most intimate part of me to his gaze.

When his tongue flicked over my entrance, I had to bite my lip to keep from crying out. My lower back arced as it dragged up to my clit. He lapped slowly over my sex, cleaning the arousal from me, and then he drew back. I was so close, my clit pulsing from his touch. He gave a flat, cold laugh as I whimpered, pushing my sex up to his mouth.

"We're done."

"Wh—what?"

"You try and make yourself come," he said, an edge to his voice. "And I'll make you fucking sorry, baby."

My mouth fell open and dead silence reigned, so intense my ears rang. He got to his feet, gathered his jacket, and left the room. My entire body burned and tingled, unsure whether to be angry or aroused. There had been an edge to those words that made my heart pound.

Maybe he was under too much pressure for me to push him the way I had.

I heard the Tesla pull from the drive as I peeled myself from the bed. My body felt weak as it always did after weathering the storm that was Lucien. The floor was cold as I padded into the bathroom and turned on the shower and went to take a long look at myself in the mirror.

My mouth was swollen and red in the left corner. That was normal, I had sensitive skin that marked easily. He'd left pink marks on my throat as well, despite his grip being gentle. The sight sent a desperate pulse down my body that burned between my legs.

Surely Lucien would never know if I just slipped the shower head between my legs. The idea of rebelling was exciting, but I knew my husband too well. The moment he took my panties down later, he would know if I'd come or not. He knew my pussy better than his own body. He could always tell when I got myself off, even if it was hours ago.

Resentment boiling in my chest, I showered, shaved, and rubbed my body down with my most expensive lotion. Whenever I was angry with Lucien, I made it my life's goal to spend as much of his money as possible even though he never responded the way I wanted him to. At least it would give me some satisfaction and take my mind off our fight.

I put on a black, lace teddy and high waist jeans, knowing full well Lucien wouldn't approve of my outfit. Then I slipped on my white pea coat and heeled boots and had my driver take me into the city. In my handbag was the credit card he left me and I intended on seeing if he'd put a limit on it.

I went to the spa first and got a massage and had my nails done. Then I got a blowout and had my makeup done at the salon next door. Just down the street was a high end lingerie boutique and I spent the next two hours picking out dozens of pieces. Lace bras and corsets, velvet panties, teddies with real gemstones between the bust, silken stockings that felt like butter sliding up my legs. I racked the credit card bill up to six thousand and then I had a coffee while my driver piled the gift bags into the trunk of the car.

I went to the Esposito family's jeweler and bought a pearl necklace, bracelet, and a set of earrings. Lucien never bought pearls—he thought they were cheap compared to diamonds. But I loved them so I decided to add a second set of black pearls as well, bringing the bill even higher.

It was getting late so I had a dinner of sashimi at my favorite sushi restaurant, which added another two hundred dollars to the card. On the way home, I leaned my head against the window and watched the lights flick by and wondered if perhaps I'd made a mistake.

Maybe I was pushing him too far.

He was gone till late and that pissed me off. I left all the bags spread out over our bedroom, stacked on the dresser, and lined up on the vanity. Then I changed into one of my new silk slips, a sapphire blue number with black lace that brushed the top of my thighs. I settled into bed with a cup of tea and a book, deciding that I didn't care what happened when he got home.

I heard the Tesla pull up and several minutes later, his footfalls echoed in the hallway. Then he walked into the bedroom and stopped, his eyes flickering over the room. His face remained stoic.

"How was your day?" I asked, not lifting my eyes from my book.

He closed the door and pulled off his suit jacket, rolling up his sleeves. My heart began thumping as he circled the bed and sat down, taking the book from my hands and setting it aside.

"Baby," he said.

"What?" I scowled.

"You're not being reasonable."

I wanted to argue with him, but I knew he was right. I was tired and frustrated, stressed out by everything that was going on. My fingers picked at the blanket idly as he gazed at me as if he wasn't sure what to do with me. Finally he stood up and sighed shortly.

"I don't care if you spend my money," he said. "But nice try though."

I sniffed. "I just thought maybe some retail therapy would help me feel less...angry."

"I think it would if you did it for the right reasons," he said.

Tears stung the corners of my eyes, but I was determined not to cry. Especially not after I'd lashed out and spent several thousand dollars. He brushed my tears away and got up, stepping into the closet for a moment. When he returned I saw him slip something into his pocket.

"What was that?"

"Your credit card," he said. "From now on, you can ask me for cash and I will let you know what you need to do to get it."

Heat flooded through my body and crept up my neck, staining my cheeks pink. Part of me wanted to accept the olive branch he was throwing me, knowing full well how much giving him sexual favors for money would turn me on. But the other part of me, the ugly part that I always struggled against, wasn't ready to give up the fight.

"Are you serious?" I whispered.

His eyes narrowed. The tiniest amount.

"Deadly."

"Fine," I snapped.

"Olivia."

"What?"

He paused in the bathroom doorway. "Watch your mouth or I'll fuck it."

I gaped at him and he sent me a look that clearly indicated the conversation was over. Seething, I rolled onto my side and turned out the light. I should have known I'd taken the wrong route for revenge. Lucien didn't care about money, he cared about me and my body. The only way to really get a rise out of him was to make him jealous, but we'd both agreed not to play with that kind of fire again.

I might be angry, but I still cared about my marriage and I loved my husband.

I was half asleep when the bathroom door opened and he slid into bed beside me. His body was warm and firm, the lines of his muscles familiar as he moved up against me. I kept still as his mouth pressed against the back of my neck. Hot and gentle. Coaxing me to turn.

"You awake?" he murmured.

"Yes." My voice was audible.

"Good," he said. "Because I'm going to give you what you wanted good and hard."

He slid beneath the bedclothes so his head was just a rise beneath them and I felt his breath ghost down my side. I rolled onto my back and my thighs brushed the sides of his face and his tongue seared hot over my sex. Heart pounding, I pushed the bedclothes aside so I could watch him tease my pussy.

"You can be such a bad girl," he murmured. "But you're so fucking pretty. I didn't think I cared about this shit—lace and silk and perfume—until I saw it on your body and now...it drives me insane."

My breath caught and he swiped his tongue over my clit.

"Maxing out your credit card was a fucking stupid way to get revenge. Spoiling you just gets me hard," he said.

He bent and covered my clit with his talented mouth, his finger slipping into my pussy and working my G-spot. My hips lifted as an orgasm burst to the surface, pounding through me in hot waves. I cried out softly and he pulled his finger out and licked my entrance clean. Making sure not to waste anything.

"If this is your way of getting revenge, it's pretty fucking stupid too," I gasped.

His mouth twitched, his intense eyes following my legs as I squeezed them together, locking my ankles. I saw his throat bob as he studied my feet and he reached out to run the tip of his middle finger under the arch.

"No, that orgasm was because I'm a fucking nice person," he said. "The rest are to remind you who owns your pretty, champagne-tasting cunt."

I blinked. "My what?"

He bent, kissing my mouth hard enough to bruise it. "Nothing. Shut the fuck up and open your legs."

Cowed and aroused, I obeyed without question. He stayed between my thighs, licking, sucking, eating, until I'd come three more times and my body tingled with overstimulation. When I hit a wall with his mouth and fingers and couldn't finish anymore, he went to the dresser and took out a pair of vibrators. My sex was so sensitive when he pushed one inside me that I cried out and wetness slipped down my ass and onto the bed. He bent, licking around the vibrator, and gave a soft growl of satisfaction.

"Expensive champagne," he breathed.

"Oh, I get it now," I panted.

Ignoring me, he pressed the second vibrator to my clit and turned them both on. My body arced and he laughed, a short, unnatural sound. A fourth and fifth orgasm rolled through me, making my vision pulse and my jaw go stiff from chanting his name.

There was nothing left in me, but he was relentless. He adjusted the angle of the internal vibrator slightly and it pushed up against my G-spot. A sudden, burning sensation, like I needed to orgasm and empty my bladder at the same time started deep inside. Those cold, dead eyes locked on mine, he turned the vibrator on my clit all the way up.

I barely felt the orgasm that washed through me, I was so overstimulated, but I did feel something gush between my legs in a warm torrent. Horrified, I shot upright and flicked on the light, bathing the bed in a dim glow. The front of Lucien's sweatpants and the silk sheets were soaked. There was an expression of satisfaction on his face, indicated only by the slight upward tilt of his mouth.

"Did I—" I stammered, flushing. "Is that...did I pee the bed?"

He tilted his head, looking down at the stain.

"Maybe," he said smugly. "Either way, I'm fucking hard from it."

"Lucien!"

"You just squirted, baby, you've done it before. Just not...so much."

Head spinning, I ran to the bathroom to wipe my legs down, but he followed me, bending my body over the sink with one firm, tattooed hand. I barely had time to grip the silver faucet to steady myself before his cock was inside me, thrusting hard. Pounding into me until I whimpered, unable to remember what words were or how to use them.

When he emptied himself into me with a noise of satisfaction, I was an incoherent mess, my eyes running and my hair tangled around his fist. He cleaned us both up and carried me back to the bed, putting a towel over the wet spot before placing me on my back. His lean fingers grazed my forehead, brushing my sweaty bangs back.

I lay there, my legs like water, remembering why I shouldn't antagonize him the way I had today.

"Sometimes I forget that you're like this," I whispered.

He gathered my body against his. "Like what?"

"This."

There was a short silence and I felt him relax against me as he stroked my hip. We were both spent, all the fight worked out of us at least until the morning.

"Think about that next time you want to act up," he murmured. "I can fight hard, but I can fuck a lot harder."

CHAPTER TWELVE

LUCIEN

Rosario Barone was a dead man walking.

A week after I'd been released from the hospital, I stood in my uptown office waiting for Cosimo. My shoulders were tense and there was a sore muscle running up the side of my neck. It had been a hot and cold week with Olivia. We went from arguing to fucking in a matter of minutes, sometimes mixing the two together. Then we apologized and made up and things would be good until the cycle started all over again.

She was back to taking her birth control. She thought I didn't know, but I wasn't an idiot. It was fucking obvious when she slipped into the bathroom at the same time every evening.

It pissed me off she hadn't discussed it with me first. But I also knew I didn't have the right to tell her not to, nor did I disagree with her choice. I needed to resolve the threat of Rosario Barone before we brought another child into our home.

Cosimo's motorcycle sounded from the street and I looked down to see him park it and pull his helmet off. He strode up the sidewalk and disappeared through the front doors. A moment later, Duran pulled up on the curb and followed him inside.

They entered the office, talking quietly in Italian. When they saw I was already waiting for them, they stopped speaking abruptly. Cosimo set his helmet aside and flopped down in the chair opposite my desk. Duran went to the corner and started making himself an espresso.

"Do we need Peregrine for this meeting," Cosimo asked.

I shook my head. Duran crossed his arms, leaning on the coffee bar. There were dark circles under his eyes and his hair was tousled. I studied him for a moment, wondering what was going on that made him so tired. Comparatively, Duran had an easy job in the outfit. He wasn't a competitive person and he preferred passing on promotions over giving up time with Iris. He worked for money so he could enjoy his life and sometimes I envied his simplicity.

"There is a fundraiser this weekend for a city councilman," Duran said. "It would be an opportune time to scout the landscape and have a chance to speak with the incumbent mayor. I think you should take Olivia and go as a guest."

"I think she's already going to represent her foundation. Will her father be there?"

Duran nodded.

"I'm not fucking letting her go alone then," I said. "I'll have to speak with her. Maybe she should stay back."

Duran's jaw worked. "I understand. But it'll look strange if you're there without Olivia."

Cosimo cleared his throat. "What if I go with Lorenza?"

"You don't have strong ties to the political class in the city," Duran said.

"Neither do you."

"I never suggested I go."

"We can send Peregrine." Cosimo shrugged. "It's kind of his job."

"No," I said quickly. "This issue is personal and I need to be there, especially if Olivia intends on going. It's a delicate situation."

There was a short silence and I noticed Cosimo's eyes were on the ground and his thumb was tapping the seat rapidly. Duran's brow rose and he jerked his head and I winced inwardly, remembering that Rosario wasn't just my wife's father.

"Do you want to discuss this issue privately, Cosimo?"

He shook his head. "I'm done with my father's bullshit. After finding out...the things that went on with Olivia, I really don't care what you do to him anymore."

His voice was thick. I was aware of his conflicting feelings, although I didn't understand them. My father was similar to his and I hadn't felt an ounce of regret when I removed his head from his body.

But then not everyone was as fucked up as I was. I knew Olivia, despite having been starved and abused by her parents, was still having a difficult time with the prospect of allowing me to eliminate Rosario.

"Alright," I said. "I'll go to the party. With Olivia. If this is the event I think it is, she has to be there anyway for the foundation."

"Better talk to Peregrine about securing an invite today," said Duran. "It's coming up fast."

Cosimo stood, flicking his wrist to check his watch. "Well, that was resolved fast. Do you need me for anything else? I have another meeting in a bit and I'd like to get something to eat first."

"You're fine to go," I said. "But stop on the way out and ask my secretary if she can get in contact with Peregrine."

Cosimo nodded and strode from the room, his helmet tucked under his arms. Duran made another espresso and sat opposite me, staring vacantly at the wall. I snapped my laptop shut and fixed him with a critical stare.

"What's going on with you?"

He shook his head. "Nothing."

"You're exhausted," I pointed out.

He hesitated and leaned forward, resting his elbow on his knees. When he met my gaze, there was a strange expression in his eyes. It was a mix of excitement and nerves.

"Iris is pregnant," he said quietly.

"Congratulations," I said carefully, trying to read him before I said anything else. Iris and Duran had gotten married seven years ago and they'd never mentioned wanting children, so I'd assumed it wasn't part of their future plans.

"It's a good thing," Duran said.

"That's good."

"It's a girl," he said.

I frowned. "How far along is Iris?"

"Twenty-two weeks," he said. "We were going to wait to tell anyone until after we found out what she was having. It was pretty easy because she only just started showing so she's been wearing big sweaters. Also, she's been pretty sick and hasn't been able to sleep at night so we've just been working on getting through that."

"It gets better as you go," I said. "Then it gets harder."

"At least sitting up all night with Iris is preparing me for being up with the baby," he said. "I don't think I've ever consumed this much espresso in my life."

I considered him for a moment. "Why don't you go home and sleep. Nothing you have on your plate right now is that pressing."

His brow rose. "Why has benevolent Lucien made an appearance today?"

"I'm actually in a fucking bad mood," I admitted. "I'm trying to knock up Olivia, but all this bullshit with Rosario has us fighting all the time and now she's back on her birth control. Fucking pisses me off."

"That...she's back on the pill?"

"No, that I can't just have things be normal for a minute."

Duran stared at me for a moment and then he laughed. I felt my brow twitch violently and I resisted the urge to scowl at him. It annoyed me when he didn't take me seriously. Most of the time, I liked my younger brother, but occasionally he could be a little shit. I crossed my legs and lit a cigarette, waiting for him to get a hold on himself.

"You have never once actually wanted normality," he said. "Not for a fucking second."

"What?"

"You love chaos," he said. "You'd shrivel up and die if you didn't have some evil plot running a hundred miles a minute in your head. You love it when the world goes up in flames around you. It's when you do your best work."

I wasn't sure how to respond to this, so I kept quiet.

"You thrive in chaos." Duran's eyes grew distant. "I don't think I ever saw you more alive than the day after you killed our father."

My body froze and our eyes locked across the desk. Up until this point, I'd assumed that Duran was ignorant of what I'd done, that he'd believed what they reported in the paper. But as he fixed his dark gaze on me, I realized that I'd never had him fooled.

"How long have you known?"

"Um...since the day after you killed him."

"And that...didn't bother you?"

"I prefer to think about it differently," he said, shrugging. "I was a kid and you did what had to be done to protect me from abuse. Our father was an abusive, volatile rapist. He had it coming. Whatever your other motivations were in killing him, I didn't care to know."

I opened my mouth.

"And I still don't," Duran said firmly.

I fell quiet, warring emotions in my chest. Of course Duran had known what I'd done. He pretended to be the carefree younger brother, but he saw everything. Five years ago, he'd been the first person to really see that Olivia was in love with me and that I was hurting her with my jealousy. Maybe I should pay more attention to the things he said.

I cleared my throat. "Does Iris need anything?"

"She needs her morning sickness to clear up so she can get her strength back," said Duran, sighing. "But it's not anything you can help with."

"Olivia had it badly up until she was twenty-five weeks along," I said. "All she ate was frozen fruit and jello for weeks."

"Iris has been throwing up water since day one, but last week she was able to keep down tea and toast," he said. "So that's all she's eating."

I got to my feet and crossed the room to where my coat hung. "There's not much you can do other than ask the doctor for some medicine for her. I know you want to help her and it's eating you up that you can't."

Duran sighed and followed me out into the hallway. "Listen, don't mention this to anyone. We're not ready to announce yet."

I nodded and we moved downstairs and Duran strode from the building and disappeared down the street. My mind was moving fast, thinking about what he'd said about me. That I was at my best when I was planning, scheming, building something.

I thrived when I was going after power.

Standing here in the luxurious lobby of my office in a city that I'd threatened, paid off, and charmed into getting under my thumb, it struck me that I was bored.

Maybe that was part of the reason Olivia and I hadn't been getting along. She always swore she didn't like the darker side of me…and yet, nothing had turned her on more than seeing me after I'd killed Romano.

Maybe we both just needed some excitement.

A common goal.

I felt the corner of my mouth turn up. Perhaps my wife couldn't admit it, but she was a bloodthirsty, little thing sometimes. She liked pretty things just as much as I craved power and control. She just preferred for the ugly parts to happen behind closed doors so she didn't have to think about them.

It was nightfall and snow had blanketed the city when I finally left the office and took the highway back to the river. As I pulled up to the driveway, I could see that Olivia had had the house decorated for Christmas.

Through the window, the enormous tree glittered white and blue. The doors were adorned with bright, silvery wreaths and lights were strung along the gutters. I parked the Tesla in the garage and walked across the dark, snowy driveway and unlocked the front door.

The hall was silent. I moved quietly upstairs to check on the nursery and found Marco fast asleep, his stuffed animal tucked under his arm. There was a light on under his nanny's door, indicating that she was spending the night. I grazed my hand over my son's back, bending to press my lips to his temple. He stirred and rolled over as I closed the door and moved up the hall to my bedroom.

The gas fireplace was burning, but the room was empty. The bed was still made and the bathroom was dark. Usually Olivia would be curled up with a book and a cup of tea, filling the room with her soft presence and the sweet scent of her damp hair after a shower. I scanned the room, thrown off, and turned on my heel. Perhaps she was downstairs making herself a snack.

The kitchen was dark, closed down for the night. I made my way around the house, checking my office, checking both downstairs living rooms. My wife was nowhere to be seen.

I called Lorenza. There was a scuffle on the other end and Cosimo picked up.

"Enza's tied up with something. What's up?"

"Is Olivia with you?" I asked.

"No," he said. "Why? Is she not with you?"

"The house was locked, the nanny is here, everything is normal," I said. "But she's not here."

"What did you do to her?"

There was an edge to his voice that I didn't like. It bothered me that after all this time, my wife's brother still didn't trust me not to hurt her. I walked into the back hallway, entering the dark corridor and paused. She'd decorated it with silver lights and candles in each window. It was a silvery wonderland, swathed in shadows, and it took me back to that night I'd let my jealousy get the better of me. The night I'd chased her up the stairs and fucked her before the mirror. The night I'd found out where the line was.

I knew then where she'd disappeared to.

"I think I found her," I said. "If I didn't, I'll call you. Otherwise, assume everything is fine."

"Alright," Cosimo said. "Don't be a dick to her, please."

I hung up the phone and slipped it in my pocket. At the end of the hall was a set of double doors that led to the ballroom. It was a huge space with marble floors for dancing and a glass ceiling I'd had made in the likeness of the Starlight Room in Viktor's house in Russia. The ceiling was made up of dozens of crystal panes that let in the stars glittering overhead. The walls were floor-to-ceiling windows that looked out over acres of snowy fields.

I moved down the hall in the dark and pushed the door ajar, stepping inside.

The room was chilly from disuse. Across the dizzying black and white pattern of the floor, beneath the starlight falling through the glass overhead, stood my wife. She had her back to me, facing the window and the record player before her, her finger trailing over the top.

She heard my steps and she set the record into place and adjusted the needle. Then she turned and a hot, ripple of desire moved down my spine and pooled in my groin.

There had never been any doubt in my mind, at any point, that my wife was the most beautiful woman who had ever lived. She was my Helen of Troy, a woman for whom I'd launch a thousand ships and burn down an empire. And every time I saw her like this, I realized it all over again.

Her beauty when she made love with me was soft and yielding. Her beauty when she went to war with me was a steel weapon. It sank between my ribs to my ice cold heart and cut me down to my knees.

And right now, she was a right on the edge of both. Sharp as a blade, but still willing to yield for me.

"Olivia," I said.

"Lucien," she said, cocking her head.

I kept my face impassive as I moved across the room and paused. Looking down at her lovely face. She'd put on that black dress, the replica of the one she'd worn to the Bolshoi theater all those years ago.

The soft fabric clung to her skin, the bodice showing a shocking amount of her breasts. The only thing it really covered were her soft, brown nipples. I cocked my head, wondering why I'd ever let her leave the house like that. She was devastating, too beautiful for regular people to lay eyes on.

"What is this?" I asked.

She swallowed and her slender throat bobbed. Her eyes were almost black in the crystal light of the chandelier and her lowered lashes were thick with blue and silver makeup. Her mouth was painted deep red, giving me flashbacks of all the times she'd left it smeared under the zipper of my pants.

Fuck, I was breaking. My resistance was weakening. I felt it splinter as I gripped her neck and pulled her close.

"No," she said softly.

"What?"

"Dance with me, Mr. Esposito."

Her voice was barely a whisper. She turned and walked to the center of the room, her hips swaying gently. She'd taken dance lessons to try to keep up with me and she'd done remarkably well. She had a natural talent for it and she improved quickly. But we'd fallen into the usual trap of our busy lives and we rarely danced together anymore.

My muscle memory took over as I stripped my jacket and rolled my sleeves up to my forearms. She watched, her eyes glittering and her full mouth parted. I knew she liked what she saw, I knew that between her thighs was a gathering wetness.

Fuck, I'd slide into her so easily after this.

The record fell silent as I slid my hand up her back and pulled her against my body. Her back lengthened and her heat crackled up my body. Warming me beneath the collar and down to my groin. From the record player came a single note from a violin. An Argentine tango.

Of course it was.

I made her wait for the first beat, then the second, then I made her fucking work for it. Her legs spun as I moved her across the floor and I noticed that she wore the gold anklet with my initial on it. Pride flooded my chest as I watched her spin on her toes, glittering so brightly I forgot there were stars in the sky overhead.

She fell back into my arms and I kissed her, pulling her back into the dance. The room swirled around us until it was nothing but a blur of darkness and warm bodies, until the only thing that existed was my wife and the beat of the music in our veins.

The music paused for a second.

Her eyes snapped to mine. Big, soft, and a little wounded.

"I know you're planning on killing my father," she whispered. "I know you'd never allow him to live if he's p lanning on challenging you."

"I don't give a shit he's challenging me," I said. "But I do think I'll kill him because he made my wife cry."

"What happens?" she whispered. "What happens if you don't kill him?"

I spun her, flipping her back over my knee. Her breasts strained against the front of her dress, barely an inch from my mouth.

So fucking distracting.

"He makes things very messy for us."

I flipped her up and pulled her back against me. Her spine arced, her ass brushing my groin. My cock twitched, roused once more by the lightest brush of her body.

"No, what really happens?"

She was so close to me, her hot breath against my collarbone, as I danced her back across the room to the center. The beat stuttered and she wrapped her leg around mine. I could barely feel the heat of her skin, but it was still pure paradise.

"He becomes mayor," I said softly. "He spills all our secrets. Then it's war. I would send you and Marco away and I would kill him. Or die trying."

She inhaled and I spun her back against my chest, my hands sliding up the sides of her body. For a second, my palms rested in the air less than a centimeter from her breasts. Then she spun to face me and I pulled her close, gripping her wrist. Making her dance backwards in a series of lightning fast movements before I abruptly pulled her against my chest.

"What happens if you do kill him?"

Her leg slid up, cocking around my waist. Her dress fell back to expose the flesh of her thigh and I glanced down at the tantalizing darkness beneath her skirt. The little rise of her sex pushed up into my inner thigh and I ached for her, wanting nothing more than to throw her down and sink inside her.

"Then he's dead," I breathed.

Her lashes fluttered.

"How can I live with myself if I let you kill him?" Her eyes were wide and glistening with shed tears. "I can't spend the rest of my life knowing I was partially responsible for my father's death, despite everything he's done. It's just...it's a point of no return."

"You just live with it," I said. "Sometimes you fucking revel in it."

Her mouth parted, glossy red. "Lucien, I'm not like you."

"Thank God for that."

"I can't just kill people and live with it," she gasped. "I'm not that person."

"Oh, I'll bet you fucking could be," I said. "So long as it doesn't ruin your manicure, you'd love it."

She gasped, fire surging in her gaze. I spun her out and let her go, watching the black chiffon of her skirt swirl around her hips and thighs. She had a second to recover her footing before I gripped her waist and lifted her and flipped her leg up onto my shoulder. The faint scent of her arousal filled my senses and I pulsed painfully, my mouth so close to paradise.

She gasped as I dropped her, catching her body at the last minute, and bringing her up against me again. My hand slipped down and pushed between her thighs. A ripple of surprise hit me as my fingers contacted the slick heat of her pussy.

"I'm not wearing panties," she whispered.

"Fuck me," I demanded. "Now."

She whirled and my arms locked around her, pulling our spines straight into position.

"No."

"No?"

"No, I won't fuck you tonight."

She was a fucking tease. My fingers tightened as I moved her across the floor, hard and fast. Spinning her, letting my feelings be known in the grip of my fingers.

"If you want to protect Marco, you'll make this choice," I said.

"You can't throw that at me, Lucien."

"I can and I will. You can take it."

"Lucien—"

I gripped her wrists, pulling her so close I could taste her breath on my lips.

"You're his mother. It's your duty to do what you must to keep him safe, just as it's mine. I've never sugarcoated a fucking thing with you, Olivia, and I'm not about to start now."

Her eyes glistened.

"I can't take this, Lucien," she said, her voice cracking.

"You've taken a hell of a lot worse, baby. Be a big girl for me," I said. "Put the knife in my hand and I'll do the dirty work."

CHAPTER THIRTEEN

OLIVIA

He was giving me a choice, but at the same time, he was forcing me to bloody my hands. I should have known I wouldn't find sympathy with him. He'd always been like this, from the first moment I'd laid eyes on his ice cold face. But I would never escape it because I loved him so deeply it hurt, so deeply that over the last week, it had felt like my soul was being torn just to fight with him.

But this...this was crossing a line.

And yet, I still craved him. My body was on fire under his lean, tattooed hands. He was slick with sweat, his white shirt sticking to his chest and the hard ridges down his stomach. The top buttons were undone, revealing the skeleton wings inked across his pectorals.

Lucien had taken all of my firsts. He'd been my first kiss, the first and only man to see me naked. He'd taken my virginity on our wedding night and I'd willingly given it to him because without knowing it in that moment, I already belonged to him.

No one could ever love me like he did. Our bodies fit together perfectly. We'd both felt it the first time we'd slid between the sheets together, despite not loving each other then. I had no experience outside of him, but I knew that there was no one else in the world who could make me feel the things he did.

I'd been innocent then, isolated from the complications of sex. But all it had taken was that night when he'd admitted he'd decapitated his father. When he'd taken the last thing I had to give up and fucked me in front of the mirror. That was the moment I'd realized what kind of man I had tied myself to.

He was the devil in disguise.

I'd come to realize that the devil was a gentleman. The devil wore charcoal gray suits, he drank expensive whiskey, he spoke French and Italian. He danced like a gentleman and, when the occasion called for it, he could fuck like one too.

Although, most of the time, there was nothing gentlemanly about the things he did.

I shivered, realizing that only I knew all of the things he'd done. Everyone else just saw Lucien Esposito, the city's millionaire bad boy, the man groomed for the public eye.

The man who held me in his arms was mine alone to contend with.

Only I had given him everything and tied myself to him forever. My husband was Lucien, the monster. The gentleman, the ice cold devil who fucked like sin and killed without remorse.

But he was the devil I needed more than anything else in this world or the next. The devil I couldn't breathe without.

"Give me time," I gasped.

The song ended and another began. This one was a slow tango, drenched with desire as it filled the room. He sank to his knees and lifted my leg to drape it over his shoulder. Our eyes locked and he bent slowly, the light glinting off his dark, slicked hair.

"Lucien," I breathed.

"It's my pussy."

"It's mine too."

He didn't speak, but his eyes glinted and he dipped his head between my thighs and pressed a brief kiss to my clit. Heat blossomed and I bit back a gasp as he darted the tip of his tongue out. Flicking it once before he lifted his head.

"Just a taste, baby," he said, his voice thick and coaxing.

"Not yet. Please, Lucien."

He relented, standing in a graceful movement and lifting me off my feet. We danced across the floor, our bodies so near, despite the barrier between our minds. The music paused for a beat. He was close, smelling of sweat and the clean scent that always followed him. His chest heaved, flushed between his collarbones.

His barren, dead eyes dragged over my face and lingered on my mouth.

I met his gaze head-on. "I won't kill my father."

He spun out and back in, gripping my shoulders. We stood frozen in the middle of the room as the music played on. His gaze bored into me, never relenting, and I shivered beneath his touch.

"You don't have to. Leave that to me."

"It's all the same thing."

"I am asking you out of respect, not because your answer will stop me."

Anger flared through my chest and I stepped back, but he held me still.

"You don't respect me," I spat. "This is fucking disrespectful. We're done here."

He began dancing again, sweeping me into his arms as though I hadn't spoken. His expression was impassive as we spun, but a muscle twitched in his jaw. Finally his gaze broke from me, fixing above my head.

"We are done when I say we're done," he said finally.

He pulled me against his hard body and I bent my leg around his waist, staining his pants with the wetness on my inner thigh. His eyes didn't lift from my face. I could tell he was deep in thought, but I found I didn't want to know what was going on inside that head.

I never truly did.

Lucien lived in a different world than I did, a world of blood, ice, and steel. When he came home at night, he left it all behind and we met beneath the white flag of our shared roof.

I needed that divide.

He bent me back until I was looking up at the ceiling and his mouth traced my cleavage. Scorchingly hot. We paused for a beat, both breathing hard.

"You're back on the pill."

I swallowed, guilt filling my chest. I'd taken it for a bit, but two days ago I'd run out and I hadn't called in my next month's supply. The fact that I'd shut him out of making the decision in the first place ate away at me, so I'd intended on telling him he should wear a condom if he no longer wanted to get me pregnant.

But every time I'd gotten drunk on his touch and completely forgotten to bring it up.

"I'm not," I breathed.

He stiffened.

"Don't fucking lie to me."

He pulled me upright and his gaze bored into me.

"I ran out two days ago."

His mouth twitched and he spun me back against him, dipping me forward so my leg slid back between his. Then he dropped me and this time, I thought he really was going to let me fall.

At the last minute, he caught me and flipped me in midair, clasping me in his lean arms. I fell into his chest, gasping. Heart hammering against my ribs. For a second, like a shadow passing through his face, I thought I saw a hint of vulnerability. He bent and his mouth grazed mine, giving me the faintest taste of him.

I strained after him as he pulled back. He clicked his tongue once.

"Needy," he said.

I winced. "You're so cruel sometimes, Lucien."

"You've always known what I am and it makes you so fucking wet for me."

We danced back across the floor as sweat trickled down my spine. I was going to have to get this dress dry cleaned.

"Give me time," I breathed. "Let me decide if I can do this."

"You can do it, baby."

I hated him in that moment, even though I loved him so much. He was so callous, so unfeeling, all the soft parts of him cut back like the dead limbs on my rose bushes in my garden.

When he got an idea in his head, he was like a bullet from a gun. Brutal, relentless, and deadly.

Unforgiving.

"If I begged you not to, would you let him live?"

"Why?" he asked, shaking his head. "Why beg for him? He did nothing but abuse you. Your parents only hurt you, Olivia, they fucked you up so badly you're still trying to dig your way out."

"They're still my blood," I whispered.

"Blood doesn't ensure mercy," he said.

"For you, perhaps not."

"What does that mean?"

He knelt and I draped my leg over his shoulder and we paused as the music slowed and flipped to the next song. He was between my thighs again, looking up at me, his fingers digging into my hips, holding me in his hard palms.

"You are a son who killed his own father in his bed. You're a murderer, Lucien," I whispered. "I'm not."

His lids flickered.

"And you're a woman who fucks a murderer," he said. "And loves it, judging by the sounds you make when I have you on your back."

My eyes stung and I swallowed, letting my head fall back. My fists clenched at my sides as I attempted not to be hurt. He sensed that he'd crossed a line and he rose, pulling me against him, and cradled my chin.

"Don't cry," he breathed.

I ran a hand over my face. "You're making me cry."

He cradled my head, turning my chin up. He had a stern expression on his face that drove me crazy. Not in a bad way, in a way that made me want to drag him upstairs so he could fuck me slowly in the dark so I didn't have to see his cold eyes while he praised me.

I steeled myself, ignoring my traitorous body.

"I'm sorry," he said stiffly. He still had trouble apologizing. "For being cruel. But I don't necessarily take back anything I said."

It was all too much. Hands shaking, I pulled from his arms and made a dash for the door, but he caught my wrist. My body tightened, trying to wrestle away, but his grip was relentless.

"I don't need your blessing to do what needs done," he said. "But I want it, out of respect."

"I'm...not ready to give it," I gasped.

He released me and I ran, my heels clattering down the hall. In our bedroom, I put on my slip before padding down the hall to the guestroom and curled up in the twin bed there. I was almost asleep when I heard the door open and I felt his arms close around me, lifting me and carrying me back to our room.

He laid me down in our bed and pulled the blanket over my shoulders. Indignation rising, I rolled over and glared at him.

"I wanted to sleep in the guestroom tonight," I pouted.

He began unbuttoning his shirt, his eyes like steel.

"Lucien!"

"No," he said flatly.

"No...what?"

"No, you may not sleep in the guestroom," he said, going to the window and opening it so he could light a cigarette. The smoke wreathed his head, drifting from his mouth and nose.

The overwhelming urge to roll my eyes moved over me. He knew exactly what I was thinking and he cocked his head, warning me not to push him. I bit my lip hard, trying to fight the urge to get the last word in.

"Olivia," he said softly.

"What?"

His brow lifted in a rare expression of emotion.

"Fucking behave."

Huffing, I threw myself down on my side with my back to him and pulled the covers up to my chin. He finished his cigarette and the last thing I remembered was hearing him turn on the shower.

CHAPTER FOURTEEN

LUCIEN

The next day, I woke to the soft sensation of her breasts against my chest. The world felt small, like the only thing in it were the four walls of our room and the naked body of my wife. Still half asleep, I flipped her onto her back and slid down her body. Down, down, easing the covers back until she lay exposed.

My brain went blank at the sight.

It was awfully inconvenient having my wife walk around with my biggest weakness between her legs. Like having a loaded gun on her hip, my name carved into the bullet.

I tasted her slowly and her lids flickered, muttering something about wanting to wash before I ate her, but I ignored her sleepy protest.

I liked the taste of her in the morning.

Sweet, natural.

I licked over her silky folds once and she moaned, opening her thighs wide. Giving into me.

Gently so as not to hurt her delicate sex, I made a V with my middle and index fingers and spread her open. There was a pink flush inside the pale brown of her tight pussy.

She was barely wet, a hint of arousal glittering along her cunt. I bent and licked it off and that tangy, expensive champagne taste coated my tongue.

My cock went rock hard.

"Fuck, lick me…daddy," she moaned.

I jerked upright. My erection disappeared as quickly as it had arrived.

"What the fuck did you call me?"

She propped herself on her elbows, her dark hair falling around her face. Right away I could tell she was still pissed about last night.

"Well, you insist on bending me to your will," she said, her voice going hard. "I thought you might like it if I called you that. It seems appropriate."

My jaw worked as I took a deep breath.

"You might want to think carefully before you say anything else, baby."

She reached down and ran her fingers through my hair. Her smile was tauntingly sweet.

"Why?" she breathed. "You don't want to be my daddy? You already order me around like you're my fucking father."

Olivia had a bit of an attitude in the right circumstances, but never in our entire relationship had she mouthed off to me like this. I took a beat to gather myself and moved up her body, pressing her down beneath me. A flicker of unease moved across her face, but she kept her frown stubbornly in place.

I slid my fingers against her scalp, gripping my fist at the root of her silky hair. Holding her head back.

"What do you need, Olivia?" I asked quietly.

"Nothing," she breathed. "Not from you."

I bent until our faces were inches apart. "No, baby, you need something. I'm not meeting your needs or you wouldn't be acting like this. So what the fuck do you need? Do you actually want me to spank you? I'd prefer not to, but you're giving me mixed signals like you're trying to antagonize me into something. Do you need more of a release than orgasm?"

Her lashes fluttered, suddenly wet.

"I'm having trouble reading you," I admitted.

"I don't need anything," she breathed.

"Yes, you do."

Her body shuddered beneath mine and my chest ached. My poor wife, caught like a fly in the web of this cruel world I'd trapped her in. Her breasts heaved, her nipples puckering, and I bent to take them in my mouth. First one and then the other. Licking those pretty, little buds until she began to soften.

Her body shuddered and I looked up, watching as a tear slid from the corner of her eye and disappeared into her hair.

She swallowed, gasping.

"Do you need to just cry it out, baby?" I whispered.

She choked on a sob and nodded. I pulled her into my arms, bracing myself against the headboard, and nestled her in my lap. The tears she'd held back broke free and flowed down her face. Her entire body went limp as she wept into my chest.

I stroked my fingers through her silky hair and let her cry it all out. After a while, her sobs slowed and she ran a hand over her face. I took some tissues out of the bedside table and passed them to her. She sat up slowly and blew her nose and scrubbed away her tears.

"Do you know what's wrong?" I asked. "Or do you need me to help you figure it out?"

She shook her head.

"What is it, baby?" I whispered.

She swallowed. "You have my blessing."

My blood pumped faster and I sat upright, turning her to face me. Her hips were soft beneath my fingers as I pulled her close. I kissed her mouth, still trembling beneath mine. She tasted faintly salty like her tears.

"That's my brave girl," I whispered.

"I hate this, Lucien," she hiccuped.

"I know."

I put on a pair of sweatpants and ran her a hot bath and went downstairs to check on Marco. He was in the kitchen with his nanny, eating breakfast at the table. The sight of his dark, tousled hair, the same color as Olivia's, made my chest clench. Fuck, I had to see this through. I had to protect my wife and son at any cost.

"Do you want to see mamma?" I asked, kneeling down.

"Yeah," he said, looking up. "I'm eating breakfast."

"I can see that."

He handed me his spoon and I took it, scooping up a piece of fruit and holding it out to him. He shook his head, grinning.

"You eat it," he demanded.

I almost shook my head, but then I obliged. He grinned and held out another bit of pineapple and I ate it. For whatever reason, he thought that was hilarious and he cracked up with laughter. I stood, tousling his hair and looked around for his nanny. She stood a few feet away in the hall, talking with our cook.

"Flora," I called.

She leaned in the door. "Yes, sir?"

"What plans did you have for Marco today?"

Flora stepped into the kitchen, wiping her hands on a towel. She was a willowy woman of around thirty with a stern face, but she had the kindest way with Marco that I appreciated.

I didn't want my son growing up the way I had. I wanted him surrounded by people who loved him, people who responded with kindness. I didn't want him to turn out like me. When he was older, he would have to face his legacy, but for now I wanted him to grow up in blissful ignorance.

"Lorenza wanted to take the babies to the zoo," she said. "I told her unless your wife objected, I would be happy to."

I stepped away from Marco and joined her by the stove.

"That would be good," I said, keeping my voice low. "Olivia is going through some things. We have some personal issues going on with her family we're trying to work through. I think it would do her good to have the afternoon to herself. Just let her see Marco before you leave, alright?"

"Of course, sir," she said.

"I'm not trying to burden you with our issues, Flora, I just want you to be aware of what's going on."

She nodded. "I appreciate it, sir."

Honesty with our hired help was a personal policy I'd forced myself to adhere to. Growing up in a volatile and violent house where my father's employees couldn't predict their environment had taught me how important discreet, professional honesty was. I wasn't going to let my home become what my father's had been.

"Are you alright, sir?"

I blinked, shaking my head. "Yes. Let me get my wallet and I'll give you cash for the trip."

"Mr. Barone is paying for it, sir." Her brows were drawn together. "And I have the credit card you gave me when you hired me on."

"Yes, of course." I ran a hand over my hair. "Mrs. Laurel?"

Our cook entered the kitchen, brushing back her graying hair and braiding it behind her ear. She reached for an apron and tied it around her waist. I kissed Marco's head and beckoned Mrs. Laurel out into the hall and closed the door.

"Can you make a breakfast tray for Olivia and an espresso for me to take to work?" I said. "I'm heading out for the morning and I need you to make sure that Olivia eats something."

Her eyes softened. "I understand."

My shoulders were tense as I moved back upstairs. When I returned to the bedroom, Olivia was dressed in a slender, black velvet dress with a dipped neckline. Traces of her breasts rose above the soft material, but it was the curve of her thighs that became her bare calves and then her slender feet. Balanced in her black pumps, my initial hanging against her ankle.

She accepted my kiss, but didn't speak. I showered quickly and dressed in one of my tailored suits. When I returned, she was sitting on the edge of the bed with her hands folded in her lap. The pink had returned to her cheeks and her eyes weren't swollen anymore. I went to her and touched beneath her chin, lifting her face.

"Where are you going looking so beautiful, baby?" I murmured.

"I wanted to go into the city." She blinked innocently. "I thought some retail therapy might help me feel a little better."

I looked around at the boxes and bags still stacked across the dresser and decided now wasn't the time to say anything.

"Whatever you need."

She bit her lip. "May I have some money?"

There was a flush at the base of her throat. I was surprised she wanted to play that game this morning. But who was I to deny my wife anything at all?

I took her purse—one of those fucking tiny bags that costed a ridiculous amount—and laid it aside. Her eyes widened as I dragged my thumb over her lower lip, painted glossy red.

"How much do you need?"

She considered it for a moment.

"Ten thousand."

"Ten thousand," I mused. "You're a fucking spoiled girl."

"I'll pay you for it," she whispered. "Tonight."

"Yes, you will."

She went pink and swallowed. "What would you like for it?"

I pushed my hands in my pockets, looking down at her, waiting for my answer like such a perfect girl. A dozen filthy images tumbled through my brain. There was one thing that got me harder than even her perfect feet, but it wasn't something I asked her for very often.

"I'll fuck your ass," I said. "It's worth ten grand."

Her mouth parted and her eyes widened. For a moment, I saw arousal and something else flicker in her gaze and then she swallowed, dropping her gaze. Her fingers twisted in her lap, covered with diamonds and gold, and manicured with dark red paint. The heavy ring on her finger glittered as she worked it anxiously.

She was so beautiful and spoiled, dressed up in designer clothes and covered with my jewels. She liked pretending she was such a good girl, so elegant and refined, but I knew how she looked when I fucked her ass. Desperate, wanton, makeup running down her face as she came again and again until she was stammering incoherently.

She just couldn't bring herself to admit it.

"Yes," she whispered. "It's a deal."

She put out her hand and I shook it. Then I counted out ten thousand dollars and tucked it into her bra, kissing her mouth before straightening. I felt her eyes on me as I left the room and I had to wait in the hall for my erection to calm down before I could go downstairs.

A hour later, I found myself walking down the hall of the country club to meet Cosimo in the restaurant. He sat by the window in a thick sweater and his leather motorcycle jacket, staring out at the snowy fields outside. I sank down opposite him and his dark eyes flicked up.

"Morning," he said. "Did you ever find Olivia?"

"I did," I said, lifting a hand to the waiter.

"I hope you were understanding with her," he said, giving me a hard stare.

"I was very understanding with her," I said. "On the bed, the floor, the couch, up against the wall."

"Jesus, why do you say shit like that to me?"

"Because it gets you the fuck out of my business."

The waiter appeared and dropped off our usual—four espressos and two plates of steak tips and egg whites. I bolted my first espresso and sipped the second, settling back in my seat.

"What do you have for me?" I asked.

Cosimo pulled a stack of paperwork from the chair beside him. "Some city permits I need your signature on. The inventory reports are sent in for the month and for the year."

"Good," I said, accepting the papers.

I leafed through them in silence, skimming the tiny print. It was the usual. Building permits, development paperwork, business licenses.

I scrawled my name on each dotted line and passed the stack back to Cosimo, who set it aside and crossed his arms.

"You're planning on killing my father," he said casually, like he was remarking on the weather.

"In this situation, I'm playing my cards close to the chest," I said.

His jaw worked and he squinted out the window. "After this bullshit is over, maybe I'll take Enza and we'll go out to Colorado for a week. I think I need to clear my head. Do a little skiing."

"Do you know how to skii?" I asked.

He shook his head. "I'm thinking of moving up in the world though, learning how to vacation like the upper classes. Maybe it's time you moved up too, Lucien."

"I'm pretty high up there already," I said.

"Organized crime is a hard place to find mobility. Have you thought about making the leap to politics?"

I paused, the espresso cup rested in my fingers. Of course I'd heard my name thrown around in certain circles and I'd mulled the idea over briefly, but I'd always considered myself too tarnished to run for office. And I wasn't confident that it was something I wanted.

"Do you mean leave the outfit?"

"Fuck no, the outfit is the best it's been with you in charge," Cosimo said. "But your illegitimate businesses are all covered by legitimate businesses. You've erased your tracks well enough that your ties to the outfit are conjecture. At least from the perspective of the outside world."

"Is it?"

"It's not provable. You're a careful person."

"What made you think of this?" I asked.

Cosimo shifted, spearing a piece of steak on his fork. "Since Olivia started her foundation, your image has shifted. You used to be shady, now you're sensational. And she is too. You should hear the things they say about her in the upper class circles."

I narrowed my eyes. "What do they say about her?"

"That she's the next up and coming thing," Cosimo said. "The rising star of high society."

"I knew that," I said. "To some degree. But I don't want Olivia in the public eye, I want her protected."

"If you're trying to keep her out of the public eye, you're doing a shit job at it."

I sent him a glance, warning him to back off, and he crossed his arms and fell silent. We finished our food and I got to my feet, lifting my hand to signal the waiter we were ready for the bill. Cosimo stood and picked up his motorcycle helmet from the floor, tucking it under his arm.

"I'm not trying to get involved in your life, Lucien," he said. "But I don't want my fucking father to run for mayor of this city. I want him out of my life, I want his seat filled by someone I trust so I never have to lie awake at night and think about him."

The emotion in his tone caught me off guard. I pulled on my coat slowly and began walking toward the door, Cosimo falling into step beside me.

"You trust me to be mayor?" I mused.

"Don't get sentimental, I might think you like me."

"One Barone is enough for me."

"Hey, you're fucking lucky to have my sister," Cosimo said, pushing through the front door and stepping out onto the porch. He started digging in his pockets until he came up with a pack of cigarettes and offered me one.

"I'm more than lucky," I said, accepting a cigarette and lighting it. "Probably shouldn't be smoking, but what the hell."

He shrugged, expelling a stream of smoke into the cold air. "Enza's satisfied if I only smoke socially."

"I'm trying to fucking cut it out," I said. "Especially now that we're trying to have another baby."

"Are you? Congratulations."

"Once all this bullshit settles down," I said, not wanting to get into the gritty details.

A strange expression crossed Cosimo's face and he squinted up the driveway to the road. We smoked in silence for a moment until I stubbed out my cigarette and descended the porch.

"Hey," Cosimo said.

I turned.

"Just think about what I said, about running for mayor," he said. "Having a kid really makes me think about the future and I don't want to worry about cunts like my father compromising the outfit. We need a foot in the real world, to keep things under control."

"I suppose you think I'm the one for that?"

"I think you'd fucking love it."

The rest of my day at the office was distracted by thoughts of our conversation. Cosimo was right in wanting more security. The world was changing fast and if I wanted to stay in total control of the city, I was going to have to make some changes.

Maybe Rosario Barone was the wake-up call I needed.

CHAPTER FIFTEEN

OLIVIA

After Lucien left for the office, I went to the dresser where he kept our intimate items and took out the little silver plug he reserved for prepping me and the slender vibrator. Lucien loved anal, but he knew it was hard for me so he didn't ask for it often. And he tried to warn me early when he wanted it so I had time to prepare to take him.

I closed the bathroom even though I was alone and worked my skirt up over my ass. For a second, I caught my gaze in the mirror and my throat was flushed and splotchy. I took a deep breath and pushed away the shame. There was no reason to be ashamed of anything he did to me. I was an adult woman and I could do as I pleased with my husband without guilt.

I closed my eyes and bent over the sink. My fingers skimmed down my thigh and slid between them, grazing the folds of my pussy. I was soaked, as I always was after having him in my mouth. I arced my back, letting a dozen images of my husband rush into my mind, and put the vibrator to my clit.

The low buzz sent a shot of heat through my pussy and a bit of arousal slipped from inside me. If Lucien were here, he would get down on his knees behind me and lick it off my pussy. He'd done so many times before and it was so sexy when he went down on his knees.

I came, gasping over the sink, my fingers curling around the faucet. Then, while I was still pulsing, I slid lube over my asshole and worked the plug inside. It popped into place and I shuddered, thinking about what would be inside me tonight.

I knelt, sitting back on my heels, and took a picture of my ass and the arches of my feet. Then I pulled my lace thong up around my hips and wriggled my skirt back down. There was a rebellious fire sparking in my lower belly as I sent the image to Lucien and set my phone aside to wash my hands.

My phone pinged as I slid into the back seat of the car. I waited until the driver had pulled the privacy curtain and then I swiped the screen. It was a message from Lucien.

Jesus fucking Christ, Olivia.

A rush of hot triumph moved through my chest as I pushed my phone back in my purse. I knew he'd expect me to show up at his office like I usually did when I sexted with him, but I wouldn't be doing that today.

He could think about that picture all day until his cock was throbbing against his zipper. I had business to take care of that didn't involve what was in his pants.

My driver dropped me off at Elliott & Lynn, one of the city's most elite designers. Alina Elliott was a society butterfly, a rare sighting at fashion shows and business events. For the last few years, I'd paid good money to have her advice and patronage for my wardrobe whenever I had to attend events. She had a keen eye, the best connections, and I trusted her completely.

I slipped through the front door with my bodyguard at my heels. Alina stood at the desk looking breathtakingly elegant in a white dress that hugged her body. Her blonde hair was pulled atop her head in a pale cloud and her eyes glittered with smoky, silver makeup.

I walked across the room, her head jerked up and she grinned.

"Liv," she said. "Come in, come in. You look stunning."

I bent across the counter and kissed the air on either side of her jaw. "Thank you. How're you, Alina?"

"Can't complain," she said. "Want an espresso? Or a vodka?"

"Let's see how the day goes," I said. "But let's start with the coffee."

She ushered me into the back room. It was a soft, feminine room done in gold and pale pink. The couches were plush, there was a crystal chandelier, and the carpet was a cream color. In the corner was a rack with a few dresses hanging on it and a privacy screen embroidered with roses. I leaned against the coffee bar while she turned on the espresso machine with a long, pink fingernail.

"Now, what do you need?" she said.

"A new dress," I said. "It's for this weekend so I can't do a custom, but I thought you might have something already here."

"What's the goal of the dress?"

I sighed. "Revenge...sort of."

"Oh?" Her mouth curved. "What's Lucien done?"

"It's not Lucien...well, maybe it's a little bit him. But there's this party that my father is supposed to attend and we have to go. I need to look like I'm confident, in control."

"Are you not confident and in control?" she asked. "You're the wife of one of the city's most powerful men."

I hesitated. Alina knew who and what Lucien was and she knew how I felt about my family. I swallowed and she passed me a foamy cup of rich espresso. I looked down at it and hesitated.

"I saw my father again after six years and I felt like a child again," I admitted. "Like all that toxicity and fear just came right back. I need something to keep me from feeling the way I felt. I need to feel like...myself."

Alina studied me.

"Show your body," she said. "But don't show it. I have the perfect dress for you."

She led the way into the showroom. It was chilly between the rows of dresses and frost decorated the large windows on the opposite wall. She went to the end of the rack and took down a dress in a white clothing bag.

"I'm dying to see you in this," she said. "Go—hurry!"

I ducked behind the curtain and wriggled into the dress. Then I turned to the mirror and my mouth fell open. The dress had an inner lining that was barely there and it clung to my skin and moved with me. Over it, the top overlay was flecks of gold, like marble. There were larger flecks to cover the parts of my body that had to be covered, but otherwise, it left me shockingly bare. I hadn't worn anything like this to an event for a long time.

Heart pattering, I ran my hands up my body. It was flattering, the perfect fit for me everywhere except the bust. I cupped my breasts and my cleavage spilled up and over the neckline that barely covered my nipples.

No, Lucien wasn't going to like that.

"Do you like it?" Alina called.

I stepped into the main area and she stood, putting a hand over her mouth.

"My God, you are gorgeous," she gasped.

"I love it," I said. "But Lucien is going to lose his mind if I wear this out in public."

She rolled her eyes. "Men can be so stupid. What does he think? That another man will look at your boobs and suddenly you'll run off and leave him?"

"He just gets jealous," I said, feeling a little warm.

"You might be the most beautiful woman I've ever dressed, but Lucien is a prime, Grade A cut of meat," she said. "Like you're going to walk out on that! He doesn't have anything to worry about."

I started laughing, unable to hold it back, and it felt amazing. I hadn't relaxed enough to really laugh in weeks. She rolled her eyes again, still smirking, and began shuffling through the racks. I struggled out of the dress and laid it aside, padding after her in my bra and panties.

She rummaged through the dresses, muttering under her breath, for several minutes. I heard her exclaim and then she twirled, a silver and white dress clasped to her chest.

"This is it," she said triumphantly.

She made me stand in the center of the room where the light hit me. Then I kept still as she pulled on the dress and zipped it up to the middle of my back. She slipped a pair of matching heels on my feet and turned me around to face the double mirrors.

It was the color of ice, the color of Lucien. The body of the dress was a simple ballroom gown with a skirt of floaty chiffon. But the elegant, V neckline in both the back and front was edged with the lightest lace and from the arms hung strands of crystals like delicate ice that reached my elbows. It was so simple, so stunning, so elegant.

I felt my spine lengthen as I turned, letting the weightless chiffon gust around my legs. Like snow blown up by the wind. When I moved, the ice crystals made a pleasant, clinking sound.

"What do you think?"

Warmth swelled in my chest.

"It's perfect."

"Wonderful!" She lifted her arms in a celebratory gesture. "Let me pack that up for you and then let's get drunk. I'm closing at noon today."

For a moment, I remembered that I had an appointment later to pay Lucien back for this dress. Then I shook my head, shrugging off the thought. No, I needed some time out of the house and out of my head. Away from my endless, churning thoughts.

"I'd love to."

We popped two bottles of champagne in the backroom. When we drank together, we always ended up telling each other far too much. Today was no exception.

I sat curled on the fluffy rug in a silk robe, my mouth ajar as she detailed her latest sexual exploit with her husband. Then she burst into laughter as I told her about Lucien's response to being called daddy in bed.

"At least it's not something I'm into," I said, shrugging. "Otherwise, I'd be disappointed."

"Too bad, he's missing out."

"He's never liked how much younger I am," I admitted. "And Lucien isn't one to play pretend. He can't divorce himself from reality well enough."

She poured another glass of champagne and passed it to me. I sipped it slowly, enjoying the taste spreading over my tongue.

"You never role play?" she asked. "We do it a lot. It's fun."

I shook my head.

"What does Lucien do then?" she said, waving a hand. "I'm disappointed with him, he needs to up his game."

I shook my head again, this time vigorously. "If Lucien ups his game anymore, I'm going to end up too sore to walk. He just...fucks the way he does everything else. You know how Lucien is."

Her eyes widened slightly. "So he fucks pretty hard then?"

I nodded, the last few weeks with Lucien playing through my mind like a reel, and her mouth broke into a grin. My face was warm and I found myself digging through my purse for a scrunchie to tie my hair up. Alina got up to get another bottle of champagne and our conversation descended into chaos and drunkenly recounting the things our husbands did to us behind closed doors.

It was the welcome release I'd needed.

The inside of the car spun as I climbed into the backseat several hours later. There were several missed texts from Lucien, nothing important, but I still felt slightly guilty. I pulled the privacy panel between myself and my driver and slid my shoes off. I knew I shouldn't do this in the backseat, but I was drunk and reckless.

I wriggled my panties down and pushed them in my purse. Then, with my skirt up around my waist, I turned my phone camera on and spread my legs beneath my coat. As my fingers slid between my thighs, I remembered the first sexual conversation I'd ever had with Lucien.

That night when he'd showed up in my room. Drunk and demanding.

"Do you masturbate, Olivia?"

He'd been so cold and casual, like it was the most normal thing to ask someone he barely knew. And I'd blushed with shame and lied, unable to admit it.

Not anymore, Lucien had cured me of that. I loved giving myself pleasure and I still masturbated almost every day alone, no matter if we had sex later. There was something so relaxing about slipping beneath the sheets alone and putting the little pink vibrator Lucien had bought for me, the one that warmed up, against my clit. It was my sacred alone time and I would never give that up.

Once, Lucien had stood in the bathroom door, his hands in his pocket, and just watched me.

"You're so pretty when you get yourself off," he said when I was done.

The back of the car swirled. I clicked the camera off and tossed the phone aside. I didn't need to record myself and send it to my husband.

I was drunk, and my pleasure was mine alone. Head spinning, I slipped to the floor of the car, rolling onto my back. Overhead, the golden streetlights swirled as they flew by, and my fingers worked between my legs.

Urging myself closer and closer to release.

It was a twenty minute drive and I took my time. My mind drifted, remembering how before my marriage doing this always made me feel confusion and shame. My parents had drilled it into my head that I needed to be pure and perfect, completely undefiled for my husband.

They'd fucked up my head and made me hate my body and then they'd dumped the entire mess onto Lucien and washed their hands of the damage.

He'd put the pieces back together slowly, giving me space to make peace with pleasure. About a year into our marriage, he'd asked if I still touched myself every day. Confusion and shame rising, I looked at the ground and shook my head.

"Why not?" he asked.

"I assumed you didn't want me to."

"Do you enjoy it?"

I nodded and he pulled me into his lap, brushing back my hair.

"Then do it," he said. "You belong to me, every part of you, Olivia. Your pussy is mine to fuck. But it's still yours. I'll get you a vibrator."

On occasion, he joined me, but most of the time he left me alone.

Now, looking back, I realized it wasn't just orgasms that he had fixed for me. He'd given me everything, but more than that, he had simply given me the space to become my own woman. Without judgement, without expectations.

If there was anyone in this world I owed a debt of loyalty, it was Lucien.

My fingers stilled and regret moved through me. I'd been so hard on him for the last few weeks about my father, about everything. He was in an impossible situation. Damned if he did and damned if he didn't.

Either he killed his wife's father or he risked his family's safety.

Out of horror and weakness, I'd blamed his brutality and his desire for revenge. But as I lay there, drunk and watching the streetlights rush by overhead, I realized why the whole situation had repulsed me and it wasn't because I cared what happened to my father.

No, I wanted Lucien to kill him.

I never wanted to have to see my father's face again, I never wanted to have to think about him. I wanted him wiped from our lives, wiped from the earth, buried six feet underground with all the ugly things he'd done to me.

And that made me irreparable.

That made me worse than Lucien because at least he took responsibility. I was too much of a coward to admit my sins.

The blood on Lucien's hands made me who I was—the lady of the Esposito house. It paid for my jewels, my manicures, my clothes, and my expensive bottles of champagne. It paid for my foundation and for the victims who had suffered the same Lucien and I had. It made things better for everyone in my small world.

It was time for me to take ownership of who I had become.

CHAPTER SIXTEEN

LUCIEN

Lucidius, my weapons expert, brought me exactly what I needed without me having to even articulate it. He knew I preferred to kill with steel over bullets. There was something satisfying, something that offered closure, about feeling hot blood against my skin.

The device strapped to my forearm and held a razor sharp, steel blade. I rolled up my sleeve and fastened it around my forearm. Sinking into my office chair, I pulled the trigger with my middle finger. The blade shot from my wrist and sank hard into the wall on the opposite end of the room.

Fuck, that was lethal.

"You need to get your hand up against him before you pull the trigger," Lucidius had said. "That way it'll sink fully into the flesh and he won't fall straight away. It gives you time after the killing to leave the body and it's not readily apparent what happened."

Gingerly, I pulled the blade from the wall and slid it back into the device. Just as I unstrapped it and slid it back into the desk, the door opened and Olivia walked in.

I hadn't seen her since she'd sent me that fucking picture earlier that had my cock throbbing in my pants for half the day. She wore one of my white, button up shirts that barely brushed the middle of her thigh and nothing else. I could see the outline of her breasts pushing against the fabric, threatening to make the buttons pull apart. Fuck me, she looked good.

"I see you're finally home," I said lightly.

She walked up to me and tilted her head back, narrowing her eyes.

"Well, I see you're finally home too," she said.

"Where were you?"

She jutted her chin. "Where were *you*?"

I took a beat, unsure what she was doing. She flicked her hair at me and sat her bare ass and pussy down on my desk and folded her arms.

It definitely wasn't the first time her ass had been on my desk, but it was the first time she'd put it there like she was trying to prove something.

I braced my hands on either side of her and looked into her eyes. "Olivia, what are you doing?"

She blinked. "I'm going through a metamorphoses."

I bit back the urge to laugh. She was drunk, I could smell the sweet scent of champagne on her breath and see the soft dilation of her pupils. Despite her earlier flirtations, I could tell right away that tonight would be spent trying to get some water and Tylenol into my wife before tucking her into bed and taking a long shower by myself.

"Like a butterfly?"

She nodded. "A chrysanthemum."

I brushed her hair back.

"Do you mean a chrysalis?"

She rolled her eyes and I resisted the urge to give her thigh a little spank. Instead I bent and pressed a kiss to her forehead and she went still, her hands clasped in her lap. When I drew back, her dark gaze was wide and thoughtful.

"I don't know why I expected anything different from you," she whispered. "You are exactly...yourself. And I think that I'm myself too."

"An astute observation," I said.

She scowled. "Don't tease me."

"I'm not."

She bit her full lower lip. "I just...I realized today how much work you've put into me...into trying to fix the things that were done to me. And I also realized that maybe you and me aren't so different."

She looked so small and hesitant that it melted me to my core. I took her chin in my fingers and turned her face up until she couldn't look away.

"You temper me, but we're two sides of the same coin."

"I know." Her voice cracked.

"Is it so terrible to be like me?"

Her voice was barely a whisper.

"No, Lucien. I love you more than I ever thought possible."

I pulled her against my chest and stroked her silky hair. It ran through my fingers like shadows slipping along the wall. Trailing down my wrist and grazing my forearm. In the distance I thought I felt storm clouds gather, menacing on the horizon.

I needed to act soon.

I hated feeling out of control and since learning what her father had planned, I'd felt my control slipping. I'd turned over Cosimo's proposal in my mind for the rest of the day and the more I thought it over, the more sense it made. Maybe it was time to stop paying off politicians and law enforcement.

Maybe it was time to step forward and take control of both the light and the dark.

She pushed the heel of her palm against my chest and I released her. Her lashes were lowered and her eyes were thick with a familiar look.

"I spent all your money," she whispered.

"Good girl."

"I'm ready to pay you back."

"You're drunk as fuck," I said, lifting her off the desk. "And you're going to bed, baby. Where the hell were you anyway?"

She tossed her hair back. "I went to Elliot & Lynn to get a dress for this weekend. You should see it, it's beautiful."

"Go put it on and show me," I said, hoping to get her upstairs.

She turned, paused, and whirled on me. "No."

"Fine, then we're going to bed."

I reached for her, but she darted back. Her shirt rode up and I caught a glimpse of that perfect, little pussy tucked between her thighs and I went rock hard. She noticed and she fucking laughed, her tongue caught between her teeth.

"Do you need something, Lucien?"

I snatched her wrist. "Yes, I need my wife to behave herself and walk her ass upstairs and get in bed."

She shook her head and scowled. "No."

"Stop saying that."

"No."

She yanked her hand from me and darted back, but I caught her with an arm around her waist. Her legs peddled in the air as I lifted her and pushed her up against the back of the door. Her thighs were so soft beneath my fingers and the thin material of my shirt was doing its best to keep her breasts contained. Fuck, the outline of her nipples pushed against the white fabric. I bent, my mouth hovering, and stopped myself.

"How drunk are you?" I asked.

"I'm not drunk," she shot back.

"Red," I said softly.

Her face sobered at once. "I'm sorry, did I do something?"

Her eyes were so wide and her lower lip trembled. I kissed her forehead and then down her neck and she shivered.

"No, baby, but I want you so fucking badly," I breathed into her ear. "But I won't fuck you the way I want to if you're not sober."

She swallowed, her hips working in my grip. "I'm a little tipsy. I had a few glasses of champagne before my driver came to get me. But I'm lucid."

"Why are you being so fucking bad if you're not drunk then?" I murmured, pressing deliberate kisses across her collarbone.

"I'm coming down from it. Just give me a glass of water and a minute and I'll be ready to take it for you," she whispered.

My cock pulsed, hot and painful against my zipper. Fuck, maybe I needed to get off alone while she was sobering up. I wanted to fuck her long and hard and right now I wasn't going to last for more than a few minutes. I kissed her mouth and set her on her feet, opening the door.

"You run to the kitchen and get yourself some toast and a glass of water. Sober up. Then meet me back here."

She obeyed, her round ass swaying beneath my shirt as she padded down the hall. I watched her go, my eyes on her pretty feet and ankles until she turned the corner and disappeared. Then I turned to go to my desk and paused.

I could make out the print of her ass and the mark where her pussy had leaked. Fuck me. My feet carried me to the desk and my hands began unfastening my belt. My cock sprang free, heavy and hard, already leaking from the tip. I bit back a groan and wrapped my fist around it, feeling it pulse beneath my fingers.

My God, she made me so fucking weak. From the first moment I'd laid eyes on her in her parents' house, standing there with big, frightened eyes, I'd been lost.

I jerked myself slowly, looking down at that little spot of wetness on my desk. She'd known exactly what she was doing, coming down here in only my shirt and no panties. Putting her naked sex right where I worked, right where I wouldn't miss it.

Leaving me a trace of her to drive me crazy.

Heat burst down my spine and pleasure surged through my groin and I came hard. Pumping my cum into a tissue. My heart was still racing as I wiped my hands and put my still hard cock away. I wasn't satisfied, but at least I wasn't in pain anymore.

I went to the corner and opened the window. There was an ashtray and a pack of cigarettes that I kept there. Mostly for when I needed a smoke after fucking my wife over the desk.

The icy air hit my face as I lit up and breathed the smoke into my lungs. Overhead, the sky was clear and the stars burned. It reminded me of when I'd taken her to Russia for our honeymoon.

She thrived in the cold, in the darkness, in the starlight, just as I did.

Perhaps when this was all over, when her father was dead in his grave, I would take her somewhere cold. Like a chalet in the mountains where there was no one to bother us. And then we could finally spend some time together without a threat hanging over our heads.

It took her a long time to come back. I finished my cigarette and took a seat at my desk to work until she returned. When I finally heard her step in the hall, it was almost midnight. She pushed open the door and I looked up, my breath catching.

She wore a set of black lingerie. The lace was so fine it clung to her like a second skin, showing me every curve of her body. The bra was silk and cupped her breasts, giving her the most beautiful overflow. I sat frozen and let my eyes trail over her garter belt, down her hips, over the silky panties that barely covered her pussy, and down to the lace stockings. Through the thin fabric, I could just make out her delicate feet, her toenails painted red.

Fucking hell.

My cock pressed hungrily against my zipper. I laid aside my book and rose slowly, beckoning my wife. She came obediently, her hands tucked behind her back. She'd done her makeup and her velvety eyes were rimmed with smoky black and her mouth was painted a deep, wine red.

Fuck me. If I hadn't just come, I probably would have finished in my pants just looking at her. Instead, I kept my face impassive as I took her by the chin.

"Are you sober, baby?"

She nodded.

"Words, Olivia."

"Yes, sir."

Pulling her out into the center of my office, I released her hand and made a slow circle around her body. Taking her in from every angle. She swallowed, wrapping her arms around her body.

"Drop your arms," I ordered.

She obeyed, straightening her shoulders. Letting me see every part of her. I made her stand there while I poured a whiskey and lit another cigarette. Then I circled her again, watching her try not to squirm. She swallowed and looked over her shoulder, but I made a noise in my throat and she corrected herself.

"Did you prep for me?" I asked, my voice hushed.

"Yes, sir," she whispered.

"When?"

"This morning," she said. "And just now."

I fought the urge to touch her, but there was something so deliciously vulnerable about seeing her standing alone in the center of the room. Looking so pretty and half naked and owned.

I took a sip of whiskey, letting it burn over my tongue and down my throat, and moved back to stand before the enormous fireplace.

"Bend over the desk and let me see."

She obeyed, moving to the desk. Her fingers hesitated at her hips and I knew she was burning up with shame.

Here she was, naked and knowing she was about to be ruined. And here I was, still fully dressed and knowing I was about to ruin her until her makeup ran down her face.

It was the most divine kind of tension. The moment before dirty, sweet pleasure, before our bodies touched.

"Don't make me wait for it," I said coldly.

She bent over and heat ran down my spine in a shock. My God, she was so fucking lovely. Her fingers hooked beneath her panties and she wriggled her ass until they slipped down just enough to see the plug in her asshole. My cock jerked and I put the cigarette between my teeth so I could adjust it through my pants.

I rewarded her with a simple, "Good girl."

She stayed as she was, her breasts pressed to the desk, holding her panties down. The soft curves of her ass, the sweet, glistening folds of her pussy, her delicate feet—they were a beautiful picture.

"You've got such a pretty pussy, baby," I said.

It pulsed and a little glimmer of wetness appeared. Sliding down towards her clit like a diamond against the soft folds of her sex. I crossed the room, unable to hold back any longer, and crouched behind her. Bending, I curled my tongue across her entrance and she whimpered. Fuck me, she tasted just like she had on our wedding night.

She shivered and released her panties and they slipped down to her ankles. Her palms went flat on the table. Another drop of arousal slipped from inside her and I flicked my tongue out to catch it.

"I've always thought you tasted like expensive champagne," I mused. "Tangy, a little tart, but so fucking sweet for me, baby."

She moaned softly. "It feels so good when you eat it from behind."

I licked her once, long and slow. "You like when I eat your expensive, little pussy like this?"

"Expensive? What does that mean?" she said, turning a little to look at me.

"Eyes ahead," I warned.

She turned back around to face the opposite wall.

I took a final drag of my cigarette and let the smoke waft up to the ceiling.

"I've always had a taste for expensive pussy," I admitted. "And you have the most expensive cunt I've ever put my mouth on."

Her pussy throbbed, the wet opening of her sex flushed with need. I put my cigarette in the ashtray and licked my fingers and dragged them through her swollen pussy to her clit. She whimpered as I pinched it gently. Torturing her as I rolled it softly between my fingertips.

"What do I get out of it?" I said, letting her go and rising until my body loomed over hers.

"Everything you want from me," she whispered.

"What did we agree on earlier in payment for the money I gave you?"

She swallowed and I saw her jaw move as she battled against herself. She swore a little here and there, but she still struggled to be as vulgar as I was with her in bed.

She struggled with other things too, despite losing her virginity to me years ago. She'd been raised to be a good Catholic girl and getting fucked in the ass by her husband, despite how much she enjoyed it, didn't fit into that image very well.

"Olivia," I said, grounding her with her name.

"What was the question?" she whispered.

"What do I get in return for the ten thousand dollars I gave you?"

"You...get to fuck my ass."

"That's a good girl."

She gave a low moan as I slipped my hand between her thighs and found her silky, soaked folds.

"I need you, Lucien," she begged, her voice cracking.

I plunged my two middle fingers into her cunt, the wet sound echoing through the room. She arced as I pumped into her, finding her G-spot and flicking it hard.

"You can take me, baby, you're so fucking obedient."

"Oh, God," she whimpered.

"No speaking," I ordered, standing. "Not unless it's your safe word."

I knew she was dying to moan, but she swallowed it back. Across the room in the mirror I'd hung there for moments like these, I could see her pretty face. Her lips open and her big eyes drunk with need. Locking my gaze on her reflection, I slapped her across the ass.

She cried out, as I knew she would.

"Oh, no, you keep your dirty, whore mouth shut," I hissed.

She bit her lip, her throat contracting as she whimpered silently. I opened the front of my pants and unleashed my cock against her cunt. Her hips startled as the hard head hit her slick folds and a shock of electricity moved down my spine.

Bracing a hand on her lower back, I dipped the tip of my cock into her and then dragged it back out, a bit of her wetness stretching between us like dew. She twitched in my grasp and pushed back, trying to fuck herself with my length. I spanked her once more and she quieted, her nails digging into the desk.

"Hold still," I said coldly.

Her lashes fluttered, but she kept quiet. I pushed the head of my cock into her, easing it in, watching her tight pussy stretch to accommodate my size. I paused, halfway inside her. My hand closed on her hip, holding her steady as I thrust gently in and out of the first inch of her cunt.

"You're such a slut," I breathed. "A pretty slut only good for my cock."

She stiffened and for a moment I thought she was offended, but then she began pulsing rhythmically around the head of the cock. A strangled gasp burst from her mouth and it hit me that she was having an orgasm without me even touching her clit. Excitement surged and I slammed into her all the way just so I could feel her come on me.

"Fuck, baby, you're fucking coming already," I breathed.

She whimpered and, fast as lightning, I slapped her across the ass. Her spine stiffened and her eyes screwed shut as she finished in wet pulses around my length. I rode her lightly and her mouth fell open, her lips trembling and her makeup already smudged beneath her eyes.

For a second, I hesitated. This was my wife, the mother of my child.

Then I shook my head.

Tomorrow she would be my wife. Tonight she was a dirty little whore.

I pulled out of her and opened the desk drawer to retrieve the bottle of lube. She stilled, her lower back arced, as I slipped the plug from her and began working lube into her asshole. A soft sigh eased from her throat. I dipped my middle finger into her, letting the tight muscles pull it up to the middle knuckle. She moaned, flushing shamefully, as the tight ring contracted.

"Are you ready for me, baby?" I breathed.

She swallowed and nodded.

I slid my finger from her and shifted over her body. Then I took the base of my cock into my hand and lined it up with her asshole. She whimpered, but she pushed back on me like such a good girl. For a moment her body resisted and then the head of my cock slipped into her heat and my vision flashed.

My God, I would never, ever grow tired of that feeling.

Relishing her groan, I let my body meld into hers, my mouth brushing her bare shoulder. Her body was stiff at first, but as I let her adjust to my size, it began to soften. I stroked her hip, whispering praise beneath my breath, and began thrusting gently. Letting her take me at her own pace.

Sometimes she could take me like this hard and fast, but I could already tell tonight wasn't one of those times. I tested her carefully, watching her in the mirror as I increased my speed. Her body stiffened beneath me and she whimpered, her dark eyes widening. I slowed and she let her head fall back, giving me access to the soft skin at the base of her throat.

"You alright, baby?" I breathed.

She nodded, her lashes fluttering. "It's a lot to take, but it feels amazing."

"That's my good girl," I murmured.

She pulsed, gripping me tightly in response to my words. I pushed my cock into her all the way and fucked her with shallow strokes, building slowly toward my climax. Her body went limp in my arms and I slid my hand up over her breasts to her throat, holding her head back against my shoulder.

When I came, I couldn't hold back the groan as I pumped my cum into her body. She gasped softly, completely given up to me. Limp and warm in my arms. I slipped my other hand down her hips and found her clit, slick from her swollen pussy, and began working it in my fingers.

"Come for me," I urged. "Come while my cock is still in you, baby."

She whimpered and I tensed, making my dick twitch inside her. It sent her over the edge and she cried out, her hands flying up to grip my wrist. Holding herself steady as she pulsed around me, getting me hard all over again. I rode her gently, despite how sensitive I was, until she was done.

Then I pulled from her and reached for the tissues, knowing we'd made a mess all over ourselves and the desk.

She released a sigh, sinking down into a heap beneath me.

"Am I paid up?" she whispered.

I bent and kissed the back of her head, letting my mouth linger against her hair.

"It's just a game, baby," I said softly. "It's me who owes you."

CHAPTER SEVENTEEN

OLIVIA

I was deliciously sore the next day. I woke early to Lucien shaking my shoulder gently to wake me. He sat down on the edge of the bed and brushed back my hair, stroking my cheek with the side of his finger.

"I'm going to the fundraiser with you tonight," he said.

I pushed myself up on the pillows. "Really?"

"I have some business to handle there as well. I'll be back to pick you up and drive you this evening."

He rose with a finalizing air and I knew it was no use asking questions so I kissed him goodbye and watched his car disappear down the snowy driveway.

I didn't understand it, but he had cleansed me of my guilt last night. Or perhaps it had been my realization in the car. Whatever it was, I felt a hundred times more at peace.

I spent the rest of the day in Marco's nursery reading him books and watching TV with him. Or rather, he watched the TV and I sat there and watched him with a faint ache in my chest. He was growing up so fast it pained me to see it. One moment he was a helpless baby wrapped in my arms and suddenly he was a headstrong toddler who looked up at me with Lucien's ice cold, hazel gaze.

We ate dinner together in the nursery and I put him to bed. Then I climbed the stairs to get ready for the party before Lucien got back from work.

The dress hung in the back of my closet. After my shower, I stood there in a towel and I ran my fingers over the fabric. The waistline was dotted with little crystals that caught the light when they shifted. My heart fluttering, I unhooked the dress and carried it into the bathroom.

I did my hair in soft waves around my neck and shoulders. Then I applied my makeup carefully, lining my eyes with dark, smoky eyeshadow, and staining my lips a deep, berry red. I rubbed lotion into my skin until it was smooth and shimmering and slipped on silver, lace panties that came up to my waist and a balconette bra.

Then I zipped up the dress and twirled before the mirror, watching as the clouds of icy chiffon floated around me.

It was perfect.

I was in the middle of pulling on thigh highs when the bedroom door opened and shut. My heart flipped and my stomach tightened.

No matter how many times Lucien saw me get dressed up, it still always gave me a little flutter of nerves. There was something about the way his cold eyes softened just a trace as he looked at me that just melted my insides.

I stepped shyly into the bedroom and he looked up. His mouth parted and I blushed, dropping my eyes. His crisp footfalls drew near and his fingertips ran up my arm and hovered over my collarbones.

"Look up, baby."

I obeyed, meeting his gaze.

He bent, sliding his hand around the back of my neck and kissing me softly. Gently enough that it didn't smudge my lipstick, but hard enough I felt hot pulses in the darkness between my thighs. He backed me slowly up against the wall and his other hand lingered on the waist of the dress for a moment before delving beneath the skirt.

I jumped as his fingers brushed over my panties, circling my clit once. Then he broke free of our kiss and took something from his pocket. Before I realized what he was doing, he'd drawn my skirts up and he was fastening something around my upper thigh. There was a brief sensation of being pinched and then cold metal and then he brushed my skirt down.

"What did you just do?"

He pulled me before the mirror in the bathroom and lifted my skirt, baring my right leg. There was a delicate leather holster around my thigh and inside it was a short knife. I stiffened, my brows drawing together. The thought of having to use a weapon made me anxious.

"I taught you how to use a blade," he murmured into my hair.

"Why do I need this?" I whispered.

He hesitated. "There's a good chance your father will be there tonight. I just want you protected."

My stomach dropped like a stone in water, but he reached around and lifted my chin. Every nerve in my body screamed to stay home, but I steeled myself and took a steadying breath.

"Won't you protect me?"

"Always," he said. "But remember where the queen stands."

"At the king's side," I said softly. "Not behind him."

He ran his open palm down the underside of my arm and lifted my wrist. Turning my hand to watch the heavy diamond glittering in the light. Then he drew my hand to his mouth and kissed the backs of my fingers.

"Will you be alright to go?"

I nodded, although I wasn't sure.

"Don't leave my side tonight," he said.

He helped me into my heels and then he went to dress in a black suit. I stood in the doorway and watched him slick his hair back and fasten a silver watch around his wrist. Then he put his shoulder holsters on and slipped his suit jacket over them.

"Are you ready?" he asked.

My mouth was dry so I simply nodded. He brought our coats, the same ones Viktor had gifted us during our stay in Russia, and helped me out into the cold. It was snowing lightly and the whole world had gone quiet. I clung to his hand, my silk glove slippery between our skin, as he helped me down the steps and into the Tesla.

I wished he'd let his driver take us. I needed the comfort of being against his body. But Lucien always drove—he wasn't the sort of man who let anyone else put their hands on the wheel. So I contented myself with weaving my fingers through his and holding his hand in my lap. He didn't speak as he pulled out onto the highway and drove into the city.

I'd been to the Grand Imperium Hotel several times for parties, but never during the holidays. We pulled up outside the towering, historic building and I found myself pressed to the window, gazing up at it with my mouth ajar. Lucien passed the keys to the valet and helped me onto the sidewalk.

"It's beautiful," he remarked.

He took my gloved hand and I paused, turning to look at him in the light spilling from the glass doors. He was the same ice cold, lethal man I'd married all those years ago, but in the soft golden glow, he comforted me.

His eyes changed just a trace as they met mine and he bent and kissed my mouth. My whole body heated like I'd taken a shot of whiskey. It was rare that Lucien was soft, but when he was...my God, nothing turned me on more.

He pulled back, lifting my chin.

"Are you ready to go in there?"

I nodded, breathless.

"That's my girl."

He tucked my hand beneath his arm and I looked up at him, noticing how handsome he looked in his suit, how the gray hairs gave him such a mature, sexy aura.

I had a sense of deep pride as my husband led me up the steps and into the lobby. Then everything was a blur of golden lights, marble floors, the soft smell of champagne and wine, and the distant sound of music from upstairs. The lobby was a dream, but the second floor ballroom took my breath away.

My mouth fell open as we entered. The floor-to-ceiling windows let in a view of the entire city, blanketed with snow and decorated for the holidays. The great chandelier was strung with lights in a canopy that covered the ceiling with strings of starlight. Every surface was entwined with holly, red berries, and silver and red ribbons.

My father, thank God, was nowhere to be seen.

"Would you like a drink?" Lucien said.

I shook my head. "No, thank you."

He cocked his head. "Why?"

I swallowed. "I didn't realize until right before we left, but I'm a day late, which is strange for me. I should have started my period yesterday."

His lids flickered. "You think you're pregnant?"

"I don't know. It could be nothing."

He pulled me against his side, his suit rough against my bare arms, and kissed my temple and the side of my neck. A warm flush crept up my throat and I pushed him back.

"Lucien, people are looking," I murmured.

"Let them look," he said. "My wife is beautiful. Of course they're staring."

He left me completely flustered by that. I let him take my hand and drew me over to the bar where he ordered me bubbly juice that looked enough like champagne.

My nerves buzzed and I wished I could drink, but after the bottle of champagne I'd consumed yesterday, I was feeling guilty. I should have stopped drinking when we'd started trying, but I'd assumed it would take longer to get pregnant.

Lucien ordered a whiskey and took my hand, leading me across the room to a group of men standing in the corner around a tall table. He cleared his throat and they all turned.

"Mr. Esposito," said a man who looked vaguely familiar. He wore a luxurious, blue suit and he had a Rolex on his wrist.

"Mr. Emerson-Green," Lucien said, extending a hand.

"Is this your wife?" he asked, his eyes falling on me. He had a pleasant face that put me at ease so I smiled up at him and he blinked, taken aback.

"This is Olivia," Lucien said, stepping aside so I could shake the man's hand. "And this is Mr. Bennett Emerson-Green. He's a relation of the man we met at the hotel. He's the second ward councilman."

"You are stunning, Mrs. Esposito," Bennett said, flashing a smile. "What has Lucien done to deserve such a lovely wife?"

I blushed, feeling a little out of my depth. I looked up at my husband, waiting for him to answer.

"You wound me," said Lucien, his mouth twitching. "But I can't disagree with you. I know I married up."

The music changed and the band struck up a quick waltz. Bennett held out his hand to me and I hesitantly took it.

"May I dance with your wife, Lucien?" he asked.

Lucien inclined his head, melting into the group of men at the table. I glanced over my shoulder as Mr. Emerson-Green led me out onto the floor and saw he was talking easily, his charm turned all the way up. His eyes remained on me and I thought I saw a hint of jealousy beneath the thick layer of ice.

Bennett was a graceful man, perhaps a decade older than Lucien, and he swept me into a waltz with ease. I wasn't sure what to say, so I kept silent and let him lead. After a few minutes, he leaned in, his eyes sober.

"You are Rosario Barones' daughter," he said.

My breath caught.

"Yes," I admitted.

His jaw tightened as he spun me out and back in again. "Lucien and I have been friends for quite a while. Do I approve of the things he does? No. But he has my trust as a friend, even though I try to keep our business separate. For my conscience's sake."

"That's good," I said hesitantly.

"Rosario is a snake in the grass, waiting to strike," Bennett said in a low voice. "I see what goes on behind closed doors. It would be better for Lucien if he eliminated the problem before it became one."

My throat went dry. "I know what my father is planning."

"He needs to be dealt with soon."

My stomach was a hollow pit and I took a moment to gather myself before speaking. There was no world in which I would admit to this man that part of me wanted my father dead, even while the other part still struggled with guilt.

"What would you do, Mr. Emerson-Green?" I asked in a low voice.

"Beg pardon?"

"He's my father."

Bennett's jaw worked as we danced gracefully across the floor. His eyes narrowed, falling on Lucien standing on the other side of the room. I traced his gaze as it moved and my spine tingled and my stomach roiled as both our eyes fell on my father. Standing with the mayor, watching me intently over a glass of wine. Bennett's grip tightened and he began steering me to the other side of the room, putting as much space as he could between my father and I.

I released the breath I'd been holding, trying not to show my fear.

"I have three daughters," Bennett said. "This is a harsh world to bring up a child in, much less a girl. It...it tugs at my heart to see you like this."

"Like what, sir?" I asked.

His mouth pressed together. "You're so young, Mrs. Esposito. Barely thirty."

"I'm twenty-six," I whispered.

"My God, you're my eldest daughter's age," he said, his voice grim. "You should be out going to parties, finding yourself. But instead here you are in the cage of Lucien Esposito."

"Lucien is a good man," I said defensively.

"Lucien is my friend, but if my daughter ever brought home a man like him, I would put him six feet under before I let him marry her."

I went still and stared at him for a long moment as the music ended. I wasn't sure if I should be angry or flattered by his concern. It took me a second, but I gathered myself, folding my hands at my waist. I had to be polite, for both Lucien and the foundation's sake.

"I think you have a soft heart, Mr. Emerson-Green, but I love and trust my husband. And, yes, I'm fully aware that he's not a good man by your standards, but for me…he's everything."

His eyes flickered and he glanced over my shoulder. I turned to see Lucien crossing the room, pausing for a brief moment to speak to two men in tuxedos at the bar. His gaze met mine, hard and cold, but somehow intimate all at once. A shiver moved down my spine.

Mr. Emerson-Green stepped closer for a second, his head lowering.

"I don't get involved in Lucien's business," he said. "Which is why I'm telling you instead of him that if he doesn't act quickly to neutralize the threat of your father, he's going to lose everything. And you didn't hear this from me."

I nodded, my heart pattering in my chest. He turned to go and I caught his elbow.

"I am not in a cage," I said. "I am more free with Lucien than I ever thought I would be in my lifetime."

There was a long silence. Conflict in his eyes, Mr. Emerson-Green took my hand, brushing it with his lips, and then he was gone. Winding his way through the crowd until I lost sight of him. I glanced over my shoulder, looking for my husband, but he was nowhere to be found.

My stomach turned over and I made my way to the bar and ordered a sparkling juice. I'd been to plenty of these fundraisers, but never one where my father was in the same room. It reminded me of another night that I'd worked hard to block from my memory, a night when Lucien had stepped out for a moment and the unthinkable happened.

My breathing came faster and I sipped the chilled juice, hoping no one noticed the flush on my cheeks.

Where was Lucien?

I turned slowly and my stomach clenched, a wave of sickness rolling through me. My father stood in the far corner, the mayor and the city commissioner at his side. He was saying something to them, but his eyes were on me. I swallowed, my body going weak and hot fear trickling down my spine.

Why was it so hard to see him?

I'd been abused by my mother, I'd been violated by Romano, but no one had ever sent such intense fear spiraling through me as my father.

Perhaps because he'd stolen so much from me. Until the age of nineteen, I'd lived under the constant threat of violence. Maybe I would wake up and my father wouldn't bother me. Or maybe I would be in the wrong place at the wrong time and he would slam my head into the wall.

That was one of my worst memories and it had taken Lucien a long time to drag it from me. One day, I was walking down the hall and Lucien reached out to touch my face and suddenly I was on the floor, hyperventilating.

He didn't say anything then. He just held me and listened, but now I realized that somewhere along the way, he had made my father his next target.

Lucien did not forgive and he did not forget.

Dragging myself back to reality, I looked down at my white knuckles. Gripping my glass so hard I was surprised I hadn't shattered it. The bartender's brows drew together and he leaned on his elbows, watching me with concern.

"You alright, ma'am?"

I stared at him, my mouth dry. At that moment, I felt a hand on my back and I jumped, whirling. Lucien was behind me, looking so perfect and solid and comforting that I almost cried. He glanced over my head, catching sight of my father, and his arm circled my waist in a possessive gesture.

I sank back against him, attempting to gather myself.

"Can—can we dance, Lucien?" I stammered.

He looked down at me and his lean fingers brushed my cheek, tucking my hair behind my ear.

"Of course," he said.

CHAPTER EIGHTEEN

LUCIEN

She was tense as I took her into my arms on the dance floor, but her muscle memory took over when the music started. It was an Argentine tango, which she knew like the back of her hand. Our eyes connected and her lower lip trembled, but otherwise she kept it together. The room faded and I lifted her chin with one finger.

"Look at me," I said, switching to French. She spoke it well enough now to carry a basic conversation with me. "Don't look away."

She nodded, biting her lip.

"I'm sorry, Lucien," she said, also in French.

"He can't hurt you."

"He actually can."

I began moving her across the floor in time with the music, sticking to the easiest steps.

"Nothing will hurt you," I said. "I promise."

She glanced over her shoulder, and I made a noise in my throat, reminding her I wanted her eyes on only me. She turned back and I spun her and her skirt moved around her like a cloud. People were beginning to notice us and I felt their stares digging into my back as I pulled her in. Shielding her from the room.

"Do you want to go?" I asked.

She shook her head. "I don't want to make a scene."

"I'll make a scene if I need to."

"Lucien," she said, turning her eyes up to me. Begging me to listen.

When we'd gotten ready, I'd strapped that little blade onto my wrist because I intended on cornering Rosario Barone in the bathroom and killing him. The image of him crumpled in his blood on the floor, slumped against the wall, was intensely satisfying. I played with it as we danced, still considering the possibility.

I needed him to suffer more than he'd ever made Olivia suffer.

And I had to be the one to do it.

It was then, staring down at my wife's face, that I made a choice. I wasn't just going to kill her father, I was going to take everything he'd ever wanted. I was going to step up and take control of both sides of the city. I was going to take all that money Rosario Barone could have made and spend it all on the woman he'd abused.

I was going to make a throne out of Rosario Barones' shattered ambitions and then I was going to fuck his daughter on it.

The restless feeling I'd ignored for a while was gone in a second and my body flooded with feral excitement. I had my target, I had my goal. I had my revenge planned out and I would get the spoils of war.

My speed increased with the music and I took her wrist and spun her in my arms. Showing her off because I knew they were all looking and we would be the topic of tomorrow morning's gossip. She gave a little gasp as I pulled her closer and her legs worked faster to keep up with mine.

All around us, the other couples cleared back to watch. The chatter in the room dulled as we became the centerpiece. Dancing beneath the gleaming lights, my wife glittering like a diamond in my arms.

I bent her back, my mouth grazing her collarbone. She stiffened.

"Lucien," she breathed.

I pulled her upright abruptly and my thigh slid between her legs, barely brushing her sex through our clothes.

"Who fucks you, Olivia," I said against her ear.

She gasped, trying to pull back, but I kept her close.

"Tell me," I said.

"You do," she whispered. "You fuck me, Lucien."

If we weren't in the middle of a crowd, I would have gotten rock hard from that.

"You don't have to whisper," I said. "I doubt anyone close by speaks French."

"Please, don't," she said, switching back to English. "Who are you jealous of?"

"I'm not," I said. "I'm angry with your father, I'm ready to burn him to the ground. I'm ready to kill him."

Her body stiffened in my arms and for a moment I thought it was in response to my words. But then her eyes locked over my shoulder and I turned, almost colliding with Rosario Barone. Steel gray eyes bored into Olivia and she shrank back, stumbling over her heels.

I released her, stepping between them.

"Fuck off," I said under my breath.

His lip curled. "What are you going to do, Esposito?" he said. "Embarrass her in a room full of people? Didn't you already do that once?"

My blood surged and I stepped closer until we stood eye to eye, our bodies inches apart. If it weren't for Olivia, I would have killed him right here. Fuck decorum, I'd have kicked him to the ground and stomped his face into a pulp with my shoe. The image was intensely satisfying, one that I'd mulled over for the last six years.

But, as much as I loathed to admit it, Rosario was right. I'd humiliated my wife in front of everyone years ago in an attempt to make Romano jealous. I wasn't going to make that mistake again.

"Walk away," I said.

Rosario's eyes dragged over Olivia behind me and an expression of faint disgust moved over his face.

"Why you have such an obsession with that little slut, I have no idea," he said. "But it makes you look fucking weak."

My vision flashed red and there was a faint roaring sound in my ears. It would be so easy just to shove my hand up against his chest and release the blade into his flesh. I would get a chance to see the panic rise in his eyes as he realized what I'd done. I'd have a moment to tell him what a piece of shit he was before all the blood drained from his face and he crumpled.

"Lucien."

There was desperation in her voice. I turned and stopped short, realizing suddenly that she'd been right in that hospital room. There were some things we couldn't come back from. Making her watch while I killed her father was one of them. Despite her reluctant blessing, she didn't want this the way I did—she didn't want it at all.

I wanted blood, revenge, and glory in that order. But Olivia was too fragile to see that kind of brutality up close.

And she didn't deserve it. She'd been through too much already.

Wrestling with my rage and my bloodlust, I turned back to Rosario. His head was cocked and he was waiting for me to lose control. He understood my weakness, he knew that his daughter was the only thing that could make me lose my head.

"I paid a lot of money for my wife's dress," I said casually, gesturing at Olivia. "I'm not getting your filthy blood on it."

His brows rose. "I'd watch how you talk to me, Esposito. I'm going to make sure you rot behind bars while I'm sitting at my desk in the mayor's office."

I stepped closer until there was barely an inch between our faces. He flinched, unnerved, but didn't break eye contact as I leaned in to whisper in his ear.

"I'm going to run for the position you want so badly," I said. "And when I win, I'm going to fuck your daughter on your desk in the mayor's office."

His mouth parted as I drew back and anger surged in his eyes.

"Well, it won't be your desk at that point," I said. "It'll be mine."

"Fuck you—"

I stepped closer and he backed up, thrown off. "Does it burn you up knowing your son is my right hand and your daughter is my wife? Haven't I taken enough from you? Because I can take everything from you, Barone, and I'd be fucking happy to."

He was on the retreat now, his lip curled back in a snarl. His eyes flashed and he whirled on his heel, striding across the room and disappearing into the hallway. Blood pounding, I pivoted to pursue him, but Olivia's hand closed on my elbow. Holding me back with desperate fingers.

I turned and froze. She stood there, her arms wrapped around her body, her eyes glittering with tears.

"Lucien," she whispered. "Please take me home."

She was poised on the edge, begging me wordlessly not to break her, and I relented at once. Every eye in the room fixed on us as I slid my arm around her waist and guided her quickly out of the room. The hallway was empty as I led her to the elevator and when the doors shut behind us, she sank against my chest.

"I should have known this was a fucking stupid idea," I said.

She shook her head. "I'm sorry."

I stroked her hair. "You have no reason to be sorry."

She pulled back, running her fingertip under her eyes to wipe away the tears.

"You always say I need to hold my head up and be brave," she said, her voice wavering. "But I just can't with him. I feel like I would rather face the ghost of Carlo Romano than my father."

"Hush," I said, my throat tightening. "You're so fucking brave, baby."

Wrapping my arms around her, I held her tightly against my body as she attempted to gather herself. There were people waiting to use the elevator when we alighted so I shielded her as I led her from the lobby, keeping her away from curious eyes.

We got in the car and I turned the heat up and faced my shivering wife. Her arms were wrapped around her body, but she didn't look as upset. I took her hand, caressing up her knuckles to her painted nails. She was embarrassed by her breakdown, even though she had no reason to be, and she kept avoiding my eyes.

"Look at me," I ordered.

She ignored me, sniffling.

I took her jaw in my grip and turned her, forcing her to look me in the eye.

"You are perfect, Olivia," I said.

She swallowed, her eyes wide and wet.

"You're a good person, a great mother, and an even better wife."

I could tell she didn't believe me. I released her chin and let my fingers slip down her neck, over her breast, and against her waist beneath her coat. She sighed as I kissed her mouth, hot and tasting like her tears. She took my tongue, her body sinking into the seat as she released a little moan, and sucked it for a moment.

I pulled away, rock hard in my pants. "And you're a good girl."

She smiled weakly, some of the redness fading from her face.

"I'm surprised you're horny," I said.

"I'm feeling a lot of things," she said, shrugging. "I'm really hungry."

I started the car and pulled out onto the dark street. "Do you know what you want?"

It turned out that she knew exactly what she wanted—a burger and a double helping of fries from a greasy fast food restaurant. I wasn't hungry so I drove in silence while she sat cross legged in the seat beside me and devoured her food. When she was done, she sat back and released a sigh. The flush had returned to her face and she no longer looked so miserable.

"God, I was starving," she said.

"Are you full?"

"Honestly...no," she admitted. "I don't know how that could be though, my stomach is ready to burst out of this dress."

"I think we'll stop at the store and get you something," I said. "And maybe pick up a couple of pregnancy tests too."

CHAPTER NINETEEN

OLIVIA

The first time I'd been pregnant, I was sick and exhausted. The second time I was ravenous and devastatingly horny.

After the disastrous fundraiser, he picked up a pregnancy test and he sat on the edge of the tub while I took it. The little positive appeared before I could even put it in his hand. His cold eyes flickered and he bent, kissing my mouth slowly.

He was elated, I could tell, even if he didn't show it.

"Good girl," he murmured, nuzzling up my neck.

I flushed, setting the test aside and crawling onto his lap. He lifted me, carrying me into the bedroom and letting me down gently onto the bed. There was a raw, pounding desire between my thighs that needed satisfied.

"Lucien, please," I whispered.

"Please?"

I parted my legs and he slid between them, catching my nipple in his mouth. I was so tender and so sensitive that I felt it in my clit as he rolled it with his tongue.

My body lit up, crying out for gratification as he slid into me. He fucked me slowly and I begged for more. We were both exhausted and slick with sweat when we finally fell back on the sheets. My last impression was of him fully naked, laying on his back, his tattooed chest rising and falling.

When I woke, the memory of the night before had faded. I rolled over and found Lucien's side of the bed empty. Pushing myself upright, my eyes fell on a sliver of light coming from beneath the bathroom door. It was early or he would be gone already. I got to my feet and remembered in a warm rush that I was pregnant with his baby.

My husband had fucked me and pleasured me until I was pregnant. And now he was satisfied with what he'd done.

I ran my fingertips over my stomach. It was another son, I could tell. I could feel it my bones, in the bottom of my stomach.

Stomach fluttering, I rose and padded naked across the dark room and knocked lightly on the bathroom door. There was a short silence and Lucien opened it, filling the doorway with his beautiful body, dotted with water and steaming from the shower. My core clenched, my hormones surging, and I pushed past him into the bathroom.

"You're up early," he observed.

I nodded, wordless. Fuck, I'd never been this horny before in my life.

His brow twitched.

"Do you need fucked, baby?"

I nodded, desperate for some relief from the rapid heartbeat between my thighs. His lean fingers drifted to his waist and unfastened the white towel, letting it fall to the ground to reveal his hard length. Then he moved close and reached up, brushing back my hair and cradling my face.

"Fuck, baby," he said softly. "You're such a needy girl. Do you need my cock so badly?"

"Yes," I breathed. "Please."

His rough hand, always calloused, sometimes cruel, sometimes tender, slid up into my hair and gripped the roots. Drawing my head back. His mouth hovered over mine and I felt his cock brush against my thigh.

"Is this how it's going to be for the next nine months?" he asked. "Will I need to get you up early to satisfy you before I can work?"

"Lucien, please," I whispered.

"Please...what?"

"Please fuck me."

He spun me around and I bent over the sink obediently, arcing my back, giving him easy access to my pussy. His fingers gripped my ass and he laughed softly, his hand tightening until pain shot up my side.

"Jesus, look at you, baby," he said, his eyes holding mine. "Needy, wet girl. Keep still for me."

I wouldn't have moved for all the money in the world. He spat into his hand and his wet fingers slid over my sex, penetrating me for a second before withdrawing. My stomach clenched and my nipples tightened as he found my clit and pinched it in a pulsing motion. Teasing, tugging slightly, giving me hints of pain with my pleasure. My God, he knew my body so well.

He entered me slowly and seated himself, taking a pause before moving. I clenched involuntarily, holding him inside my body. My eyes practically rolling back in my head from the sensation of having him fill me. He was so thick and hot and he fit inside me like we'd been made for each other, filling the parts of me that were difficult to define.

He took a short breath, but he didn't move. I lifted my lashes and met his gaze in the mirror. For the first time in a long time, there was a flicker of emotion in his eyes.

"You belong to me," he said, as if tasting the words.

"Yes, sir," I said obediently.

He made himself twitch inside me, sending a shock of desire through my hips.

"Every part of you."

He brushed his fingers through my hair, gathering it in his square, hard fingers. His touch skimmed over my throat and traced down my collarbone to my right breast. He cupped it, squeezing it hard enough to spark pain. Then he let go and began running his thumb around my nipple, coaxing it until it went hard.

"Your soft, tight cunt," he said reflectively. "Your ass, your tits, your legs. Your mouth. Every part of you belongs to me. I'm the only man who's ever had you."

"Yes, sir," I breathed.

Our eyes locked and a shudder moved through my body. My pussy pulsed, the slick muscles gripping him. A muscle twitched in his jaw and I knew it was taking everything he had not to thrust.

"Who takes my cock like a good whore?" he said, his voice going cold.

"I do." The words caught in my throat. Thick and choking me.

He growled with approval, low and deep in his throat. His middle finger touched my nape, dragging down my spine. Caressing my lower back with slow strokes.

"Who do you come for?"

"Y—you."

"Say it loud and clear. You're not ashamed of me. Who do you come for, Olivia?"

"You," I said, letting my voice ring out. "Only you."

He dragged his cock halfway out and slammed it back in.

"That's right, baby."

I clung to the sink and he fucked me and stroked my clit until we both shuddered as one. Lost in each other. Then we showered together and he left for work, his jaw set in a grim line. I knew he had something on his mind, but I also knew better than to ask him about it when he was in a mood. And I was sick of resisting, tired of fighting.

He existed in shades of gray and I'd accepted that, but I hadn't realized I would need to keep accepting that. That I would have to keep choosing him every day despite the things he did. Despite his terrifying hunger for revenge and power, despite his mercilessness.

I was his wife, the mother of his children.

The queen on his chessboard.

And that was enough.

Determined to make today better than the last few weeks, I went downstairs and made myself breakfast. I rarely had problems with food while I was pregnant because I knew I wasn't eating for myself, so I took advantage of it.

Marco sat in his high chair, jabbering about how apparently Lucien had promised him a sleepover with his cousin later on in the day. I made a mental note to call Lucien because I hadn't made plans to send

Marco over to Lorenza and Cosimo's house. It bothered me when Lucien arranged my schedule without asking me.

I prepared us both avocado toast with soft boiled eggs and bacon on the side. Marco made an enormous mess on his tray while I reveled in eating three pieces of loaded toast without a trace of guilt. Then I had a cup of hot chocolate with whipped cream and sat on the bathroom floor while Marco played in the tub.

"Mama, look," he said.

I turned to look at the pile of bubbles on his head.

"That's amazing, baby," I said, smiling.

He went to look in the mirror over the tub, admiring his bubble hat. My stomach tightened at the reflection of his hazel eyes. They already had a trace of that disconnected, flat expression I'd grown to love on his father's face. But if I could have given Marco my eyes, I would have. He looked so much like his father that sometimes it hurt my heart.

As much as I loved my husband, I didn't want my son to be like him.

I wanted him to be his own man. Free of ice, free of scars.

My phone rang just as I laid Marco down for his nap. I kissed his forehead and ducked into the hall, shutting the door quietly. My screen flashed, signaling a missed call from Lucien. I went down to the kitchen and made tea and settled on the stool to call him back.

"How are you feeling?" he asked.

"Fine. Really good, actually," I said. "I was starving. Maybe a little tired, but way better than I did with Marco at this stage."

"Did you eat?" His voice was clipped.

"I haven't eaten lunch yet, but I ate a big breakfast."

"Do you need me to order food to the house for you?"

"No, I have a smoothie bowl in the freezer," I said, my chest warming. My hand slid down to my lower stomach.

"That's not enough. I'll order you something."

"Lucien, I don't need that."

"What I said was a statement, baby, not a question. And I expect you to eat what I order."

"Alright, fine." I rolled my eyes.

"I heard you roll your eyes, baby."

"How—"

"I can hear it in your voice."

"Fine, I'm sorry."

There was a short silence and papers shuffled and then I heard his footsteps and a door shut. I could tell he was in the downtown office.

"I'm taking you out tonight for dinner," he said. "Then I'd like to fuck you to sleep. How does that sound?"

I took a minute to gather myself. Of course I was excited that Lucien had time to take me out. Usually he was too busy for that sort of thing unless it was a special occasion we'd planned days in advance.

"It sounds good," I said, unable to hold back my smile.

"Oh, and Marco is going over to Lorenza and Cosimo's house," he said briskly. "I've already set it up. They're going out of town to the cabin in the Adirondacks for the next couple of days."

I frowned. "I was actually going to call you about that. Can you please talk to me before you arrange my son's schedule."

"Our son," he corrected.

"I'm the one who's with him all day and I need to be able to organize his schedule," I snapped. "Just consult me next time, please."

"Watch your tone, baby," he said, not unkindly.

I took a slow breath and a sip of my tea. Today was going to be good and nothing was going to mess it up. I was not going to fight with my husband.

"Yes, sir," I said.

"Good girl," he said absently. "Also I made a doctor's appointment for you this Wednesday. Does that work for you?"

"That's fine."

"Alright, make sure to wear something nice tonight. It's an expensive hotel and we'll be staying the night, so pack a bag. I'd like a short distance between getting you fed and getting you fucked."

"Lucien!"

"Oh, I've said much worse things to you, baby," he said, a hint of warmth in his tone. "I'll be back at six to pick you up."

I hung up and went upstairs to pack, but I couldn't shake the feeling that something else was going on. Lucien spoiled me, he bought me gifts, and took me on anniversary and birthday trips. But there was something odd about his plans for the night and I didn't like it.

He was there to pick me up at six sharp, already dressed in one of his fine, gray suits. I wore a slinky, silver dress, that I wouldn't be able to wear for much longer, and a pair of matching heels. He walked into the bathroom just as I fastened the heavy sapphire necklace around my throat. His eyes fell on me and his mouth twitched.

"You're so fucking lovely," he murmured.

He kissed the back of my neck and my body shuddered. My anxiety about the evening had vanished at the sight of him, handsome and stoic as ever. He slid his tattooed hand down my stomach, lingering on my lower belly. When he raised his eyes to mine in the mirror, there was a distinct glimmer of satisfaction in them.

"What?" I asked.

"Nothing." He shook his head. "I love you."

He didn't tell me he loved me often, it wasn't a natural part of his vocabulary, so it felt like a gift when he offered it unprompted. My body warm, satisfied, and happy for the first time in weeks, I kissed him.

He gazed down at me as I stroked my fingers through the gray flecks of hair at his temple and his ice melted just a little.

He brought me to a hotel on the northeast side of town. We rarely ventured this way together so it was a little strange that he'd picked it. The hotel was beautiful and modern, the way Lucien liked it. Everything was black glass, shining surfaces, and pure elegance. All the seasonal decorations were silver and white and glittered like starlight.

Instead of leading me to the dining room, Lucien went to the front desk. The woman behind the counter took one look at him and paled, scrambling to her feet.

"Mr. Esposito, sir," she said. "What can I do for you?"

"You must be new," Lucien said.

"Yes, sir," she stammered.

"Started today?"

"Yes, sir."

His lids flickered, his hand settling on my waist. "You'll want to talk with your manager about my request for tonight. Understood?"

She nodded vigorously. "I will, sir. Is there anything else I can do? We have your table reserved for anytime you like."

"Is the honeymoon suite all booked?" he said.

She looked down at her computer and I thought I saw a flicker of confusion pass over her face and then she nodded. She went and took down a set of brass keys tied with white ribbon and handed them over.

"Let me just have your things brought up," she said.

"Thank you," Lucien said, passing her the Tesla key card. "They're in the car just outside the door. If the valet wouldn't mind to park for us, that would be good."

"Of course, sir," she said.

"Thank you," he said. "We're going to have dinner. If you could check the notes under my name, it has room instructions."

She nodded and he thanked her again, leaving her a substantial tip. I frowned as he led me into the darkened living room and helped me sit down at a table in the middle of the front room.

"Lucien, I don't think the front desk clerks are allowed to accept tips," I said quietly. "You could get her fired."

He sat back in his chair. "I own the hotel, baby."

Of course he did. I rolled my eyes before I realized what I'd done and froze. His head cocked slowly and his gaze narrowed, but I was saved by the arrival of our waiter. He exchanged pleasantries with Lucien and laid down our menus and tucked his hands behind his back.

"May I start you out with a wine, Mrs. Esposito?" he asked.

"My wife is pregnant," Lucien said. "Do you have anything nonalcoholic?"

"Of course, sir, we have a delicious champagne that's totally alcohol free," he said. "And congratulations, sir."

"I'll have that," I said.

"I'll take the Bordeaux," said Lucien. His eyes lifted and fixed on me with intensity. "What would you like for a starter, baby?"

I glanced down at the menu, my stomach rumbling. There was a lot of fancy things I couldn't pronounce that didn't sound like they'd fill me up. I hesitated, afraid to say what I was really hungry for.

"If you have any cravings, we'd be happy to make anything you'd like," our waiter said. "When my wife was pregnant, she used to eat loaded fries every night for dinner."

My stomach growled and twisted at the mental image. A twinge of guilt moving through me. I took a quick breath and calmed myself, remembering I had to eat despite what I was feeling. And tonight I wasn't going to struggle with my food.

I was going to fucking eat it and enjoy every minute.

"Yes, please," I said, smiling up at him. "Steak fries. And could I have them loaded with cheese, bacon, and....extra cheese?"

"Anything, ma'am," he said.

Lucien's eyes flickered with rare warmth. "I'll skip the starter."

The waiter nodded and gathered up our menus, but before he left, he leaned in and said, "It's not listed, but there is a burger with sweet balsamic glaze. It's served with whipped potatoes and gravy."

"I want that," I said.

Lucien laughed softly. "I suppose we can order our main course. I'll take the steak, very rare, with mixed vegetables."

After our waiter left, Lucien leaned his elbows on the table and looked at me for a long moment. I blushed, taking a sip of my water.

"Sorry if I embarrassed you," I said. "I know french fries aren't exactly sophisticated."

His brow twitched.

"I fucking love watching you eat and enjoy it," he said. "I'm proud of you for taking care of our baby."

His lids lowered and I wasn't sure what to do as he studied me in silence. Finally he reached across and took my hand, fingering the heavy diamond ring on my finger. There was a trace of wistfulness in his eyes.

"What is it?"

"I'm fucking obsessed with you."

I was speechless. He looked at me without a hint of embarrassment, or anything for that matter. His face was blank again, impassive as the day he'd walked into my house and stolen me away.

"So is everyone else. They love the work you do at the foundation. Hell, you have our waiter wrapped around your little finger without even trying. You're a natural."

I swallowed, my fingers clenching in his.

"How would you feel about me going into politics?" he asked.

Politics? I stared at him, a thousand mental images spinning through my mind. I'd thought he wasn't interested in entering that arena.

"Are you sure that's what you want?" I asked.

"No. I'm thinking about it. There would be something satisfying about getting the position your father is vying for. I feel like moving into city politics is the natural next step for me. I'm well liked, I have money, I have a beautiful, articulate wife who made a reputation for herself running a charitable foundation."

I bristled a little.

"I run the foundation because it helps people," I said. "The way you and I should have been helped."

"I know, I didn't mean it like that."

I sighed. Lucien would never stop reaching for the moon and the stars. He had no concept of a plateau and nothing would ever be enough for him. His mind worked quickly and ruthlessly and it would never be satisfied. I knew better than to stand in his way at this point.

"As long as our children are shielded, I'm fine with it," I said. "And the foundation continues to be mine to oversee."

"Really?"

"Far be it from me to keep Lucien Esposito back."

His brow twitched. "Good girl."

Our waiter appeared, cutting our conversation short. The champagne and fries appeared and I inhaled both, eating the entire plate of fries while Lucien watched me with satisfaction in his glittering, hazel eyes.

For one moment, the world felt overwhelmingly perfect. Lucien sat across from me, his handsome face half lit by candlelight. Outside, it was snowing gently and the city glittered quietly like a painted backdrop behind him. And inside, I was warm and fed with his baby growing in my stomach.

I swallowed, hoping that when this moment broke, the waiting storm would be gentle.

CHAPTER TWENTY

LUCIEN

The moment she placed that positive test in my hand, I knew I had no other choice. Her father had to die and I had to make sure nothing like this ever happened again. I had power in the underground, in the darker parts of the city, but I needed to step into the sunlight. I had to take a step beyond paying off politicians and become one. I needed to be truly untouchable, not reliant on anyone but myself.

My wife and children's safety depended on it.

After she was finished eating, we retired to the lounge in the hotel. I let her curl up against me and I stroked her hair gently and watched the snow pile up on the street. Then I carried her up through the lavish hallway and into the honeymoon suite.

Her eyelashes fluttered and opened wide. She wriggled out of my grip and began circling the room, her lips parted as she took everything in. It was modern, but lavish, and it looked out over the city. In the center of the room was a coffee table with six dozen white roses, a bottle of nonalcoholic champagne, and chocolates. In an open, velvet case was a sapphire bracelet to match the stone hanging from her pretty throat.

"Lucien," she said quietly.

"Yes, baby?"

"What...what is all this?" Her dark eyes were concerned. "It's not a special occasion."

"Do I need a special occasion to spoil my wife?"

I was a fucking liar. Of course Olivia deserved to be spoiled, but that wasn't what tonight was about. I'd brought her here to keep her safe in case things didn't go as planned, just as I'd sent Marco out of town. I'd fed her well to make her sleepy so I could exhaust her body until she passed out. So she slept through the ugliness, oblivious and protected.

Because no matter what, I would always keep her safe.

I saw a million thoughts pass like ghosts behind her dark gaze. Then she shook her head and smiled, holding her hands out to me. I went to her and caught her fingers in my grasp, pulling her against me.

"Shall I make love to you?" I said, half joking.

She pulled back, smiling, and looked up at me. I brushed a tendril of hair back, tucking it behind her ear, and stroked her cheek. I saw her throat bob as she swallowed and a pang of guilt went through me.

This was for her protection. I had to follow through.

"I want it gentle," she whispered.

My chest tightened. My poor wife, she was so brave in the face of everything I put her through. I bent, kissing her forehead, lingering with my lips against her skin. I felt the tension in her body ease and she sank into me, her fingers gripping my jacket.

I took her into the bedroom and stripped her clothes from her body. She lay in the center of the velvet and silk bedclothes and watched me take off my suit, a glimmer of desire in her heavy eyes.

I bent over her pussy to taste it, but she shook her head and pulled me up to kiss her mouth. She gripped my side gently, guiding my body between her thighs. Her wet pussy accepted my cock, wrapping it in total bliss.

I made love to her, even though it wasn't what I usually did. Usually I fucked her, but tonight wasn't the moment for that. She took me, her lids heavy, her eyes holding mine. Then I reached between us and stroked her clit until she shuddered and came apart around me. My orgasm followed soon after and I rolled off her body and drew apart her legs. I loved the sight of her pussy, just used, wet with my cum.

"You've got a lovely cunt," I murmured against her neck.

"Hmm, thank you," she said sleepily.

I filled the tub and we bathed together. She sat in my lap in the hot water and let me wash her with lavender scented wash. Then I dried her body and laid her down in the bed and gently rubbed her hips and lower back until her lids closed and her breathing evened.

I slid from the bed. She was completely passed out, snoring a little under the covers. I was careful to make no noise as I dressed in casual pants, a shirt, and my shoulder holsters. My guns lay heavily against my ribs as I pulled on my jacket and buttoned it tightly. Then I slipped two knives into my forearm holsters and covered them with my sleeves.

One of my bodyguards stood in the kitchen. I wasn't sure when he'd arrived, but he was ready, his gun strapped to his thigh. I locked the bedroom door from the outside and he moved to stand before it, his hands tucked behind his back. Out in the hall, I locked the main door and another bodyguard took his place before it.

The hotel staff and my security had done an excellent job carrying out my requests. I could tell every camera in the hall and the lobby was disconnected and the street around the hotel was cleared. It was cold and the air bit my face savagely as I began walking toward the historic district where Rosario Barone worked.

He would leave his office around eleven and take his car home. Except, tonight his driver was unconscious in the trunk of a car in the parking garage. I'd pulled some strings with all three taxi companies so they wouldn't respond to any calls from Rosario. And I'd made sure that all of his close friends had been given tickets to the opera house tonight.

He would have to walk to his hotel four blocks away. Vulnerable. Ready for me to do what needed done.

I paused across the street, keeping my hat pulled low. The secondary mayoral office was in a tall, historic row house with an iron fence across the front garden. I checked my watch, my palm itching. Five more minutes. My senses heightened, taking in the falling snow, the streetlights, the faint sound of ice forming on the gutters.

The front door opened and I recognized Rosario's figure. Inwardly, I was deadly calm. Just as I'd been when I killed Romano and my father. But in the silence, I felt my heartbeat increase just a trace. Like a wolf lifting its face to smell the wind.

Rosario paced back and forth on the sidewalk for several minutes. He paused on the curb and began searching his clothes for his phone and came up with nothing. Swearing softly, he turned and went back up the walkway to find the door was locked. Of course it was, anyone could be bought out for the right price.

He beat on the door for a moment, but the office was empty. Finally, he kicked the door in a fit of anger and whirled, striding down the sidewalk to the street. For a moment, he looked back and forth for a taxi and then he gave up and began walking down the street.

Perfect. Caught like a fly in my web.

I slipped out into the road and began following him, keeping to the shadows when I could. The snow was soft and made my footsteps almost soundless, not that Rosario was listening anyway. He was stalking down the sidewalk quickly, his head bent, briefcase hanging from his right hand.

We approached a fork in the road where he could stay to the main street or take a shortcut through the alley. I hung back a few blocks, watching his figure hesitate and look back and forth. Then he turned and disappeared past a iron fence and into the alleyway.

My heartbeat increased as a surge of predatory arousal moved through me, making the hair stand on the back of my neck. I ducked into the alley, drawing the knives from beneath my sleeves. The metal glinted and my blood mounted, pumping through me until I swore I could see and smell everything. Up ahead, Rosario slowed as the light dimmed further into the alley and I increased my speed, gaining on him.

He turned at the last moment and I struck him in the chest with my elbow, throwing him against the wall. All the air left his lungs in a sick sound and he rolled to the ground twice.

Not missing a beat, I flipped him onto his back and put my boot on his neck, keeping him still.

"Just take my wallet," he said, squirming. "Just take whatever."

"I knew you were a cunt," I said. "But I didn't think you were a pussy."

He stopped wriggling and the clouds shifted, letting a shaft of pale light into the alley. His eyes widened as they fell on my face and I cocked my head, flipping the knives once and catching them again.

"Lucien," he breathed.

"In the flesh."

He bared his teeth, pure hatred filling his gaze. "You going to kill me like you killed Romano, you fucking traitor?"

Slowly, I knelt until his face was purple from the pressure on his throat. I played with it for a moment, grinding my heel, and then shifted my weight just enough so he could breathe.

"Do you know why I killed Romano?" I asked.

"Because you wanted power," Rosario snarled. "And everyone knows the story of what he did to you, I'm not an idiot."

My chest went tight, remembering the pain in Olivia's eyes the night she confessed she'd been sexually violated by Romano. The fact that I hadn't protected her, that I hadn't known what had happened until it was too late, still haunted me. Rage flared in me and I brought the blade up to his throat, pressing it into his flesh just enough he winced.

"I killed Romano because he assaulted your daughter."

He spat at me and I leaned back to avoid it.

"My daughter is a fucking whore," he snapped. "She always has been."

It took everything I had not to sink the knife into his throat and watch the blood bubble out of his mouth. I took a quick breath and released it slowly, grinding my foot just enough to make him wince.

"Of course you wouldn't care," I said flatly. "You beat her, you hit her. And I want to know why."

"Why?" he breathed, staring up at me like I was insane.

"Why did you hurt her?" I said. "Olivia is...kind, she's obedient. Why would you beat her the way you did? I doubt she ever once disobeyed you."

He opened his mouth and shut it, a flicker of doubt passing through his eyes. I swallowed, forcing my face to remain impassive.

"You did it because you like hurting small, weak things," I said quietly. "Because it's the only way you can feel like a man."

My stomach churned as I recalled all the things she'd told me. How he'd kicked her in the ribs until she vomited because he thought the condom her friend had left in her wallet was hers. The time she'd walked by him in the hallway without greeting him and he'd taken her by the neck and slammed her head into the wall. The time Cosimo had driven her to the hospital because she'd lied and said she'd fallen on the sidewalk, but really her father had brought his fist down on her hand and broken her wrist.

Olivia had grown up thinking that men would always abuse her and it had taken me years to break her of that idea.

And now, the reason for all her pain was at my feet.

Helpless.

I shifted, straddling his chest, and dug the knife deeper into his flesh. Blood slipped out and he squirmed, but I hushed him.

"Do you like this?" I asked. "Do you like being helpless? Do you like feeling small and weak?'

"Fuck you," he spat.

"I'm going to kill you," I told him flatly. "Not because you're trying to challenge me or because you threatened my family. No, there's only one reason you deserve to die."

His eyes were wide like a panicked animal. I let the knives fall with a clatter and moved closer, pinning his arms down beneath my knees. He made a faint strangled sound as I slid my hands up the sides of his throat and cradled his head in my fingers. My grip hardened, trying to force him to meet my gaze.

"No, I want you to hear this."

He gasped, his glazed eyes darting to mine before flicking away.

"Look at me," I growled, my voice splitting the silence.

Panting, he obeyed.

"You put your hands on my wife," I said. "I'll see you in hell, motherfucker."

The sound his neck made when I snapped it healed the rage in the bottom of my soul. It put out the fire that had burned there since Olivia had told me what he'd done.

Justice was done. The light faded from Rosario's eyes and I released his head and it fell back at an awkward angle. I sat there, still straddling his body, and looked up at the sky.

I took a deep breath of icy air and held it. Reveling quietly in what I'd done.

Overhead, the snow still fell even though the moon shone full through the clouds. It landed on my skin and melted, dripping down my jaw and throat. In my chest, there was peace and the warm glow of victory. I got to my feet slowly and gathered my knives, stained with blood from where I'd cut the side of his throat. There were crimson smears on my hands and I knew I needed to get back to the hotel and clean every bit of his DNA from me.

I took his wallet, emptied the money, and tossed it by his head. There had to be a shadow of a suspicion his killing was a mugging gone wrong. Then, without looking back at the limp body already covered in a thin layer of snow, I strode down the alley toward the hotel.

My heart rate increased as I walked down the center of the road. The moon had disappeared and snow fell thickly around me, but inside I was burning with a purpose I'd not felt in a long time.

This was my fucking city.

And that was the last time anyone would challenge me in it ever again.

I made it to the hotel in record time and circled around to the steel door of the back entrance. It opened as I approached and Peregrine stood there, his face sober.

"Come," he said, jerking his head.

I followed him down the dark hallway and he pushed open the door to the meat locker. In the corner of the room was a shower head coming out of the wall, presumably to wash away animal blood. Beside it stood a table with a metal surface.

"Table is for your clothes," Peregrine said. "And weapons."

I nodded, crossing the dark room. All around me, frozen carcasses of pigs and cattle hung like silent guardians. The room was chilly, making the hair prickle on the back of my neck. Peregrine followed me, pulling on a pair of rubber gloves that reached his elbows.

I stripped my clothes off and Peregrine took them, setting them on the table. Then he turned on the faucet and ice cold water sprayed out, dousing me. My senses roared back to life, shocking me, and my dick retracted into my body faster than I knew what was happening.

"Jesus—fuck!" I swore. "Couldn't have been warm?"

"You said you wanted no traces," Peregrine said. "This is how we're doing it."

I gritted my teeth and scrubbed my body in the icy water over and over again until every fleck of blood was gone. Washed down the drain at my feet. From the corner of my eye, I saw Peregrine drag the table to the middle of the room and light my clothes on fire on the metal top. The combination of the thick smoke, the scent of blood, and the icy water made my stomach churn.

Fuck, I needed a drink to calm my raging adrenaline. But more than a drink, I needed my wife. I needed to fall into the quiet world where only she and I existed, wrapped up together in our bed.

I stepped out of the cold water, my entire body numb. Peregrine returned and passed me a pair of sweatpants. My hands were so stiff it took me almost five minutes to dry off and get my clothes on. Peregrine tossed the towel onto the metal table and it began smoking, fire curling around the edges.

"I'm good?" I said, keeping my jaw stiff so it wouldn't chatter.

"You're good," Peregrine said. "I'll make sure everything else gets cleaned up."

"Thank you," I said. "And, I don't need to tell you never to mention this. You're the only person outside of my bodyguards and the hotel staff that know something went down. You're the only person other than me who knows who I killed tonight."

"You know you can trust me," said Peregrine.

"I know," I said. "Goodnight."

The kitchens were empty and the security cameras were dead as I passed by them. I was barefoot so I moved silently out into the main lobby. The clerk behind the counter kept their head down, busily typing on their computer. I walked by them and took the stairs up to the honeymoon suite.

My bodyguards left silently and I bolted the door. Still shivering, I went to the bathroom off the kitchen and took a hot shower, scrubbing my skin until it was impossible for any trace of blood to remain on it.

Then I went out into the living room in a clean pair of boxer briefs and poured a glass of whiskey.

I hadn't felt this good in years. Having Rosario alive and unpunished for hurting Olivia had rested like a thorn on my side for the last six years. Now he was gone, freezing slowly in the dark. Dead, as he deserved.

The scales of the world were balanced. I moved to the window, looking out over the city. I'd always run it from the inside, handing out bribes, blackmailing, and threatening influential people to keep my power.

And I wasn't about to stop.

But stepping into the mayoral race would let me operate on both levels. It would tighten my grip, give me power like I'd never had it before.

My blood pumped faster and I took a sip of whiskey. It had a smooth take and a savory aftertaste. It was expensive, almost twenty thousand a bottle. For a fleeting moment I fantasized about pouring the whiskey all over my naked wife, hundreds and hundreds of dollars dripping down her bare stomach. Licking it from her tits, shooting it out of her navel, dripping it from my mouth to her waiting tongue.

That was the kind of fuck-you power and money I wanted for her.

The bedroom door creaked and I turned to see Olivia standing there in one of my t-shirts. Her hair was rumpled and she blinked up at me confusedly, rubbing her face. I eyed her, fully and deeply satisfied with myself.

"What are you doing?"

I held out my arm and she slid beneath it, letting me pull her against my side. She turned her face up and I kissed her mouth, savoring every bit of her taste.

"I couldn't sleep," I said. "So I got up and took a shower and I'm having a drink."

She rubbed her eyes. "We could watch some TV? Maybe that would help."

I shook my head. "No, let's go to sleep. I'm ready to get some rest. Tomorrow is going to be a good day, baby."

CHAPTER TWENTY-ONE

OLIVIA

The nagging sense of something being wrong had lifted when I opened my eyes. Lucien was gone, his side of the bed creased in his wake. Rubbing sleep from my eyes, I padded out to the kitchen to find him making espresso. I paused for a moment in the doorway, looking at him through my rumpled bangs. He was so gorgeous, all lean muscles and tattoos. The way those sweatpants hung off his hips drove me crazy.

His eyes lifted and I saw something in them that was new. It looked like anticipation...and almost like peace.

"Good morning," he said pleasantly.

I crossed to the kitchen and stood on my toes so he could kiss my mouth. He brushed his fingers through my tangled hair and cradled my face.

"Listen, I have something to tell you," he said.

My stomach twisted.

"Your father was found dead this morning."

My whole body went stiff and there was a faint roaring in my ears. I barely felt his hands slip down my sides and linger on my waist, stroking in soft circles. I'd never had so many conflicting feelings rush through me at once and I was struggling to maintain control of myself. My lashes were wet and there was a dull ache in my chest, but there was also an overwhelming feeling of relief.

I didn't have to fear him anymore. He wouldn't hurt our family. I never had to worry about running into him and having to relive the trauma of his abuse. I swallowed.

Was I a sick, evil person for being happy that he was gone?

"Are you alright, baby?" Lucien asked.

I raised my eyes to his and nothing but barren, frozen wasteland looked back at me. My stomach tightened as I remembered how I'd awoken to find him gone. How I'd padded out to the living room to see him freshly showered, looking out over the city like he owned it.

Lucien had gotten up at some point and left. But how long had he been out of bed? And what had he done while I slept?

"What happened?" I whispered.

"Mugging gone wrong," he said. "I don't mean to sound cruel, but this does eliminate the threat of him hurting our family. And it protects the outfit."

"He got mugged?"

"On his way home from work last night," said Lucien. "It's all over the news this morning."

I narrowed my gaze, wishing I had the ability to see past the stone wall of his face. But, as it always was, there was nothing in those cold eyes. Perhaps he was telling me the truth.

Or perhaps whatever really happened was locked away for good, in his brutal mind.

And I was grateful for it.

My throat closed and a tear slipped down my cheek and lingered on my jaw. He had absolved me of any blame in my father's death. I would never know for sure what had happened so I would always be innocent. My husband had taken the burden of guilt solely onto himself to protect me and our family.

"Are you alright?" he asked.

I drew myself up. I was Olivia Esposito, wife of Lucien Esposito. I was the queen on his chessboard, the mother of his children, the other half to his whole. I wasn't scared. I was the wife of the most notorious man in this city. And if Lucien had anything to do with it, he was about to get a lot more powerful.

"Lucien," I asked. "If you run for mayor, will you quit the outfit?"

"Fuck, no," he said. "This is everything I've built. I'm Lucien Esposito, I can have my fucking cake and eat it too."

The idea of him like that, soaked in power, like a god ruling over his own personal universe, sent a surge of warmth between my thighs. My breath came faster and I slid my hands up, digging them into his forearms until he winced. I wanted him to take what my father had coveted.

I wanted my husband to burn down the memory of every man who had hurt me so I could rise like a phoenix from his flames.

"Then you'd better fucking win," I said.

His brow twitched. "I have no doubt I will."

"I'll stand by your side, I'll wave for pictures, I'll cut ribbons," I said. "But promise me that at the end of the day I'll always be fucked by the most powerful man in this city."

He picked me up and pushed me onto the counter. His head dipped, his fingers yanking down my slip, baring my breasts to his mouth. Behind us, the coffee pot bubbled wildly on the stove, but we were too drunk on excitement to notice.

He pulled me to the edge of the counter and got down on his knees. His eyes locked on mine as he pressed kisses with his open mouth up the inside of my thighs. Drawing nearer and nearer to the wet, slickness between my legs.

"I'm the only one you need to get on your knees for," I whispered. "Ever again."

He'd said it to me once, years ago, and I knew he remembered because his eyes flickered. Then he bent his head, burying it between my thighs, and ate me like I was his last meal. I writhed and moaned for him and came on his tongue. Then he fucked me on the kitchen floor, our clothes pulled aside, and our eyes locked.

Never breaking, never letting go.

I loved seeing him in action and today he was in top form. After we'd fucked in the kitchen once and in the bed twice, he left me panting and slick with his cum and went to call Peregrine. By the time we were cleaned up and I'd dressed in heels and a sleek, white pencil dress, Peregrine and Duran had appeared in the doorway.

They got to work immediately. The election was in a year and it was going to take every minute of that time to rebrand Lucien as a mayoral candidate. Peregrine was already pacing back and forth with his phone to his ear and Duran was cursing at the printer in the corner, trying to get the documentation in order. Lucien had Bennett Emerson-Green on the phone and they were conversing urgently by the window.

I made them coffee and set it out and excused myself. Then I went to the bedroom and slipped on the sapphire necklace and bracelet. I looked at myself in the mirror and I looked young and eager, which wasn't the look I was going for at all. Frowning, I brushed my bangs aside and pulled my hair back into a low bun at the nape of my neck. No, too severe. I brushed my bangs back over, but kept the low bun.

Perfect.

Then I went downstairs to the restaurant and had a decaf coffee and breakfast alone. I sat there for a long time and watched the pale sunlight glitter off the snow piled in the streets. I knew I needed to call Cosimo, but I was afraid he knew too much.

But it was inevitable. The topic would come up one way or the other.

He picked up on the third ring.

"You heard?" he asked.

"Yeah," I said. "Yeah, I did."

There was a long silence. Then he cleared his throat.

"Am I a sick bastard if I admit that I'm relieved?" he said.

"I'm relieved too," I said.

He released a pent-up sigh that reached down to the soles of his feet. "I'm glad you're safe. And I'm glad the outfit is safe."

"Me too."

"And...um, I can't tell you what to do, but maybe don't ask Lucien about it," Cosimo said. "There are some situations where ignorance is bliss."

I nodded and then remembered he couldn't see me. "Yeah, I won't. I don't think you should either. Our problem is solved and we don't have to worry about him ever again. That's enough for me."

"It's enough for me too," he said. "Listen, the kids are going wild and Enza's tearing her hair out, so I have to go. Love you, Liv. You call me if you need anything."

"Love you," I said, even though the words felt unnatural. Neither of us had grown up in a home where expressing affection was encouraged, but we were learning.

Healing was a forever process.

Three days before Christmas, I woke to find Lucien already sitting up in bed, his computer in his lap. I rolled over and sat up, brushing back my messy bangs. Even though I was less than two months along, I swore I was already showing. My lower stomach pressed against my silk slip. Lucien noticed and his hand drifted down to rub my belly absently.

"How're you feeling?"

"Hungry and horny," I said. "The usual."

He picked up an envelope from his bedside table and passed it to me. I turned it over and tore open the top, pulling out some kind of legal document. I skimmed it, too lazy to read all the tiny print.

"What is this?"

"I want you to have a haven," he said. "Somewhere we can go where there's no work, no outfit, no foundation, no tabloids."

I stared at him. "Yes, but what is this? A ticket?"

"Read it, baby," he said. "It's a deed to a chalet in the Adirondacks that now belongs to Olivia Esposito."

"It's mine?" I felt my eyes widen. "Can we go?"

He set aside his laptop and bent to kiss my forehead. "I thought we would spend Christmas there. Just you and I and Marco."

I stared up at him. "Really?"

He took my throat gently in his grip, caressing it with his thumb.

"I'm sorry I'm not always here," he said. "Going forward, especially as our lives get busier, I swear to make as much time as I can for you and Marco. And the new baby."

We left for the chalet early the next morning and Lucien drove us upstate. We could have taken a private plane and our trip would have been cut in half, but I knew my husband preferred to be the one with his hands on the wheel, so I didn't point that out. Instead, I spent the next few hours entertaining Marco and playing his favorite song so many times Lucien's jaw started twitching.

We arrived late in the evening. The two story, spacious chalet sat near the top of the mountain, overlooking a frosted valley. It was beginning to snow again as Lucien took my hand, hoisting a sleeping Marco into his other arm, and led us up the walkway. He punched in the code and ushered me inside.

We laid Marco down to sleep in the downstairs bedroom. Then I padded barefoot over the pine floors and up the staircase to the lofted bedroom. My stomach fluttered as I paused at the top, looking over the A-frame room with floor-to-ceiling windows. There was a huge bed, almost twice as big as the one we had back home, by the window.

The view was breathtaking and I found myself entranced, taking in the falling snow.

"Do you like it?"

I jumped, turning to find Lucien with the suitcases. He set them aside and pulled me in for a kiss.

"I love it," I breathed.

His eyes, the same color as the frozen landscape around us, fixed on my mouth.

"Marco is fast asleep," he said.

I knew what he wanted because I knew him. He was an insatiable force in every aspect of his life. Breaking out of his embrace, I reached for the suitcase.

"Let me shower first."

When I slipped from the bathroom, he was already in bed. Laying on his back on the pillows with the rumpled, white sheet across his naked lap. I crossed the room, suddenly shy, and paused at the edge of the bed. His eyes skimmed over my body and lingered on the little rise of my lower belly beneath my silk slip.

"What do you want tonight?" I whispered.

Instead of replying, he pulled me onto the bed, flipping me to face the window on my hands and knees. I knew then what he wanted, what Lucien always wanted deep down.

Compliance, obedience, the willingness to be conquered.

My stomach fluttered and heat blossomed between my legs as his mouth brushed the arch of my foot. Kissing slowly, leaving little wet spots on my skin as he worked his way up to my thighs. By the time he got to my ass, I was dripping down the inside of my leg.

"Who fucks you?" His voice was hard.

"You fuck me, Lucien," I gasped.

I felt him on his knees behind me as he lined his cock up with my wet entrance and pressed into me. Stretching me slowly as he pushed his hot length into my pussy. I clenched my muscles around him and he growled softly.

"Who got you pregnant, baby?"

A shock of arousal tightened my nipples.

"You did," I gasped. "You got me pregnant, Lucien."

He made a low noise of appreciation and took my hips in his lean fingers and began fucking me hard. I gasped, gripping the sheets to hold on. He was quiet as he took me, the only sound our slick bodies hitting together. After a while, he spat on his fingers and began working my clit as he thrust into me.

He kept me on the edge, desperate to come for several minutes. His strokes were hard enough I felt the shock of impact, but slow enough I felt every inch of his cock drag in and out of me.

"Lucien, please," I begged.

"Hush, baby," he said. "I'll let you come when I feel like it."

He tortured me for a while longer and then he pulled me to the end of the bed so he could stand and take me from behind. I braced on the heels of my hands, anticipating that he would fuck me hard, but he was surprisingly gentle.

Forceful, but still gentle.

He put one hand on my hip and the other on my shoulder to keep me still and thrust with aching slowness. When I glanced over my shoulder, I saw him there, his tattooed body glittering with sweat. His eyes fixed to the place where we joined, where our bodies became one.

I was shaking by the time he finally let me come and I couldn't bite back the cry that burst from me. He flipped me onto my back and pushed his fingers into my mouth to silence me. My eyes rolled back as I shook and writhed beneath him and he tensed, emptying himself into me with a quiet groan.

The next morning I padded downstairs in a set of flannel pajamas printed with snowflakes. Marco was already awake, running around yelling at the top of his lungs in the living room. I crossed the room to the kitchen area where Lucien stood, making him a bowl of cold cereal, and wrapped my arms around his waist.

"Good morning," I whispered.

He turned and warmth stirred in my chest. He was shirtless in only gray sweatpants that showed the faint outline of his dick. I knew he'd gotten up early to read or do paperwork because he still wore those slutty reading glasses I loved so much. My hormonal body raged.

He kissed me. "Good morning."

"You look good," I breathed.

"So do you."

He carried the bowl of cereal out and turned the television to the cartoon channel. Marco sat on the floor and accepted the bowl, his eyes gluing to the screen.

"Sit tight, son," Lucien said, ruffling his hair. "Your mother and I have to do the laundry and then we'll go for a walk after breakfast. Alright?"

"Okay," said Marco.

I frowned as he took my hand and ushered me to the other side of the room and opened a door in the far corner.

"The laundry?" I asked.

He pulled me into the tiny, dusty room. "It shouldn't take long."

A shot of warmth moved down my spine as he took off my slippers and tossed them in the dryer. They began thumping rhythmically and he turned me around, bending me over, and pulling down my pajama pants just enough to bare my pussy. I gasped as he pushed into me in one controlled thrust.

"Good girl," he breathed.

We fucked quietly and quickly and washed up in the sink. Then I went out to sit on the couch and watch cartoons with Marco while Lucien showered upstairs. Marco finished his cereal and crawled onto the couch to cuddle and I took him in my arms, stroking my fingers through his dark curls.

Lucien returned and made himself an espresso and me a decaf tea and sat down on the couch. Abandoning me for a chance to be with his father, Marco scrambled into his lap and perched cross legged, his eyes still fixed on the television. The sight of my husband and my son filled me with a warmth and contentment I hadn't felt in a long time.

CHAPTER TWENTY-TWO

LUCIEN

A YEAR LATER

It was three in the morning and we'd won the election. We were in my new downtown office I'd bought for my mayoral run and everyone in the main room was drunk and celebrating.

I was locked in my office, sitting at my desk, watching my wife's lovely eyes water as she struggled to get my cock down her throat. She pulled back to catch her breath and when she took me again, she swallowed the tip. I moaned softly, cradling her head.

She was getting off on it. But then she'd always loved power and pretty things and she was about to get a lot more of both.

The only reason I'd won this election was on the floor between my knees, her mouth wrapped around my dick.

In the last year, she'd become something more than I'd anticipated. She was elegant and adored now, a pillar of the community.

A goddess of philanthropy, a bleeding heart with a pretty face.

Once Olivia decided she was going to be the first lady of the city, she didn't stop. Even through her pregnancy with our second son, Hugo, she'd accompanied me to every event, she'd danced with every senator, she'd stood beside me for every photo shoot. And she'd run her foundation all while carrying my child and getting back on her feet just a week after giving birth to attend a gala with me.

She was born for this. My decision to run for mayor had allowed her to become the woman I'd only been able to see glimpses of before. And she had made everything possible. Without her, I never would have won the election.

Seeing her grow into power at my side only made her private submission to me sweeter. I'd watched as she charmed crowds, held babies for pictures, and greeted city officials until she was exhausted. And now I got to watch her get down on her knees with a wicked glitter in her eye and blow me with that talented mouth.

It was the most beautiful thing I'd ever witnessed.

She pushed her elegant fingers into my pants and stroked the base of my cock, sucking hard as I came down her throat. Then she rose and fixed her lipstick and patted down her hair. Her nipples were hard beneath her dress, but I could tell she wasn't in the mood to come. That didn't bother me.

She would have time for me later, tangled up in my bed. But right now, she had too many stars in her eyes.

"We should go," I said. "I have to make my victory speech."

She nodded and crossed the room to look in the mirror. Her lovely, curvy figure was wrapped in a tight, blue dress with a V neck and her soft, dark waves were pinned at the nape of her neck. She looked demure and sexy in a tasteful, soft way.

Warmth stirred in my chest as I watched her, amazed. Every time I pushed her, she blew me away with the way she rose to the occasion.

I pulled on my jacket and went to kiss the back of her neck. Her eyes met mine in the mirror and she smiled.

"We look good," she said softly.

"We do."

She turned and adjusted my tie. "Alright, let's go out there and face the crowd."

I took her hand and led her out into the main room to a roar of applause. All of our friends and allies in the city government and my underbosses were here tonight. All drunk and high on the euphoria of victory. I found myself being swept up in the crowd, shaking hands and greeting city officials. At some point, Peregrine, who had acted as my right hand through this all, gripped our elbows and dragged us out into the hall.

"Sir, you need to be in the event room now," Peregrine said. "You too, Liv."

I took my wife's hand and let Peregrine lead the way down the stairs and through the lobby of the Grand Imperium Hotel. Olivia gave a little gasp as she looked over her shoulder and I turned, taking in the sea of bodies outside the glass doors. It didn't bother me, but I could tell it was making Olivia nervous. I glanced down at her, lifting my chin. She smiled and copied me, letting her shoulders drop and her chin come up.

"Get back," Peregrine snapped, waving at a group of journalists. "Get to the press section. The mayor-elect isn't speaking to anyone in the lobby."

Olivia's eyes were wide and she moved closer to me, clinging to my hand. I slid my arm around her waist and kept her near as Peregrine ushered us into the back of the event room behind the curtain.

"There's a lot of fucking people out there," I said under my breath.

"It's definitely more attention than I anticipated, but then you were a popular candidate," said Peregrine.

He flicked his wrist and checked his watch. "Alright, Liv, we're actually sending you out separately. I want Lucien to go out and let things die down a little and then you'll be announced. Got it?"

She squared her shoulders. "Got it."

Everything moved in a rush and suddenly I was striding across the stage and the room shook with applause. The lights were blinding and I felt sweat drip down my back as I paused at the podium. It took the announcer a minute to quiet the crowd down and I turned to meet my wife's eyes from where she stood behind the curtain.

Her brows drew together as Peregrine stepped around her and joined me at the podium. He bent into the microphone.

"And of course, please welcome the lovely first lady of your city," he said. "Olivia Esposito."

The crowd was on its feet, roaring with twice the energy they had for me, but I didn't care. Pride swelled in my chest. There was nothing else in the world except my wife stepping out onto the stage like a piece of pure light flickering across the darkness of the room. My God, she was breathtaking in her dress, my jewels glittering like ice around her throat, and her lovely face framed by her soft waves.

I expected her to freeze, but she didn't. Instead she lifted her hand and waved, her face breaking into a smile as she crossed the stage. The crowd was beside themselves, shouting for her, stamping their feet, clapping for what seemed like an eternity.

I bent to kiss her as she took my hand and let my mouth linger over her ear.

"That's my good girl," I murmured.

She blushed.

The crowd began chanting something and it took me a moment to realize they were calling her name. She stepped closer to me, caught off guard. I slipped my hand around her waist to reassure her and she raised her hand and waved again. The light caught the ring I'd placed on her finger almost seven years ago and I heard every camera in the room click.

It took Peregrine several minutes to get the room to quiet. I delivered my speech to a warm response, but I was distracted. Every nerve in my body was electrified and in my chest was a deep hunger.

Now that I'd tasted this kind of power, I was never going to get enough.

We both answered questions from the press and Olivia did beautifully. Then we stood together as the cameras clicked away. They were in love with her and it made my chest swell with pride. I took her hand and spun her once, letting them all watch her glitter in the hot lights, and pulled her in for a kiss. Lights flashed and the crowd broke into applause. Then I led my exhausted wife off the stage and through the back hallway to the elevator.

As soon as the doors slid shut, she sagged against the wall. I kept my hand on her waist, feeling territorial. I didn't like sharing her, not even with a crowd. She was mine, my wife, my woman, no matter what roles we occupied outside the four walls of our bedroom.

I stroked her face with my thumb and she gazed up at me, exhausted.

"I know you're tired, baby," I said. "But I need to fuck you."

She smiled sleepily. "I know."

I pressed her against the elevator wall and kissed her mouth slowly. Exploring the sweet taste of her lips and tongue. Kissing her, eating her, licking her until her eyes were drunk and her nipples were pebbled beneath her dress.

"They loved you, baby," I breathed.

"I know," she panted, letting her head fall back so I could kiss up her throat. "They love you too."

"But no matter how much they love you, you are mine," I reminded her. "My wife."

Her lashes fluttered. "I could say the same for you."

"I've always been yours," I said.

I lifted her in my arms and carried her down the hall and into our suite. Our bodyguard let us in, keeping his eyes averted as he locked us into the room. Then we were alone and I wasted no time stripping my clothes off as she attempted to get her zipper down. Spinning her around, I tugged it open, baring her smooth back, and pulled it from her body.

Beneath it, she wore the sluttiest set of black lace lingerie. My cock throbbed in my boxer briefs and I shoved her against the couch, bending her over it. She gasped, gripping it to steady herself, as I tugged down her panties and pushed my groin against her ass. Grinding into her desperately.

"Fuck me, baby," I breathed. "You looked so perfect out there, so beautiful."

"You have no idea how sexy it is to see you on the stage in a suit, looking all presidential," she panted. "And all I could think about was how I had your cock down my throat less than an hour ago. I want you, Lucien, I need you inside me."

I shoved down the front of my boxer briefs, unleashing my cock. She gasped, whimpering as I pushed it past the entrance of her silky, wet sex and into her heat. Even after all this time, she still sometimes had to breathe through that first thrust.

Once I was seated in her, buried to the hilt, she shuddered and gripped me like such a good girl.

"I'm going to fuck you hard," I said.

"Please," she begged.

I thrust, pleasure moving like a shock through my groin. She went limp, sagging over the back of the couch, her head back. I gripped her hips and pounded into her, filling the room with the sounds of our bodies meeting and her soft gasps.

A rush of ownership moved over me and I took her body with mine. The world could adore her and call her name, but it would never mean anything in comparison with how she cried mine as I filled her with my cock. To them she was the first lady of the city, but to me she would always be the beautiful slut who had come for me like such a good girl on our wedding night.

No one else would ever know her like this. So deeply and intimately that it broke through all my ice.

I fucked her again in the bed and she rode me slowly, shaking as she finished. High on power, high on me. Then we slept hard, a euphoric mess in the sheets.

Triumphant. The king and queen entwined.

CHAPTER TWENTY-TWO

OLIVIA

THREE MONTHS LATER

It was the inaugural ball and every important person in the city was packed into our house. Light spilled from the windows, glittering on the snow. Outside the driveway was lined with cars and the ground marked with footprints. Inside, it smelled of crisp pine, whiskey, wine and the hopeful anticipation of the coming year.

"Feeling alright?"

I turned to find my brother standing behind me, his hands tucked behind his back. He had grown into his own since becoming Lucien's right hand and we'd only become closer over the last few years. Now, there was a glint of pride in his eyes as he looked down at me.

"Dance with me?"

I set aside my wine and accepted his hand. I wore a black dress that hugged my body and long, white gloves that reached to my elbows. Sapphires glinted on my throat, my ears, and my wrist.

As we stepped onto the dance floor, every eye dragged over us. I kept my back straight and my chin up as Lucien had taught me, offering everyone a tempered smile. The music struck up after a moment and we fell into step, gliding across the dance floor.

"Lucien is really working the room tonight," Cosimo remarked.

"He's on a mission," I said. "He has been for the last year."

We moved gracefully back and forth, sparkling beneath the starlight and the heavy chandelier overhead. I knew we were being watched so I kept that pleasant smile fixed to my face.

I was good at that now.

"There's only one place a man like Lucien goes," said Cosimo. "Up."

"He has a talent for it."

Cosimo's dark eyes fell to mine with a thoughtful expression.

"I'm sorry I never saw what our parents did to you," he said. "I wasn't looking. But I should have been there for you."

My throat tightened. "It's not your fault. We were both victims."

He was quiet as he steered me in smooth circles over the marble floor, riding lightly on the swelling music coming from the orchestra.

"My little sister, the mayor's wife," he said. "I never thought I would see you like this. Confident, collected, and happy."

I nodded, smiling honestly this time.

He cocked his head. "What's next for Olivia Esposito? You've become the first lady, a philanthropist, a mother, the most adored woman in the city. Where do you go next?"

He was complimenting me, but it still made me uncomfortable. There was a hint of a warning in his tone, a reminder to be cautious. For a second, I allowed the mask to fall from my face as I looked up at him.

"Wherever Lucien goes," I managed.

He shook his head, spinning me and pulling me back.

"No," he said. "I don't believe that for a moment. You want to see the world at your feet just as much as Lucien does. I didn't see it back when you married him, but you and Lucien are one and the same. Two halves of a whole."

I swallowed, unsure how to answer him. He was right, I knew that now. But I still wasn't sure if that was a good thing.

"No," Cosimo said slowly, looking out over the crowd. "I have a feeling there's no stopping you now, Liv. All I can do is stand back and watch you go."

The music ended and we stood there, staring at each other for a long moment. Then someone cleared their throat and I turned to find Lucien standing beside us, his hands behind his back.

"Mind if I take my wife back?" he said, glancing at Cosimo.

"If you can keep up with her," he said. He bent and kissed my cheekbone. "I'm heading out soon. Goodnight, Liv, and be careful."

He shook Lucien's hand, congratulating him, and disappeared into the crowd. The music struck up a waltz and Lucien took me in his arms, his hand sliding down to my lower back. His icy, hazel gaze locked with mine and he bent to kiss my forehead briefly, murmuring my name under his breath.

"Are you alright?" I asked.

"I am more than alright," he said. "I'm the husband of the first lady."

I laughed, letting my head fall back. The unease slipped from me as I looked up at the lights whirling overhead as my husband spun me slowly in his arms. We moved across the floor, beyond the bar stacked with a tower of champagne glasses, beyond the swan made of ice, to the center of the glittering room.

I glanced across the room and saw our reflections in the big mirror on the wall. Lucien caught my eye and the corner of his mouth twitched. I followed the lines of his body with my eyes. He had changed a little in the last year and he'd abandoned his habitual gray attire for sleek, fitted, black suits. His hair was a little shorter and the lines of his body were leaner.

He'd become a man in the public eye.

I had changed too.

Was this who I wanted to be? For a moment, I faltered as I stood looking at my reflection.

"Eyes on me, baby," he said softly.

Mouth dry, I locked my eyes with his and my confidence flooded back. His hand pressed to my spine, straightening it, and his other hand touched my chin. Lifting it. Then he bent and briefly kissed my mouth in a discreet gesture.

"I'll always protect you," he said softly. "No matter what."

Heat flooded me and I wanted to fall into his arms, to kiss him, and fuck him. To drown in the lean, heat of his body and the safe bubble of his protection. But I knew that hiding would never satisfy me now. Lucien had put my shattered pieces back together and given me a taste of something new, something I would always crave.

The freedom of power.

There was no retreating now. There was only Lucien and the bright, glittering future he had built for us.

With him by my side, there was nothing to do but rise.

THE END

Continue Lucien & Olivia's story! The third book in the King of Ice & Steel Trilogy can be found on Amazon KU after August 25th 2023.

OTHER BOOKS BY RAYA MORRIS EDWARDS
All on Amazon KU

KING OF ICE & STEEL TRILOGY READING ORDER

Captured Light

Devil I Need, the sequel to Captured Light

Ice & Steel, the Conclusion to Captured Light & Devil I Need

(August 25th 2023)

CAPTURED STANDALONES READING ORDER

Captured Desire - Iris & Duran - out September 5th 2023

Captured Light - Lucien & Olivia

Captured Solace - Viktor & Sienna

Captured Fantasy - Cosimo & Lorenza

Captured Ecstasy - Peregrine & Rosalia

THE WELSH KINGS TRILOGY

Paradise Descent, Book 1 in The Welsh Kings Trilogy

Prince of Ink & Scars, Book 2 in the Welsh Kings Trilogy (out April 2024)

Printed in Great Britain
by Amazon